MORE THAN MONEY

Campaigning American Style
Series Editors
Daniel M. Shea, Allegheny College
F. Christopher Arterton, George Washington University

Few areas of American politics have changed as dramatically in recent times as the way in which we choose public officials. Students of politics and political communications are struggling to keep abreast of these developments—and the 2000 election only fed the confusion and concern. *Campaigning American Style* is a new series of books devoted to both the theory and practice of American electoral politics. It offers high-quality work on the conduct of new-style electioneering and how it is transforming our electoral system. Scholars, practitioners, and students of campaigns and elections need new resources to keep pace with the rapid rate of electoral change, and we are pleased to help provide them in this exciting series.

Titles in the Series

Campaign Mode: Strategic Vision in Congressional Elections
by Michael John Burton and Daniel M. Shea

The Civic Web: Online Politics and Democratic Values
edited by David M. Anderson and Michael Cornfield

High-Tech Grass Roots: The Professionalization of Local Elections
by J. Cherie Strachan

Political Polling: Strategic Information in Campaigns
by Jeffrey M. Stonecash

Dancing without Partners: How Candidates, Parties, and Interest Groups Interact in the Presidential Campaign
edited by David B. Magleby, J. Quin Monson, and Kelly D. Patterson

Fountain of Youth: Strategies and Tactics for Mobilizing America's Young Voters
edited by Daniel M. Shea and John C. Green

More than Money: Interest Group Action in Congressional Elections
by Richard M. Skinner

Forthcoming

The Rules: Election Regulations in the American States
by Costas Panagopoulos

Negative Campaigning
by Richard R. Lau and Gerald M. Pomper

MORE THAN MONEY

INTEREST GROUP ACTION IN CONGRESSIONAL ELECTIONS

Richard M. Skinner

ROWMAN & LITTLEFIELD PUBLISHERS, INC.
Lanham • Boulder • New York • Toronto • Plymouth, UK

ROWMAN & LITTLEFIELD PUBLISHERS, INC.

Published in the United States of America
by Rowman & Littlefield Publishers, Inc.
A wholly owned subsidiary of The Rowman & Littlefield Publishing Group, Inc.
4501 Forbes Boulevard, Suite 200, Lanham, Maryland 20706
www.rowmanlittlefield.com

Estover Road
Plymouth PL6 7PY
United Kingdom

British Library Cataloguing in Publication Information Available

Library of Congress Cataloging-in-Publication Data

Skinner, Richard M., 1970–
  More than money : interest group action in congressional elections / Richard M.
Skinner.
    p. cm. — (Campaigning American style)
  Includes bibliographical references.
  ISBN-13: 978-0-7425-4720-9 (cloth : alk. paper)
  ISBN-10: 0-7425-4720-5 (cloth : alk. paper)
  ISBN-13: 978-0-7425-4721-6 (pbk. : alk. paper)
  ISBN-10: 0-7425-4721-3 (pbk. : alk. paper)
  1. Pressure groups—United States. 2. Lobbying—United States. 3. Political
campaigns—United States. 4. United States. Congress—Elections. 5. United States—
Politics and government—1989– I. Title. II. Title: Interest group action in congressional
elections.
  JK1118.S585 2007
  324.973—dc2   2006030201

Printed in the United States of America

♾™ The paper used in this publication meets the minimum requirements of American
National Standard for Information Sciences—Permanence of Paper for Printed Library
Materials, ANSI/NISO Z39.48-1992

In memoriam Gerson Lisman Skinner, 1922–2002; Elizabeth McGrath, 1909–2004; and Alison J. Meloy, 1972–2001.

Contents

Part IV: The Context

Acknowledgments

I WOULD LIKE TO THANK THREE MENTORS for their guidance over the years: Theodore Eismeier, James Ceaser, and Michael Malbin. I hope to prove worthy of their confidence.

I would like to thank the staff, board of trustees, and academic advisory board of the Campaign Finance Institute. Special thanks are due to Anne Bedlington, Mark Rozell, and Clyde Wilcox, whose cooperation was essential to this project. Several other political scientists provided valuable advice, including Larry Sabato, Katie Dunn Tenpas, Paul Herrnson, Burdett Loomis, Diana Dwyre, and Robin Kolodny.

Gratitude is also owed to the faculty and staff of the University of Virginia, Randolph-Macon College, the State University of New York, Geneseo, Hamilton College, and Bowdoin College. Special thanks to Steven Finkel, Paul Freedman, Sarah Corse, Martha Derthick, Carol Mershon, Gerard Alexander, Matthew Holden, Edward Drachman, Alan Cafruny, Philip Klinkner, Peter Francia, and Quin Monson. Janet Martin and Chris Potholm provided invaluable help in guiding me through the publication process. I must also thank several of the brightest minds of my generation: Elizabeth Skinner, Dennis Logue Jr., Brian Menard, Tim Hulsey, John Froitzheim, Julie Biskner, and Muge Kokten. Thanks to the staff at Rowman & Littlefield (including anonymous readers), as well as to those with the other presses with which I worked.

I thank the participants in my interviews, who gave to me much time and insight without compensation.

I must also thank my family for their love and support.

List of Tables

I

THE PERSPECTIVE

1

Groups and Parties in the Political World

W ITH ITS SPANISH MISSIONS and awe-inspiring views of the Pacific, California's central coast is one of the most beautiful parts of the state, but it
rarely attracts much attention. While some of America's most famous people,
from William Randolph Hearst to Ronald Reagan, have owned homes in this
area, its small population is dwarfed by those of Southern California and the
Bay Area. But for a few months in 1997 and 1998, California's central coast
was at the heart of American politics.

In its 1990s configuration, California's Twenty-second District comprised
most of San Luis Obispo and Santa Barbara counties. It included the scenic
community of Santa Barbara as well as Vandenberg Air Force Base. Far from
the liberal influences of Hollywood and San Francisco, this is traditionally Republican territory, though not overwhelmingly: Bob Dole carried the district
by just 514 votes in 1996. Until that year, the district had not elected a Democratic congressman since 1944.

The 1990s had brought political turmoil to this placid country. In 1992,
multimillionaire Michael Huffington ousted longtime congressman Robert
Lagomarsino in a Republican primary. Two years later, Huffington ran unsuccessfully for the Senate; he was replaced by Andrea Seastrand, a far more conservative Republican whose outspoken Christian Right views created some
controversy in this swing district. In 1996, Seastrand lost to Walter Capps, a
liberal Democrat and a theology professor at the University of California,
Santa Barbara.

Capps died suddenly in October 1997. His wife Lois became the presump-
tive Democratic nominee. The Republicans, however, had a contested primary

between assemblymen Brooks Firestone, a moderate, and Tom Bordonaro, a conservative. Because he is an heir to the Firestone tire fortune, Firestone had a huge financial advantage. Bordonaro, however, had strong support from religious conservatives. One of them was Gary Bauer. Bauer, a former Reagan White House staffer, had become president of the Family Research Council, a prominent conservative group, and was planning his own bid for the Republican presidential nomination. Bauer had formed a political action committee, the Campaign for Working Families (CWF), which financed his own activities and supported sympathetic candidates.

The CWF spent $100,000 on radio and television advertisements praising Bordonaro for his support for banning "partial-birth" abortion, a controversial late-term procedure, and criticizing Firestone for his opposition to such a ban. Both Bordonaro and Capps denounced Firestone's campaign and Bordonaro claimed that it undermined his own appeal. But the CWF effort was widely credited with helping Bordonaro defeat Firestone. In the January 1998 all-party primary, Capps won 45 percent, Bordonaro 29 percent, and Firestone 25 percent (Berke 1998a, 1998b). Peter Dickinson, executive director of the CWF, declared, "This is our mandate. We are trying to put conservatives into Congress" (Purdum 1998).

The CWF effort continued into the general election. Once again, it spent $100,000 on a broadcast campaign on the "partial-birth" issue. This time, its advertisements attacked Capps: "Tom Bordonaro and the American Medical Association support banning this terrible procedure. Unfortunately, Lois Capps doesn't" (Cannon 1998a). This campaign brought swift opposition. NARAL Pro-Choice America produced radio and television advertisements attacking Gary Bauer, without mentioning either Capps or Bordonaro. The spots criticized Bauer for opposing family leave legislation and AIDS funding, and for supporting an absolute ban on abortion and the abolition of the Department of Education (Cannon 1998; Edsall and Spurgeon 1998). Capps herself made a television advertisement responding to the CWF's charges; the CWF countered with a spot featuring Senator Rick Santorum (R-PA) affirming its position (Hallow 1998).

The CWF and NARAL were not the only groups that participated in this contest. Americans for Limited Terms spent $185,000 on radio and television advertisements attacking Bordonaro, who had refused to limit himself to three terms in office, and praising Capps, who said that given that she was sixty years old, a three-term limit was no problem for her. Ironically, Bordonaro supported a term-limits amendment to the U.S. Constitution while Capps opposed it (Cannon 1998). The Christian Coalition said it distributed 100,000 voter guides and made 15,000 phone calls to mobilize its supporters (Hallow

1998). Planned Parenthood made radio advertisements praising Capps for her support of legal abortion. Other groups that got involved included Americans for Job Security, a probusiness group that backed Bordonaro; the Sierra Club, which campaigned for Capps; and the American Federation of Labor-Congress of Industrial Organizations (AFL-CIO), which sent a pro-Capps mailing to its members (Purdum 1998).

In the March 1998 runoff, Capps defeated Bordonaro by 53 percent to 45 percent. Some ascribed Capps's victory to a backlash against the CWF campaign. John Davies, an adviser to Firestone, said, "The impact of the ads was to remind Firestone voters that he (Bordonaro) was the guy who had punched their friend in the face." Bauer retorted, "We brought him from nothing to beat a Republican who outspent him 5 to 1. Bordonaro got 29 percent in the primary, and this time, in the final, he got 45 percent. We still feel it's a net plus. We are putting the conservative agenda front and center" (Cannon 1998). Media accounts of Capps's victory dwelled on the role played by the CWF, NARAL and other outside groups. During the campaign, Bordonaro bemoaned the impact of this activity: "Is this the future of campaigns? Pretty soon, all we're going to have to do is file and sit back and let all those independent expenditures run the show. It's going to be rolling the dice whether you get into office or not" (Berke 1998a)?

This level of outside involvement was unusual. As a special election, the contest in the Twenty-second District would inevitably attract more attention because it was not competing with dozens of other races for media coverage, as it would have had it been held in November. The Twenty-second was a competitive district that saw several close races in the 1990s. But the November 1998 election in that district, which was a rematch between Capps and Bordonaro, attracted far less attention, both by the media and by outside groups. (Capps won, 55 percent to 43 percent.) In the 1990s, the Twenty-second District coincided almost perfectly with the Santa Barbara–Santa Maria–San Luis Obispo television market; this makes it a cost-effective area for broadcast advertising. Had this race instead taken place in a district in the nearby Los Angeles market (which then included all or part of twenty-five House districts), it is doubtful that so many groups would have been so active.

But if this race was unusual, it was symptomatic of a broader trend: an expansion of interest-group activity in congressional elections. For example, in 1996, in Pennsylvania's Twenty-first District, parties and outside groups spent $1.4 million, while the two major-party candidates spent $1.7 million (Beck et al. 1997). In 2002, in Pennsylvania's Seventeenth District, parties and interest groups spent more than twice as much as the two major-party candidates did; interest groups alone may have spent more than $1 million (Medvic and

Schorson 2004). Interest groups have been increasing their involvement in campaigns, especially since the 1994 Republican takeover of Congress. Organized labor, which had enjoyed a warm relationship with the Democratic leadership for decades, was thrust into an icy world ruled by Republicans hostile to unions. Not surprisingly, labor leaders have sought to change this state of affairs. Environmentalists and pro-choice groups have joined this effort. This mobilization has led to a countermobilization by business and conservative groups. By 2004, Republican control of Congress seemed sure enough that groups on both sides focused their energies on the presidential contest.

Interest groups are fulfilling new roles in our political system, both on their own and in combination with one another and with the political parties. This work attempts to better understand this activity, and put it into the broader context of political parties, interest groups, and congressional elections. It is also important that we understand that our interest groups differ: in their relationships with the political parties, in the nature of the incentives they offer to members, and in the resources that they can deploy for political action.

Interest Groups in Congressional Elections

Interest groups have long been active in congressional elections. From early in the twentieth century, the American Federation of Labor (AFL) sought to defeat unsympathetic members of Congress. Responding to the Smith-Connally Act's ban on the use of union dues to fund federal campaigns, the Congress of Industrial Organizations (CIO) created its Political Action Committee in 1943. The CIO-PAC played a major role in the congressional elections of the 1940s, so much so that it engendered fierce denunciations by such conservatives as Richard Nixon, who based much of his first congressional campaign on criticism of the PAC. The AFL soon established its own political organization, Labor's League for Political Education. When the AFL and the CIO merged in 1955, they also merged their political operations into the Committee on Political Education, which still exists today (Taft 1964).

The passage of amendments to the Federal Election Campaign Act in 1974 led to the widespread creation of political action committees (PACs) by corporations and trade associations (Sabato 1984). A few years later, "New Right" organizations claimed credit for the defeats of such liberal stalwarts as George McGovern, Birch Bayh, and Frank Church. Some of these groups, such as the National Conservative Political Action Committee and the Moral Majority, faded from the scene quickly. Others, such as the National Right to Life Committee, remain potent political players. More recently, Balz and Brownstein (1996) partially attribute the Republican takeover of Congress in 1994 to the activities of a "conservative populist" coalition that included the National Rifle Association (NRA), the National Federation of Independent Business (NFIB), and the Christian Coalition.

Since 1994, many observers have noted increased involvement by interest groups in congressional elections. They focus their attention mostly on the explosion of "issue advocacy," but many also note the importance of group-sponsored voter turnout operations in recent years (Edsall 1996; Rozell and Wilcox 1999).[1] In his sample of seventeen competitive House and Senate races in the 1998 election, Magleby (2000) finds 111 outside groups electioneering; these groups ran phone banks, conducted voter turnout efforts, aired broadcast advertisements, and distributed direct mail. Some groups, such as labor unions, have been active for decades, while others, such as Americans for Job Security, came into existence only a few years ago.

Rozell and Wilcox (1999) assert that direct communication by interest groups offers several advantages over PAC contributions. It allows groups to concentrate their resources in a few races. There are no limits on direct spending by groups. They also highlight issues of concern to them: unions can focus on the minimum wage, feminists can dwell on abortion, small-business groups can denounce taxes. Rozell and Wilcox point to several causes for increased group involvement in elections over recent decades: the increasing number of interest groups, the increased role of government, and the rise of single-issue organizations. Dwyre (1997) argues that unregulated spending has boomed in part because most contribution limits did not increase after 1974 (until they were increased by the Bipartisan Campaign Reform Act of 2002) and because of the unusually high stakes in 1996 (control of the presidency and both houses of Congress was being contested).

Several factors shape groups' decisions about political activities. The political context—the closeness of partisan competition, the number of contested seats, the groups' own political orientation—determines their opportunities for electoral involvement. Their resources—money, membership, expertise—determine how they can respond to this context. The nature of their membership—why people join the organization in the first place and whether it is easy for them to leave—helps determine the resources groups can deploy (see Hirschman 1971; Wilson 1973). While these factors are not always determinative, they do define the parameters for political action. Although groups are affected by the political context, their resources shape how they can respond. Different groups have different resources: business groups are often money heavy; unions, membership heavy. There are highly ideological groups with small, influential memberships; there are material-incentive groups with millions of members who have little interest in a broad ideological agenda. Some groups focus their efforts on turning out members to vote; others talk more to sympathetic nonmembers. But all of these strategies are dependent on the resources available to groups.

While relatively little has been written on interest groups' role in elections, for decades scholars have been studying their behavior in the political world. An impressive body of work has grown up to explain how interest groups form, how they gain members, how they hold on to their members, and why they engage in political activity. Most of the political activity described in these works has been lobbying or the operation of a political action committee (PAC). There have been several treatments of PAC decision making (Sabato 1984; Eismeier and Pollock 1988; Biersack, Herrnson, and Wilcox 1994, 1999). These studies have found that the PACs vary in their strategies and decision-making processes depending on their size, their institutional affiliation, and their goals.

In the 1950s, pluralist writers such as Truman assumed that people formed groups naturally out of a shared interest or as a response to a threat. But Olson (1965) upset this consensus by arguing that large numbers of rational, self-interested individuals would not form groups unless there was "coercion or some other special device" to make them work together. Olson claimed that attempts to form large groups succeeded usually when leaders could force potential members to join, as is the case for labor unions, or when they could offer them some material benefit unavailable otherwise, such as discounts on insurance. If there is no such coercion or benefit, people will not join groups because they can potentially enjoy the results of a group's activity without having to pay the cost of membership. Any political activity that a group may conduct is simply a by-product of the selective benefits provided to its membership.

Olson smashed the pluralists' assumption that groups would form naturally. But the publication of his work coincided with a huge growth in group membership during the 1960s and 1970s. Many of the groups that sprouted during this era were aimed at social change and did not offer any significant material benefit to their members. Political scientists sought to explain this development. James Q. Wilson devised a taxonomy of incentives that groups offered to members. *Material incentives* are tangible benefits of some sort: a free magazine subscription, discounts on travel, a professional license. *Purposive incentives* offer members the chance to express their views or work toward a common goal: to protect the environment, to oppose gun control, to support lower taxes. (Purposive incentives tend to appeal to high-status individuals socialized into political awareness by their parents and peers; see Verba, Schlozman, and Brady 1995; Berry 1997.) *Solidary incentives* give members the opportunity to interact with others: to socialize at a club, to win esteem by being elected to office, or to go on trips with fellow members, for example (Clark and Wilson 1961; Wilson 1973).

Moe (1980) expands on Olson's work by relaxing his assumptions: individuals are rational, but not exclusively materialistic. This allows greater roles for purposive and solidary incentives. Moe also points out that individuals who join groups because of these incentives are more likely to participate in organizational affairs; those who join because of material incentives will probably remain passive. Interest-group entrepreneurs can use this to their benefit by encouraging members to volunteer on behalf of the group's goals; indeed, such participation can be a benefit in itself. Walker (1991), among others, shows that Olson's "by-product" theory could not account for most group political activity: people really do join groups in order to receive purposive benefits. But Hansen (1985) finds that demand for such benefits is highly responsive to changes in fashion. The presence of a threat is necessary to keep old members and win new ones.

For most groups, political activity means lobbying or otherwise monitoring legislative activity. But for some, it can mean involvement in elections. Schlozman and Tierney (1986) argue that groups have four main resources for political action: money, membership, information, and expertise. Organized interests choose their tactics based on their resources, their legal (especially tax) status, the nature of their cause (whether it can appeal to the wider public), and their past efforts. They may either seek to influence the outcome of elections or influence officeholders' behavior, or both. If they are seeking to influence the outcome of elections, they will allocate resources into close races and assume that supportive officials will back positions. If they are seeking to influence officeholders' behavior, they will aid certain winners so as to persuade them to support the group's positions.

While Hirschman (1971) does not specifically address interest groups, he does introduce an important concept: exit. Groups are constantly under the threat of losing their members. If groups cannot provide a sufficient level of benefits, their members will leave. This constrains groups' activity, especially if they are not able to discourage members from leaving. Schlozman and Tierney (1986) assert that because exit from trade unions is unrealistic (it would require workers to quit their jobs), labor leaders are less constrained than their counterparts in other groups. Rothenberg (1988) suggests that groups that require only a small contribution are especially likely to lose their members should the members become dissatisfied.

Groups and Parties: Rivals or Allies?

Political scientists have argued for years that interest groups undermine the party system. Portraying groups as being unable to assemble the broad coalitions that parties can build, political scientists also argue that groups reinforce elitist biases of the American system (Schattschneider 1942, 1948, 1960; Walker 1991; Schier 2000). Berry (1997) asserts that parties are broad "vote-maximizers," while groups are narrowly focused "policy-maximizers." But what if the best way of maximizing policy outcomes is by maximizing votes for one party?[2] When a group's preferences overlap strongly with a party's platform (for example, organized labor and the Democrats), there is an incentive for such a group to support a party's candidates. When control of a house of Congress depends on the outcome of a few races, this incentive becomes even stronger.

Nor are groups and parties easily disentangled. In her study of the Illinois Republican party, Schwartz (1990) describes a "party network" that includes elected officials, party officers, contributors, and interest-group leaders. Members of this network work together to help party candidates win office. They also share common ideological values. The network can adapt to a changing environment and can admit newcomers. Schlesinger (1985) argues that our concept of "political party" needs to encompass more than simply the formal party apparatus; he calls on us to understand the close links that parties have developed with PACs and other groups. Aldrich (1995) describes contemporary political parties as "parties-in-service" that provide assistance to candidates. Bedlington and Malbin (2003) find members of the House of Representatives operating as part of this network, using their PACs and personal campaign committees to help their party's candidates win close races. Members can do this both by contributing directly to candidates and by giving to the party campaign committees. Not surprisingly, party leaders strongly encourage such giving. These close races will determine which party will control the House, who will chair committees, and who will run the floor. Perhaps we now have party-networks-in-service: amagalmations of party institutions, interest groups, and individual activists all working together to elect candidates under a single banner. (Also see Kolodny 1998; Monroe 2001; Cohen et al. 2001, 2003, forthcoming.)

The relationship between groups and parties may be analogous to that between parties and political consultants. Early treatments of political consultants, such as that by Sabato (1981), emphasize the damage the consultants were inflicting upon parties. Consultants were making parties almost irrelevant by assuming the parties' traditional roles, such as communicating with voters or helping candidates raise money, and were enabling candidates to run campaigns without party assistance.

But more recent studies of political consultants have painted a more complex picture. Parties rely on political consultants to provide services to candidates that they cannot provide well themselves: media, direct mail, polling. Party officials often refer candidates to preferred consultants who can provide the necessary services and have established relationships with the party. Kolodny and Dulio (2001) find that much of party spending goes to consultants, who provide the same services they perform for candidates. Consultants often have strong links to the parties: many began their careers working for party committees. Rather than weakening the parties, consultants are valuable members of the "party network"—"subcontractors," as Kolodny and Dulio (2001) call them. (Also see Dwyre and Kolodny 2001; Dulio and Kolodny 2003.)

Interest groups may also function as "subcontractors" for the parties. If campaign finance laws limit the degree to which groups can coordinate their actions with candidates, they certainly can perform functions for the parties for which they have special expertise: the National Rifle Association can contact gun owners, the Sierra Club can run advertisements about environmental issues, unions can communicate with their members. Group and party leaders know each other and work together for common goals. Since 1993, Grover Norquist, head of Americans for Tax Reform, has held a weekly meeting of conservative activists, including representatives from the Christian Coalition and the National Rifle Association; one of the meeting's main purposes is to plan strategies for the election of Republicans. Even before George W. Bush announced his presidential candidacy, his campaign sent a staffer to the meetings; since Bush became president, a White House aide has been in attendance. Similar gatherings take place among liberal activists. For the 2004 election, a new entity called "America Votes" sought to coordinate the political activities of many liberal/Democratic groups (Barnes 2001; Drew 1997; Dreyfuss 2001; Page 2001; Hadfield 2004).

Such party-group ties are not entirely new. Dark (1998) describes the decades-long alliance between organized labor and the Democratic Party. In a survey conducted in the early 1980s, Schlozman and Tierney (1986) found that of groups seeking to influence the electoral process, 59 percent preferred a party. In recent years, the party system has been changing in ways that should encourage groups to strengthen their ties to the parties. Party unity in Congress, after bottoming out in the 1970s, has rebounded to levels similar to or even higher than those seen in the 1940s and 1950s. The gradual realignment of conservative white southerners from the Democrats to the Republicans has pushed southern Democrats to the left, moved the national Republican party to the right and sharpened party differences in Congress and elsewhere (G. C. Jacobson 2000).

While elites have polarized more dramatically than the masses, voters are increasingly divided by party, too. The National Election Studies show a steady increase since the 1970s in the correlation between party identification and issue positions among voters in House elections. Voting in congressional and presidential elections has become more consistent; ticket splitting peaked in 1972 and has declined to the levels of the Kennedy years, while voters have become better able to distinguish between the two parties ideologically. Although this trend has been obscured by the third-party candidacies of recent years, partisans have become less willing to defect to presidential candidates of the other party (G. C. Jacobson 2000; also see Bartels 2000, Fleisher and Bond 2001, Hetherington 2001, Lawrence 2001). According to the National Election Pool exit poll, just 11 percent of Democrats voted for George W. Bush in 2004 while only 6 percent of Republicans voted for John Kerry. This is a far cry from the one-third of Democrats who backed Richard Nixon over George McGovern. This growing polarization makes it more feasible for groups—particularly those that are strongly ideological—to increase their ties to the parties.

If interest groups pose a threat to the existence and well-being of political parties, party leaders do not seem to have received this message. When the National Republican Congressional Committee gave $250,000 to the National Right to Life Committee, they were acting as partners, not rivals (Leavitt 2000). Leaders of the AFL-CIO planned their 1996 political efforts in consultation with President Bill Clinton, his chief of staff, and his labor secretary. This seems like a textbook example of a "party network" at work (Dark 1998). When the Republican National Committee assisted in the formation of the Christian Coalition, they presumably were helping to create an ally, not a rival (Sabato and Simpson 1996).

The leadership of the so-called 527 organizations formed after the passage of BCRA—America Coming Together, the Media Fund, America Votes—included not only veterans of the Clinton White House and the Democratic National Committee, but also longtime officials of the AFL-CIO, EMILY's List, and the Sierra Club. This "shadow party" could also be called "The Democratic Party Network, Inc." Both former president Bill Clinton and Democratic National Committee chairman Terry McAuliffe strongly encouraged the formation of these entities (Skinner 2005).

The Strategic Context

The 1994–2000 era was the first four-election cycle in which partisan control of the House of Representatives was seriously contested since 1950–1956—when television was still in its infancy and therefore part of electoral ancient history. Every competitive House race could conceivably tip the partisan balance; in 1998 and 2000, the number of genuinely competitive House races was small. Such a situation increases the incentive for groups and parties to pour money into these contests.

Long before the first ballots were cast, pundits proclaimed 2000 to be an unusually important election. As it happened, the presidency was decided by a few hundred disputed votes in one state; the two parties finished in a dead heat in the Senate, while the Democrats came within only a few thousand votes of taking over the House. Not surprisingly, the 2000 elections broke all records for campaign spending. Estimates of total spending by candidates, groups, and parties ranged as high as $3 billion. A study by the Brennan Center for Justice found that group spending on candidate-specific advertisements in 2000 totaled at least $56 million, about evenly divided between pro-Democratic and pro-Republican groups. The parties spent at least $147 million, surpassing candidate spending for the first time (Brennan Center for Justice 2000). Citizens for Better Medicare, a group created by the Pharmaceutical Research and Manufacturers Association (PhRMA) to present its views on Medicare coverage of prescriptions, allegedly spent $50 million on broadcast advertisements, although not all of them mentioned candidates (Miller and Miller 2000).

In 2002, the pharmaceutical industry continued to funnel money into "front groups," including the United Seniors Association, the Seniors Coalition, and the 60 Plus Association, which were active in numerous competitive congressional races. While by most measures, the funds spent by interest groups in 2002 did not match the totals seen in 2000, they were still impressive by historical standards. (For example, $20.3 million was spent on independent expenditures in 2002, down from $22 million in 2000, but still well above the $13 million spent in 1998. See Magleby and Tanner 2004.)

Given the increasing partisan polarization of Congress, party control matters more than ever before (Aldrich and Rohde 2000; Cox and McCubbins 1993; Rohde 1991; Sinclair 2000a). Groups with strong partisan/ideological ties, such as organized labor or small-business associations, therefore have a special incentive to be involved in congressional elections. There is a strong impetus to concentrate efforts in a few races that can determine control of Congress. In a political system where party leaders play an enormous role, where members of the two parties vote dramatically differently on key issues, and where margins of control are narrow, groups that care about party control have powerful incentives to increase their involvement.

The Legal Context

The legal context for political activity by interest groups turned notably more permissive in the 1990s. A series of court decisions and Federal Election

Commission (FEC) rulings fell on the side of the so-called magic words definition of express advocacy. In *Buckley v. Valeo* (519 F. 2d 821 (D.C. Cir. 1975)), the Court of Appeals for the District of Columbia overturned the definition of independent expenditure in the 1974 amendments to the Federal Election Campaign Act of 1971 as being too broad. The Supreme Court then ruled (424 U.S. 1 (1976)) that such government regulation must be limited to communications that explicitly advocate the election or defeat of a candidate. After *Buckley*, lower courts issued conflicting opinions on the meaning of *express advocacy*. Some opinions have stuck to a definition based on the so-called magic words ("vote for," "vote against," "elect," "defeat," etc.), while others have allowed a broader definition that includes nonverbal cues and contextual factors. But *Federal Election Commission v. Christian Action Network* (1995) was widely interpreted as confirming the dominance of the "magic words" interpretation and so opening the gates to greater use of "issue advocacy."[3] During the 1996 elections, the Democratic National Committee and the AFL-CIO used issue advocacy extensively; conservative groups followed on their heels.

The legal context, however, changed dramatically in 2002 with the passage of the Bipartisan Campaign Reform Act, which redefined electioneering in a more inclusive fashion. These changes come at the end of the period included in this study and will probably increase the importance of tendencies described within it. They may well accentuate the roles played by interest groups within the party networks. Certainly this is suggested by the rise of the so-called 527 organizations, such as America Coming Together and America Votes, which have close ties to organized labor and other Democratic-leaning interest groups. (See Boatright et al. 2003 and Potter 1997 for much more thorough discussions of this topic.) Republican 527s, such as Progress for America, were also run by consultants and funded by donors who were well enmeshed in their own party networks (Weissman and Hassan, forthcoming).

Herrnson (1998) and Jacobson (1997) demonstrate that parties tend to concentrate their resources in the closest races in order to maximize their strength in Congress; Bernstein and La Raja (1999) show that this holds true for outside groups engaging in issue advocacy. This is not true for PACs, especially those interested in pursuing access. PACs instead concentrate their giving to safe incumbents, especially those who are committee chairmen or party leaders (Sabato 1984; Eismeier and Pollock 1988). Congress's shift to Republican control has led many corporate PACs to shift from bipartisanship to a distinct Republican tilt, but they remain cautious and rarely help challengers (Boatright et al. 2003).

Rozell and Wilcox (1999) identify several resources that interest groups may possess: money, membership, and expertise in such areas as polling and candidate training. Jacobson and Kernell (1983) argue that political actors behave strategically, seeking the best use of their resources. Parties and sympathetic PACs, for example, help strong challengers during favorable years and defend weak incumbents during unfavorable years. Walker (1991) finds that resources possessed by groups are an important influence on the strategies those groups pursue. These resources are, in turn, partially determined by what incentives groups offer and how they are structured.

Money

For many organizations, their most important asset is money. Most politically active groups are content to simply create a PAC that contributes to campaign committees of favored candidates. If they are primarily concerned with securing access to policymakers, they may choose to make small donations to a number of candidates (usually incumbents). Often, they do not contribute enough to be concerned with the $10,000 overall limit on gifts to a single candidate ($5,000 each for the primary and general elections). Over half of political action committees did not contribute more $5,000 to all federal candidates during the 2001–2002 cycle, while only about one-eighth gave more than $250,000.[4] This elite group gave 82 percent of PAC contributions.[5]

But for some larger, better-financed groups, those limits do constrain their giving. If they are concerned mostly with electing friendly members, they may wish to concentrate their giving in a handful of close races. If they have a great deal of money, they may wish to spend more than the caps allow. Two means of getting around these caps are independent expenditures and issue advocacy.

Political action committees can spend unlimited funds on independent expenditures; these must be made without any coordination with candidates. PACs must disclose their spending. The National Conservative Political Action Committee (NCPAC) engaged in independent expenditures extensively in the 1980 election against such liberal senators as George McGovern and Frank Church. But the use of independent expenditures skyrocketed after the Republicans took control of Congress in 1994. During the 1995–1996 cycle, independent expenditures by PACs in congressional races set a new record, totaling $9.14 million. This figure was almost matched in 1997–1998, with an equivalent figure of $13 million. But in 1999–2000, independent expenditures set another record, hitting $22 million. This cycle also marked the first in which more money was spent on independent expenditures supporting Democrats (or opposing Republicans) than on those backing Republicans (or attacking Democrats [Magleby and Beal 2003]). In the 2001–2002 cycle, independent expenditures reached $20.3 million, down from two years before, but well above the total seen in 1997–1998 (Magleby and Tanner 2004).

Because it was not regulated before the passage of BCRA, issue advocacy offered many advantages to political actors. They did not need to disclose their expenditures or their sources of funding. There was no limit to the amount of money that they could spend. Corporate treasury funds and union dues, off limits to most political activity, could be used for issue advocacy. Groups could rely on a small number of very large donors (for example, Jane Fonda, who made a huge gift to Planned Parenthood in 2000) rather on than the much broader base mandated by the limits on individual donations to PACs. Parties could use "soft money" for issue advocacy; independent expenditures (which include express advocacy) must be funded with "hard money."[6] Tax-exempt organizations that are either forbidden from partisan activity or are not supposed to have it as their main purpose could engage in issue advocacy without upsetting the IRS (Potter 1997). Issue advocacy can take many forms: television and radio commercials, direct mail, voter guides, and so on. Broadcast advertisements are probably the most visible means of issue advocacy.

Membership

For some groups, their principal asset is a large membership that they can mobilize in support of favored candidates. Rosenstone and Hansen (1993) argue that groups can decrease the costs of political participation for their members. Activists will mobilize their constituents when they believe that it can help them win political battles: "Citizen participation is a resource that political leaders use selectively in their battles for political advantage" (Rosenstone and Hansen 1993). Mobilization can be vital, since many citizens will not participate unless encouraged to do so: "Most people, most of the time, are able to find better things to do than participate in politics" (Walker 1991).

Organized labor has several strong incentives to mobilize its membership. First of all, despite years of decline, unions still have many more members than similar organizations. With 13 million members, the AFL-CIO dwarfs such groups as the National Rifle Association (4 million), the U.S. Chamber of Commerce (215,000), and the National Federation of Independent Business (600,000). The National Education Association, the largest union not affiliated with the AFL-CIO, boasts 2.3 million members. There are, however, some groups with larger memberships than either the AFL-CIO or the NEA. The American Association of Retired Persons (AARP) has 32 million members. But unlike unions, the AARP has a fairly weak hold on its members. It cannot prevent them from leaving to protest policies they dislike. Unlike unions, the material benefits the AARP provides are, while not trivial, certainly not as essential as a job or a health insurance policy. It also has a limited ability to shape its members' attitudes.

Second, union members are different from the constituents of other interest groups. Unions are purposive organizations whose members join for non-purposive reasons. As Wilson (1973) notes, such groups may feature especially large gaps between their staff's opinions and those of the rank and file. Indeed, the views of labor's leadership are often much more liberal than those of its members (see Mundo 1992). Unlike many political groups, organized labor cannot assume that its constituents will vote as it wishes. It must persuade them to back its political program.

Unions are also able to take advantage of "solidary networks," webs of family and friendship binding people together. Unlike members of many other organizations, unionists work together and know one another. Unions can turn this to their advantage by encouraging shop stewards to mobilize their constituents (Rosenstone and Hansen 1993). Unions are not the only ones who use such networks to their advantage. Christian conservative and right-to-life organizations take advantage of the networks created by churches, often using them to distribute voter guides favorable to their positions or to recruit volunteers (Guth et al. 2002). Verba, Schlozman, and Brady (1995) find religious activity to be the principal means by which less-educated people acquire civic skills. More recently, the Business Industry Political Action Committee (BIPAC) has conducted the Prosperity Project, which helps corporations communicate with their members about candidates and issues to the extent that they legally can do so. While they generally cannot tell their (nonmanagement) employees how to vote, corporations can produce voter guides, invite candidates to visit their facilities, and encourage workers to register to vote (Hamburger 2000, 2001, 2004; L. Jacobson 2000; Miller and Gross 2001; Stone 2000).

Some groups encourage their members to volunteer in support of favored candidates. Labor unions have long provided an army of envelope stuffers and doorbell ringers for Democratic candidates. Purposive groups may have highly motivated members whom they can mobilize as activists; indeed, participation can serve as an important incentive to remain in the organization (Moe 1980). The National Federation of Independent Business encourages its members, many of whom are well placed in social networks, to volunteer for favored candidates. Sympathetic office seekers can usually count on volunteers from pro-life or pro-choice groups. Some groups even supply field coordinators to manage their efforts at voter mobilization (Biersack, Herrnson, and Wilcox 1999).

Expertise

There are many services that groups can provide to candidates, provided that the groups have developed expertise in particular areas. AMPAC does polling for pro-doctor candidates; the National Committee for an Effective Congress provides demographic information to Democrats while the NFIB trains conservative office seekers (Biersack et al. 1994; Biersack, Herrnson, and Wilcox 1999; Rozell and Wilcox 1999). Groups may also have expertise in speaking out on certain issues, for example, the Sierra Club and the environment, the National Rifle Association and gun control, and Planned Parenthood and reproductive health.

The Theoretical Framework

We need a theoretical framework that will help us better understand this range of interest-group activity. This framework should comprise three concepts: the *incentives* that groups offer to potential members, the *resources* that they possess for political action, and the legal and political *context* that shapes their activities.

We also need to rethink our understanding of political parties. Political scientists have long conceived of parties as formal organizations that may be helped sometimes by interest groups, but that are usually in competition with them. In this study, it will become clear that *some* interest groups have close, long-standing ties with one party or another. Indeed, we can speak meaningfully of such groups as parts or members of party networks. The party can then be reconceived as a web of continuing relationships between political actors who share goals and values.

Legal changes such as the varying status of soft money and a more permissive environment for issue advocacy have contributed to the importance of groups in the party networks. The effect of these changes has most likely increased the tendency of the parties to become more ideologically polarized, because the groups that develop long-term ties to the parties are on balance more ideological than the formal party organizations themselves. This said, there have been many other factors leading to ideological polarization—the political realignment of the South, the widespread use of gerrymandering, the emergence of stronger party leadership in Congress, to name a few—and it would be an error to attribute this result solely to the increased influence of these groups.

This combination of context and resources shapes group activity; groups should behave strategically within these limits. If groups care about the partisan control of Congress, they should deploy their resources so as to maximize the number of seats held by their favored party. Groups have different resources that can be used in congressional elections; they should use those that are most electorally effective for them.

Drawing on the previous observations, I suggest that increased partisan competition for control of Congress with only a small number of seriously contested seats raises the significance of each such election. Therefore, partisan groups should seek to become involved beyond the limits on PAC contributions. Nonpartisan groups, which do not care which party controls Congress, and which may be interested primarily in pursuing access, should not become involved to such an extent. Partisan groups should be more likely to engage in independent expenditures and to be involved in activities such as issue advocacy, voter mobilization, and the provision of campaign services.

Groups will seek to deploy their resources most efficiently in this effort: money, membership, and expertise (Bernstein and La Raja 1999; Biersack, Herrnson, and Wilcox 1999; Herrnson 1998; Jacobson and Kernell 1983; Scarrow 1996). They will use those resources that they possess in a manner most likely to achieve their objectives. We can expect labor unions to be especially likely to mobilize their memberships.

Membership incentives should constrain groups' actions and autonomy in politics. Groups based on purposive incentives will attract an ideological membership that may push for a more strident approach to elections (Moe 1980). Groups based on material incentives that are able to prevent exit will have enormous autonomy. Within reasonable limits, they will not have to consider membership views when making political decisions (Hirschman 1971; Wilson 1973). Groups based on material incentives that are unable to prevent exit will be under serious constraints in their political activity. Staff will fear making political decisions that could alienate some of the members (Hirschman 1971).

Decisions about activating nonmembers will be shaped by the nature of a group's membership and issue platform. Groups with a strongly purposive membership may steer their resources toward activating nonmembers to vote since their membership is already politicized. They may also encourage their members to become activists. Groups with a nonpurposive membership will instead focus on activating their members. Groups that stress issues that appeal to a broad segment of voters will use these issues to attract support among the general public. Groups that stress issues that appeal only to their memberships or to well-defined demographic segments will be more likely to "narrowcast" (Moe 1980; Schlozman and Tierney 1986).

TABLE 1
Predictions

Incentive	Likely resource	Likely nature of membership
Material	Membership, money	Heterogeneous, large, apathetic
Purposive (narrow)	Expertise: activating nonmembers, narrowly targeted issue credibility. Membership as activists.	Homogeneous, small, highly motivated
Purposive (wide)	Expertise: widely targeted issue credibility.	Moderately homogeneous, moderate sized, moderately motivated

Notes

1. *Issue advocacy* is speech that does not expressly call for the election or defeat of a candidate. Courts have repeatedly ruled that government regulators cannot control issue advocacy in the same fashion as express advocacy. In *Buckley v. Valeo* (519 F. 2d 821 (D.C. Cir. 1975)), the Court of Appeals for the District of Columbia overturned the definition of independent expenditure in the 1974 amendments to the Federal Election Campaign Act of 1971 as being too broad. The Supreme Court then ruled (424 U.S. 1 (1976)) that such government regulation must be limited to communications that explicitly advocate the election or defeat of a candidate. Since *Buckley*, lower courts have issued conflicting opinions on the meaning of *express advocacy*. Some opinions have stuck to a definition based on the so-called magic words ("vote for," "vote against," "elect," "defeat," etc.), while others have allowed a broader definition that includes nonverbal cues and contextual factors. (The Supreme Court has yet to issue a definitive ruling on this subject.) Rulings supporting the "magic words" definition include *Faucher v. Federal Election Commission* (928 F.2d 468 (1991)), *Federal Election Commission v. Central Long Island Tax Reform Immediately Committee* (616 F.2d 45 (2d Cir. 1980)), *Federal Election Commission v. Christian Action Network* (894 F. Supp. 946 (W.D. Va. 1995)). The principal opinion supporting a broader definition is *Federal Election Commission v. Furgatch* (807 F.2d 857 (9th Cir. 1987)). Recent studies found that few candidate advertisements met the "magic words" standard and that study participants who viewed candidate-specific "issue ads" mostly perceived them to be primarily aimed at persuading them to support or oppose the named candidate. (Brennan Center for Justice 2001; Magleby 2001a) The Bipartisan Campaign Reform Act (BCRA) defined an "electioneering" communication to include advertisements that mention the name or likeness of a candidate, are targeted to that candidate's constituency, and air within sixty days of a primary or ninety days of a general election.

2. One might question whether parties are always "vote-maximizers": were Republicans vote maximizing when they voted to shut down the government in 1995 or to impeach President Bill Clinton in 1998?

3. Besides Christian Action Network (894 F. Supp. 946 (W.D. Va. 1995)), rulings supporting the "magic words" definition include *Faucher v. Federal Election Commission* (928 F.2d 468 (1991)) and *Federal Election Commission v. Central Long Island Tax Reform Immediately Committee* (616 F.2d 45 (2d Cir. 1980)). The principal opinion supporting a broader definition is *Federal Election Commission v. Furgatch* (807 F.2d 857 (9th Cir. 1987)).

4. Federal Election Commission; Campaign Finance Institute.

5. Federal Election Commission; Campaign Finance Institute.

6. "Hard money" is raised according to a federal law that limits the size and sources of contributions. It may be used to expressly advocate the election or defeat of federal candidates. "Soft money" is not federally regulated. It may not be used for express advocacy. There are no limits on the size of contributions, and corporations and labor unions may give "soft money." Congress and the Federal Election Commission established "soft money" through a series of actions in the late 1970s. In 1978, the FEC released an advisory opinion (Advisory Opinion 1978-10) that found that party committees could fund voter registration and other turnout activities, as well as administrative costs, through a combination of state and federal money. Since most states do not forbid corporations and labor unions from contributing to parties, this opened a new avenue for them to engage in otherwise prohibited political activity. In 1979, Congress, responding to criticism that campaign finance regulations overly restricted party activity, amended the Federal Election Campaign Act of 1971. These amendments excluded state and local expenditures for grassroots political activity from the rules governing party contributions to candidates. Such activity included voter registration and the distribution of grassroots campaign material such as slate cards. In 1990, the FEC established formulae for the use of federal and nonfederal (soft) money to fund various permitted party activities. The use of "soft money" increased dramatically in 1996 when both parties used it to fund "issue ads" that praised their candidates without actually urging a vote for or against them. See Corrado (1997).

II
THE GROUPS

2

Studying Groups through Case Studies

A<small>LTHOUGH INTEREST GROUPS HAVE BECOME MAJOR PLAYERS</small> in congressional elections, studying them is not as easy as one might assume. If groups contribute directly to candidates or engage in independent expenditures, they must form a political action committee (PAC) to do it; in turn, the PAC must report its activities to the Federal Election Commission (FEC). Membership groups must also report their spending on internal communications supporting or opposing specific federal candidates. But doubts have been raised about the usefulness of internal communication and independent expenditure data: that they are often misleading or downright meaningless. Internal communications must be reported only if a membership group expressly advocates or opposes the election of a federal candidate and such a message is the "primary" focus of the overall communication. (Labor unions have long dominated internal communications [see Magleby and Beal 2003].)[1] Another major area of interest-group involvement is issue advocacy, which is not reported to the federal government. There have been efforts to track broadcast issue ads, most notably by Kenneth Goldstein for the Brennan Center for Justice and the Wisconsin Advertising Project (see Brennan Center for Justice 2000; see also the Wisconsin Advertising Project at polisci.wisc.edu/tvadvertising/Index.htm). David Magleby (1999, 2001b, 2004) has supervised three collections of case studies on "outside money" in hotly contested House and Senate races. But these works have focused on races as units of analysis, and have not attempted to investigate groups' decisions about political activity.

Another option is to conduct a survey of interest groups. But the response rate would almost certainly be low. A survey would also be of limited utility because relatively few groups engage in these sorts of activities. For example, one study found that nearly all issue ads in 2000 House races during the last five months of the campaign were funded by six groups: Citizens for Better Medicare (primarily funded by the pharmaceutical industry), the AFL-CIO, EMILY's List, the Business Roundtable, and the Coalition for American Workers (Brennan Center for Justice 2000).

Case studies are the best method for examining interest-group activity for a number of reasons. They allow for intense study of a small number of groups; this is appropriate for a small universe of actors. They allow for greater insight into strategy and motivation. They are less dependent on the "hard" statistical data that is so difficult to come by in this area.

These case studies were chosen according to a variety of factors. I sought to create a mixture of groups. Factors considered included size of membership, nature of membership, issue area, and partisanship. While groups were chosen with a bias toward activity, I also made sure to pick some groups that are less active than others. Because of my interest in the role of group membership, I chose only "real" groups, those with a continuing existence and multiple supporters, as opposed to "shell" groups: those whose existence is fleeting and have only one or a very few supporters (see Boatright et al. 2003 for a discussion of "shell" groups such as Citizens for Better Medicare and the United Seniors Association). The case studies are based on a series of interviews with key actors, but also include Federal Election Commission data as well as the work of other researchers.

The groups selected for inclusion in this study are:

The American Federation of Labor–Congress of Industrial Organizations (AFL-CIO)
The National Rifle Association (NRA)
The National Federation of Independent Business (NFIB)
The Sierra Club
The National Abortion and Reproductive Rights Action League (NARAL Pro-Choice America)
The National Right to Life Committee (NRLC)
AARP (formerly known as the American Association of Retired Persons)
The Association of Trial Lawyers of America (ATLA)

Two other groups were asked to participate; they declined. They will be included to a limited extent:

EMILY's List
The American Medical Association (AMA)

TABLE 2
Groups Included in Study

Group	Incentive	Exit	Partisanship	Size	Heterogeneity	Appeal of issue
AARP	M, S	Easy	Nonpartisan	Very large	High	Wide
AFL-CIO	M, S	Difficult	D	Very large	Moderate	Moderate
AMA	M, S, P	Moderate	Mixed	Moderate	Moderate	Narrow
ATLA	M, P	Moderate	D	Small	Low	Narrow
EMILY's List	P	Easy	D	Small	Low	Narrow
NARAL	P	Easy	D	Moderate	Low	Narrow
NFIB	P, M, S	Easy	R	Moderate	Moderate	Moderate
NRA	P	Easy	R	Large	Moderate-low	Narrow
NRLC	P, S	Easy	R	Moderate	Low	Narrow
Sierra Club	P, M, S	Easy	D	Moderate	Moderate-low	Wide

Incentive: M = material, S = solidary, P = purposive. When a group employs more than one incentive, the incentives are listed in rough order of importance.

Exit: Exit was judged as "difficult" if leaving the organization would entail severe material or psychic hardship, for example, loss of a job. Exit was judged as "moderate" if leaving the organization would entail significant hardship, for example, loss of a material benefit helpful to the conduct of one's business. Exit was judged as "easy" if leaving the organization would entail loss of a benefit not central to one's well-being, for example, loss of the ability to go on group-sponsored trips, loss of the satisfaction gained by supporting a political cause.

Partisanship: D = Democratic. R = Republican. The AMA's partisanship was judged as "mixed." AARP was judged as "nonpartisan" since it does not endorse candidates.

Size: Very large = over 10 million members. Large = 1–10 million. Moderate = 100,000–1 million. Small = fewer than 100,000.

Heterogeneity: Groups were judged to have "high" heterogeneity if their members had little in common with one another except for a demographic coincidence, for example, AARP's members are all over fifty, but are otherwise diverse. Groups were listed as having "moderate" heterogeneity if members had certain material or purposive interests in common—the occupational interests of physicians or small-business owners—but also significant differences—the division of physicians into specialties, the wide variety of businesses owned by NFIB members. The NRA and Sierra Club were listed as "moderate-low" because while their members are bound together by strong purposive incentives, they are also organizations with histories of significant internal strife. Groups with few obvious internal divisions were listed as "low."

Appeal of issue: A group's issue appeal was listed as "wide" if it was concerned primarily with issues that interest the general public or a large fraction thereof, for example, AARP and the senior issues, the Sierra Club and the environment. Issue appeal was listed as "narrow" if the group was concerned primarily with issues that interest its members or a well-defined demographic segment of the electorate, for example, ATLA and civil justice, the NRLC and abortion. It is important to note, however, that none of these groups are primarily concerned with the sort of minutiae and technical matters that often dominate the agendas of corporations and trade associations.

The rest of this part is devoted to background essays on each group that was selected: its formation, its organizational maintenance, and its political activity.

Notes

1. For example, in 2004, the AFL-CIO led all groups in making internal communications by spending $3,043,331. Seven groups spent more than half a million dollars on internal communications. One was the National Association of Realtors. The other six were labor unions: the AFL-CIO; the National Education Association; the American Federation of State, County and Municipal Employees; the Service Employees International Union; the American Federation of Teachers; and the International Association of Firefighters. Data for the three previous election cycles show similar patterns, with unions absolutely dominating internal communications. The only nonunion organizations that regularly spent large sums on internal communications were the National Association of Realtors, the National Rifle Association, and the National Federation of Independent Business (Center for Responsive Politics).

3

Material Giants: The AFL-CIO and AARP

THE AFL-CIO AND THE AARP HAVE MUCH IN COMMON: Both rely on material incentives, both have huge memberships, both have formidable reputations for lobbying. But they behave in strikingly different ways in elections: the AFL-CIO and its member unions are among the most active groups, while the AARP refuses to endorse candidates or make contributions. Organized labor has been central to the Democratic coalition since the New Deal, while the AARP has shied away from partisan politics. "Union shop" contracts free organized labor from concern that its members will bolt due to political decisions; the AARP can benefit from no such assurance. The AARP has a remarkably heterogeneous membership that includes men and women, whites and blacks, rich and poor, Glenn Miller fans and Led Zeppelin fans; the organization lacks much ability to shape its members' identities. Unions face their own problems of heterogeneity, but have a greater capacity to form bonds among their members, who work together and know one another. Many unions were built by leftists who sought to change American society and who understood the importance of the political process. The AARP, by contrast, entered politics relatively late in its history, and political activity has often taken a backseat to providing member services.

The American Federation of Labor–
Congress of Industrial Organizations (AFL-CIO)

With 13 million members, the AFL-CIO is the primary labor federation in the United States. While union membership has fallen dramatically since the

1950s, from about one-third of the workforce to only about 13 percent, the AFL-CIO saw its overall membership remain relatively constant, until the formation of the Change To Win coalition in 2006. Unions such as the Teamsters, the United Automobile Workers (UAW), and the United Mine Workers (UMW) that had either left the federation or had been expelled rejoined the AFL-CIO in the 1980s. This greater unity allowed the AFL-CIO to keep its total membership high.

As a federated organization, the AFL-CIO has some special characteristics. The president of the AFL-CIO is elected by representatives of the affiliates, so he must satisfy them if he is to remain in office. Dissatisfied affiliates also have the option of withholding their political contributions or leaving the federation altogether. The AFL-CIO's federated structure also makes it vulnerable to internal fractures. Indeed, the AFL-CIO has seen a series of divisions, between unions that had belonged to the AFL and those that had belonged to the CIO, between those that approved of George Meany's leadership and those that disapproved, and between private-sector and public-sector unions. Finally, the federated structure limits the power of the federation president: while he plays a leading role in the AFL-CIO's political activity, he is not the only relevant actor, and he has little control of the affiliates' economic resources. Workers join and employers negotiate with individual affiliates and their locals, not the AFL-CIO.

A Movement in Transition

The union movement has seen dramatic changes over the past half century. Such stalwarts as the UAW, the United Steelworkers, and the International Association of Machinists (IAM) have seen their memberships cut by half from their peak totals in the 1960s and 1970s. Unions based in the public and service sectors, such as the American Federation of State, County and Municipal Employees (AFSCME) and the Service Employees International Union (SEIU), now dominate the politics of the AFL-CIO. Not surprisingly, the demographics of the union movement have changed significantly. Union members are much more likely to be women, minorities, public-sector workers, or college graduates than they were in the 1950s or 1960s. The rate of unionization differs by sex, but by less than it once did: in 2002, 14.7 percent of male workers belonged to unions; 11.6 percent of female workers did. In the 1960s, about one in five unionists were women; by 2002, 42 percent were. African Americans are more likely to belong to unions (16.9 percent) than whites (12.8 percent) or Hispanics (10.5 percent).

One-quarter of New York State workers belong to unions, the highest figure in the nation; just over 3 percent of North Carolinians do, the lowest in the nation. Over half of union members live in just six states, reflecting a geographic concentration that has long limited labor's political effectiveness, especially in the Senate.[1] In 1964, 8 percent of union members worked in the public sector; by 1996, 42 percent did. (Only 16 percent of all U.S. workers are employed by the government.) Similarly, the percentage of public-sector workers who belonged to unions rose from 15 percent in 1964 to 37.5 percent in 2002. In the 1950s, hardly any union members were college graduates; by the 1990s, 25 percent were (Asher et al. 2001; Bureau of Labor Statistics 2003). Indeed, with the exception of the overrepresentation of public-sector workers and African Americans, union members essentially "look like America," in Bill Clinton's phrase.

These changes may have had differing impacts on the labor movement's political effectiveness. The college-educated are more likely to vote and otherwise participate in politics; the increase in the percentage of unionists who are college graduates may give unions more political clout. Similarly, government employees have a more obvious stake in elections than their private-sector counterparts. African Americans and working women both lean more toward the Democratic Party than average; this may make it easier for union leaders to mobilize their members to vote for Democrats. On the other hand, union members are now much more likely to live in the suburbs and to identify as middle class than they were in the 1950s. They are also more likely to identify as Independents, though not as Republicans (Asher et al. 2001).

A Movement Divided

To make some generalizations, there are essentially two segments of the labor movement. One is composed of public-sector and service unions (such as SEIU, AFSCME, American Federation of Teachers [AFT], and the National Education Association [NEA]). These unions are growing or at least maintaining their strength. Their members are more likely to be women or minorities, and are probably more likely to be Democrats. The leaders of these unions are almost unanimously Democrat and liberal; they are more likely to mobilize their workers as political activists. The other segment is composed of craft and industrial unions. They have suffered catastrophic losses of membership. Their members are more likely to be white men, often culturally conservative, and are perhaps less loyal to the Democratic Party than their predecessors were in the 1950s and 1960s. (Although they are still more likely to vote Democrat than white men who do not belong to unions. See Sousa 1993.) The leaders of these unions follow a variety of political strategies, although almost all strongly favor the Democratic Party. These strategies range from the liberal activism of the UAW and the IAM to the low-key pragmatism of some craft unions.

Organizing for Power

Unions have particular organizational characteristics that have important political implications. Olson (1965) and Wilson (1973) both note that unions' power depends upon their ability to coerce workers into joining them by making membership a condition of employment (the "union shop"). This allows them to overcome the "free rider" problem, in which people see no reason to join a group if they can obtain its benefits for free. The passage of the National Labor Relations Act (also known as the Wagner Act) in 1935 made it possible for unions to greatly increase their membership during the following decade by providing for the union shop, collective-bargaining procedures, representation elections, and a ban on company unions.

Unions' ability to use coercion not only allows them to build large memberships; it means that union leaders can operate with much greater freedom than their counterparts in other groups since they need not worry about members' leaving. But it also poses a challenge: union members often hold different (usually more conservative) opinions than their generally liberal leaders. This holds true even in some highly politicized unions such as the United Automobile Workers and the International Association of Machinists (Wilson 1973; Mundo 1992). Because of coercion, unions have larger memberships than they might have otherwise; also because of coercion, their leaders must invest substantial resources in mobilizing their members for political activity. They cannot simply assume that their members will vote according to their leaders' preferences.

Unions are also highly distinctive in their political activity. They have long sought to turn out their members to vote for their preferred candidates (almost always Democrats), and they encourage them to contact fellow workers by phone, at home and at the workplace. Union PACs favor Democrats overwhelmingly, concentrate their giving in close races, and often help nonincumbents. This differs from the behavior of corporate PACs, which either favor Republicans or incumbents of both parties, and prefer to bet on sure winners as a way of securing access (Rozell and Wilcox 1999; Herrnson 1998; Sabato 1984; Eismeier and Pollock 1988; Sorauf 1992). Most endorsement decisions begin with state and local labor councils, but are ultimately approved by the Committee on Political Education, the AFL-CIO's political action committee. COPE acts as a "lead PAC" for other labor unions; they usually follow its course. COPE is also able to exploit its ties to other liberal groups in order to help favored candidates (Wilcox 1994). The AFL-CIO itself is led by a president who is elected every two years by a convention of delegates from affiliate unions.

A Brief History of the AFL-CIO

The American Federation of Labor was founded in 1885. While the AFL did occasionally endorse candidates, it did not make political activity one of its principal missions. Its membership was dominated by skilled workers; its unions often excluded blacks and opposed immigration (Francia 2000; Taft 1964). In the 1930s, a new "industrial unionism" movement challenged the AFL's conservatism. Led by the United Mine Workers, these unions formed the Committee for Industrial Organization. Unlike the AFL "craft" unions, these organizations sought to organize entire industries, including unskilled workers, and adopted more openly leftist ideologies, ranging from support for the New Deal to sympathy with Communism. They formed Labor's Nonpartisan League to support Franklin Roosevelt's reelection in 1936. The AFL expelled the members of the CIO in 1938; these expelled members subsequently formed the Congress of Industrial Organizations. CIO unions organized the automobile and steel industries during the following years, raising the percentage of the workforce that belonged to unions from 13 percent in 1935 to 35 percent in 1945 (existing AFL unions such as the Teamsters also contributed to this growth).

The CIO unions were more politicized than their AFL counterparts for several reasons. Organizers at large employers such as General Motors could not count on the sort of solidary incentives that help support craft unions. Instead, UAW organizers tended to be motivated by purposive incentives, usually political radicalism, whether Communist or non-Communist. Since the CIO was organizing large corporations with facilities around the nation, union leaders had to be concerned about federal politics. Since their organizing efforts followed the passage of the Wagner Act, CIO leaders were also acutely aware of the importance of having friends in the White House and on Capitol Hill (Wilson 1973).

After the Smith-Connally Act (1943) banned direct union contributions to candidates, the CIO formed the CIO-PAC to elect Roosevelt and other prolabor politicians in 1944. The AFL, which was becoming more politicized and liberal, formed the Labor League for Political Education in 1948. A year before, the Taft-Hartley Act allowed states to ban the "union shop"—the ability of unions to require workers to enroll as a condition of employment. Known as "right-to-work" laws, these rules helped put an end to the growth of labor unions.

The Meany Era

The AFL and CIO merged in 1955. George Meany, president of the AFL, became president of the new AFL-CIO. Despite his craft union background,

Meany held liberal views akin to those of the CIO leadership. Through his alliances with CIO leaders, Meany was eventually able to win secure control of the AFL-CIO's executive committee. His autocratic manner, however, often grated on some other labor leaders, especially Walter Reuther of the United Automobile Workers (which left the federation in 1968, rejoining in 1981 [Dark 1998]). As part of the merger, the AFL-CIO created the Committee on Political Education (COPE), a PAC that would make contributions to candidates and coordinate union political activity.

Over the past forty years, the AFL-CIO has seen a progression from strong centralized leadership to internal conflict to weak leadership and finally back to strong centralized leadership. Dark (1998) argues that labor performs best under conditions of "centralized pluralism," when a small number of actors can develop long-term relationships of trust and when these actors can deliver on their promises to one another. The AFL-CIO arguably reached a peak of political power during the mid-1960s, when Meany enjoyed a close relationship with President Lyndon Johnson. Meany provided Johnson with critical support for the passage of Medicare, Medicaid, and civil rights legislation. But Meany was unable to secure passage of labor law reform that would make it easier to organize workers. Union membership had peaked during the postwar era at about one-third of the workforce, but was beginning to fall, especially as economic growth shifted to right-to-work states in the South and West.

Leadership Under Fire

The 1970s were a difficult time for the AFL-CIO. Meany disliked the "New Politics" activists who rose from the civil rights and antiwar movements, and who demanded procedural changes that disturbed him. They achieved greater openness in political decision making through the McGovern-Fraser Commission's drastic remodeling of the presidential nomination process in 1971 and a series of congressional reforms during the mid-1970s that reined in the power of committee chairmen. While many of these changes had the effect of bringing greater power to prounion liberals, they offended Meany's belief in quiet, behind-the-scenes decision making. They also threatened Meany's traditional role as a power broker and gave greater opportunities for his left-liberal rivals to exert influence (Dark 1998).

Meany's battle with the Left reached a peak in 1972, when he refused to endorse Senator George McGovern (D-SD), the antiwar Democratic presidential nominee. Four years before, Meany had conducted a highly effective labor campaign in support of then vice president Hubert Humphrey, who nearly defeated Richard Nixon in the presidential race. But in 1972, Meany failed to grasp the changes the McGovern-Fraser Commission had wrought; the AFL-

CIO ran slates of unpledged delegates in several primaries. Few voters backed the slates, preferring to support delegates pledged to particular candidates. Accustomed to a dominant role in Democratic back rooms, Meany found himself shut out. Under his direction, the AFL-CIO Executive Committee voted to remain neutral in the 1972 presidential election (Dark 1998).

Meany's shunning of McGovern angered more liberal labor leaders, especially Jerry Wurf of the American Federation of State, County and Municipal Employees (AFSCME). In the wake of new guarantees for collective bargaining by government employees, the 1960s saw an explosion in the number and activism of public-sector unionists. Between 1968 and 1974, the percentage of public-sector workers who were unionized roughly doubled; growth then leveled off as state and local governments retrenched (Lewin 1986). The new public-employee unions had significantly more nonwhite and female members than many of their private-sector counterparts. They did not share Meany's suspicion of the antiwar movement, the women's movement, and other "New Politics" elements (Dark 1998). Public-employee unions, as well as the more leftist industrial unions such as the UAW and the International Association of Machinists, supported the reforms of the McGovern-Fraser Commission. They also conducted their own campaigns to support McGovern after he was nominated.

Split along ideological lines, the AFL-CIO's political clout diminished. Jimmy Carter campaigned for president as an anti-Washington populist and owed little to the AFL-CIO. Conflict over Carter's attempts to control inflation only alienated labor further and many unions backed Edward Kennedy for president in 1980. Kennedy's inability to defeat Carter in the Democratic primaries, and the election of a conservative Republican president, Ronald Reagan, seemed to confirm reports of labor's political decline (Dark 1998).

Responding to Reagan

Twice over the next two decades, organized labor was forced to respond to political body blows from the Right. Ronald Reagan and the two presidents Bush proved to be much more hostile to organized labor than their Republican predecessors Dwight Eisenhower and Richard Nixon. In response, the AFL-CIO strengthened its ties to the Democratic congressional leadership and to other liberal groups, including those with a "New Politics" heritage. Organized labor also successfully adapted to the McGovern-Fraser reforms, and once again became a key player in the picking of Democratic presidential nominees. (See chapter 8 for a more complete discussion of this period.) In 1992, Bill Clinton was elected president, with strong support from organized labor.

But the AFL-CIO was not able to turn around the declining rate of membership in labor unions, especially the industrial unions that were devastated by the recession of 1981–1982. AFL-CIO president Lane Kirkland helped heal ideological wounds and bring back wayward affiliates (the UAW, UMW, and Teamsters all rejoined the federation during his time in office). But he did not provide the kind of strong leadership that many thought necessary to revive labor's fortunes (Dark 1998).

The AFL-CIO generally enjoyed a good relationship with the Clinton administration, except on the issue of foreign trade. But organized labor was hit hard by the results of the 1994 congressional elections. Not only did Republicans take control of Congress for the first time in forty years, but the new congressional leadership was adamantly antiunion (Dark 1998; Gerber 1999; Asher et al. 2001). Most Republicans elected in 1994 opposed organized labor on virtually all issues; the average COPE rating for congressional Republicans, which had hovered around 30 percent in the 1980s, fell below 15 percent during the 104th Congress and did not significantly increase during the following years. Since many newly elected Republicans replaced moderate Democrats from the South and West, the parties experienced the same polarization on labor issues as they did on other matters (Francia 2005).

Fighting Back After '94

It was against this background that Kirkland resigned in October 1995; he was facing a campaign for his removal led by the Service Employees International Union (SEIU) and AFSCME. Kirkland was replaced by John Sweeney, president of SEIU. Sweeney had close relationships with other liberal activists and his union was one of the few to have gained members in recent years. Sweeney soon announced the launching of a $35 million campaign to elect a Democratic Congress that included $25 million in "issue ads" as well as $10 million on grassroots organization (Dark 1998). (Outside estimates of labor's total spending put the figure much higher.) Labor's grassroots activity included voter registration, voter education, get-out-the-vote drives and training for local activists (Gerber 1999). Labor's campaign contributed to the defeat of several Republicans, but it failed to deliver control to the Democrats.

There were several postmortems on the AFL-CIO's 1996 effort. Most suggested that large expenditures on broadcast advertising were no substitute for strong, well-funded candidates (Business Industry Political Action Committee 1997, 1998; Gerber 1999). G. C. Jacobson (1999), however, finds that the AFL-CIO's campaign was responsible for defeating seven of the twelve Republican freshmen who lost in 1998. The AFL-CIO conducted studies that reportedly showed that personal contact was the most effective way to persuade members to back union-endorsed candidates (Edsall 2000 [AQ: This source is not on ref list.]).

Organized labor had another reason for changing its strategy. After the 1996 election, many Republicans vowed revenge for the AFL-CIO's attacks on them. While their efforts to limit union power on the federal level failed, Republicans succeeded in placing on the California ballot Proposition 226, a referendum on "paycheck protection." This would require labor leaders to get the consent of their members in order to deduct money from members' paychecks for political purposes. While this proposition failed (in large part, thanks to a huge turnout by union members), labor strategists realized that they needed to find ways to achieve political victory without unduly alienating potential Republican allies. Their success in mobilizing union members in California against Proposition 226 also convinced them that they had a resource their opponents generally lacked: an apparatus capable of turning out thousands of supportive voters (Dark 1999).

In the 1997–1998 cycle, organized labor reallocated its resources away from broadcast advertisements to member mobilization. This appears to have paid handsome dividends for Democratic candidates; unions were credited with reelecting Senators Harry Reid (D-NV) and Russell Feingold (D-WI) and with creating a Democratic sweep in California that rivaled that of 1958 (Dark 1999; Magleby 1999). Lefkowitz (1999) claims that organized labor and other liberal groups were responsible for the Democrats' five-seat gain in the House, the first such victory for a president's party in a midterm election.

Fighting the "Ground War"

Since 1996, organized labor has shifted to a strategy of mobilizing its members to vote, although it has not entirely abandoned broadcast advertising. (See chapter 5 for a much more extensive treatment of this topic.) This strategy appears to have succeeded; since 1998, exit polls have indicated that union members compose a higher percentage of the electorate than in prior elections (Abramson, Aldrich, and Rohde 1999; Dreazen 2000; Francia 2000; Monson 2004). The AFL-CIO spent $46 million for its 1999–2000 political activities, targeting seventy-one congressional districts for special attention (Lawrence 2000; Swoboda 1999). While the AFL-CIO concentrated on the "ground war," it also conducted an "air war," reportedly spending $9.5 million on TV ads after Super Tuesday (Annenberg Public Policy Center 2001). Unions did not increase their PAC contributions: between 1997–1998 and 2001–2002, overall labor PAC giving remained stable at around $50 million (Boatright et al. 2003).

The AFL-CIO's political activities were widely credited with Al Gore's surprisingly wide victories in such strong union states as Michigan, Pennsylvania, and Washington State, as well as the Democrats' winning of previously Republican Senate seats in Delaware, Missouri, Michigan, Missouri, and Washington State.

Unions continued to be politically active in 2002. One source estimated the AFL-CIO's political spending at $33 million (Biersack and Viray 2005). The AFL-CIO spent at least $3.6 million on TV advertising ("One Billion Dollars Spent" 2002). Steve Rosenthal, political director of the AFL-CIO, estimated that there were 225,000 union members involved in turning out the vote (Kiely 2002). But while organized labor continued to wage an effective "ground war"—an AFL-CIO survey found that 93 percent of labor households received political information from a union source—the Republican Party managed to catch up in 2002 through "The 72-Hour Project." Union turnout was similar to that found in 1998 (Monson 2004). But despite an extensive "ground war," the AFL-CIO was unable to rescue such union stalwarts as Senator Jean Carnahan (D-MO) and Rep. Jim Maloney (D-CT) from their own weaknesses. Republicans also made gains in areas where unions are weak, such as Georgia, Mississippi, and other southern states.

In 2004, the AFL-CIO continued to focus on mobilizing its members to vote, primarily for the presidential election. (There were few closely contested House races, and most of the "hot" Senate contests were in right-to-work states.) During the Democratic nomination campaign, the AFL-CIO failed to unite behind one candidate, as it did in 1984 and 2000. AFSCME and the SEIU put aside their rivalry to back former Vermont governor Howard Dean, while the IAM, the Teamsters, and the Steelworkers ardently supported Rep. Richard Gephardt (D-MO) (A. C. Smith 2004a; Walsh 2003; Farhi 2003). Once Kerry became the certain nominee, the AFL-CIO formally endorsed him (Harris and VandeHei 2004). The divisions during the nomination battle hurt the AFL-CIO's reputation for effectiveness. It also undermined the influence of Gerald McEntee, leader of AFSCME and chairman of the AFL-CIO's political committee; McEntee vacillated for months, flirting with Kerry and retired Gen. Wesley Clark, then endorsing Dean, whom he abandoned after Dean performed poorly in early contests (Greenhouse 2004b).

The AFL-CIO claimed to have spent $45 million in sixteen states on phone banks, worksite leafleting, and door-to-door solicitation. The SEIU spent $65 million on its own political operation, including $40 million to cover the salaries and relocation costs of more than 2,000 members who took time off from their jobs to volunteer on the elections (Williams 2004). Despite their divisions during the nomination season, labor leaders united in support of

Kerry for president, bonded by a belief that the Bush administration was relentlessly hostile to the interests of workers. One estimate claimed that unions spent $100 million in the 2004 elections. The AFL-CIO focused on many of the same states it covered in 2000: Pennsylvania, Ohio, Michigan, Wisconsin, Missouri, and West Virginia.

Survival in a Hostile Environment

In light of the labor movement's inablity to reverse its decline in membership, and its having lost some high-profile strikes, dissatisfaction has grown with Sweeney's leadership in recent years. Andrew Stern of the SEIU and James Hoffa of the Teamsters have emerged as the primary spokesmen for this discontent. (Stern actually had served as the SEIU's recruitment chief when Sweeney led that union.) Stern and Sweeney share a common left-liberal political orientation, but Stern, a onetime Ivy League student radical, prefers confrontation while Sweeney has a more consensual, discreet style of leadership (Bernstein 2004). Bruce Raynor, president of the textile workers union UNITE (which has now merged with the Hotel and Restaurant Workers, or HERE), explained that Sweeney has "done an outstanding job in the political arena. But in the area of organizing, it's clearly been disappointing" (Greenhouse 2003c).

Now challenging Sweeney as the nation's most visible labor leader, Stern leads a collection of union leaders known as the New Unity Partnership, which also includes the presidents of UNITE-HERE, the Carpenters, and the Laborers. The partnership shared Stern's belief that the AFL-CIO needs stronger centralized leadership, that many smaller unions need to merge, and that affiliates must reemphasize organizing new members. To do so, the AFL-CIO should rebate dues to affiliates. (The SEIU is one of the very few unions that has gained members in recent years, rising to a new high of 1.8 million workers [Birnbaum and Edsall 2004; Edsall 2004]). In July 2005, both SEIU and the teamsters left the AFL-CIO. Along with several other unions (most notably UNITE-HERE and the United Food and Commercial Workers), they founded the Change to Win Federation in September. Despite the organizational split, AFL-CIO and Change to Win affiliates continue to cooperate in political activity.

In recent years, the AFL-CIO appears to have become a more effective actor in elections. This is due primarily to its increasing skill at deploying its most effective resource, its ability to mobilize its members to vote and volunteer. In turn, this shift results from changes in the union's external environment and its internal structure. The Republican takeover in 1994 provided a threat to

which the AFL-CIO had to respond. It also eliminated organized labor's traditional "inside strategy" of cultivating relationships with congressional leaders. The triumph of the liberal-activist wing of the labor movement has largely
eliminated the ideological divisions that plagued the AFL-CIO in the 1970s. It
has also brought a leadership to power that is more attuned to electoral politics and is more committed to membership mobilization. The reentry of the
UAW, UMW, and Teamsters into the AFL-CIO has strengthened the role of the
AFL-CIO as the leading voice for unions.

Yet the AFL-CIO continues to face very serious challenges. Despite a few
prominent organizing victories, the decades-long decline in union density
shows no sign of ending. Indeed, the fastest-growing industries in recent
years, such as information technology, have also been the most resistant to
unionization. If organized labor remains a formidable force within the Democratic Party, it wields little influence with Republicans, except in the Northeast and a few western states.

Union membership remains highly concentrated in a few large industrial
states, putting the AFL-CIO at a disadvantage in the Senate and, perhaps, in
the Electoral College. As the nation's population continues to shift south and
west, unions may find it difficult to maintain their influence. Should these
partisan and geographic trends continue to frustrate the AFL-CIO's attempts
to wield political power, the labor movement may become divided and demoralized. Some craft and industrial unions may seek to reach accommoda-
tions with Republicans, though some attempts have already been frustrated by
the GOP's basic conservatism. The hard fact is that there is little most unions
can do to win the support of a Sun Belt Republican with a safe seat. They cannot threaten his chances at reelection, they cannot endanger his career in the
House, and they cannot appeal to shared values.

AARP

The AARP (formerly the American Association of Retired Persons), whose
membership is open to all Americans over age fifty, is the principal organization representing senior citizens in the United States. In fact, with 36 million
members, the AARP is the second-largest membership organization in the
United States, after the Roman Catholic Church. Members pay dues of $12 a
year; the AARP receives only 29 percent of its budget. Most of the remainder
of its budget comes from sales of advertising space in its publications and roy-
alties from companies that market their products to AARP members; income
from these sources obviously depends on the AARP's maintaining a large
membership (Vaida 2004). Its annual budget of $636 million is more than

three times that of the National Rifle Association, although only 10 percent goes to lobbying (Holmes 2001; Kondracke 2001).

But the AARP has encountered difficulties in recent years. During the late 1970s and 1980s, the seniors' organization saw its membership grow at 20 percent a year. But more recently, its annual growth has slowed to 1 percent. The AARP has also encountered legal trouble with the Internal Revenue Service and the U.S. Postal Service (Holmes 2001). In 2001, it lost its long-standing rank as Washington's most effective lobby in *Fortune*'s annual survey of insiders. AARP's staunch nonpartisanship and membership diversity were cited as hurting its effectiveness (Birnbaum 2001). A House Democratic staff member told the *New York Times*, "I've almost stopped thinking of them as a lobby. They have all kinds of valuable member services and do really good research work. But in terms of being a tough lobby, they're not what they used to be" (Holmes 2001).

A Cautious Giant

Indeed, despite the AARP's enormous size and clout, it has been surprisingly cautious about its political involvement. It does not operate a PAC. It does not endorse candidates. It does not adopt formal positions on legislation, only "principles." The AARP does have a program, AARP-VOTE, which seeks to educate voters and organize volunteers. AARP-VOTE distributes nonpartisan voter guides (about 1 million in presidential years) that list candidates' positions on such issues as Social Security and long-term care as well as the organization's "principles." It also conducts candidate forums, registers older Americans to vote, and lobbies legislators on senior issues. The AARP is a 501 (R) 4 tax-exempt social welfare organization. It may not engage in partisan activities, but it may speak out on issues. Its voter guides must treat all candidates equally.[2]

The AARP's reliance on material incentives (including publications, investment advice, and travel and insurance discounts) has allowed the organization to develop an unusually large membership, which has in turn given it a huge budget. But those material incentives, combined with AARP's inability to prevent exit, also constrain the organization's staff. A wide variety of older Americans find AARP's benefits to be attractive, but this very diversity keeps AARP from following a more assertive course that might increase its political effectiveness. More than once, AARP's staff have had the impact of membership diversity brought to their attention in an unsubtle fashion.

The AARP had maintained its nonpartisan stance despite holding many positions that are much closer to the Democrats than to the Republicans. The AARP supported a Medicare benefit for prescription drugs, a cornerstone of

Al Gore's presidential campaign (Serafini 2000a). In February 2001, the AARP board adopted its principles for the year; these included "balanced" use of the federal budget surplus, with enough money available for a prescription drug benefit and new education spending. It opposed eliminating the inheritance tax, although it supported reducing it. It supported other "targeted" tax cuts, including a credit for caregivers and an expanded IRA. It opposed any privatization of Social Security, although it supported a new voluntary savings plan to Social Security. All of these principles stood in opposition to the Bush administration's agenda of across-the-board tax cuts, partial privatization of Social Security, elimination of the inheritance tax, and controlling the cost of Medicare (Kondracke 2001).

Problems of Mobilizing Seniors

Many serious challenges face one who seeks to create an organization of older Americans. The first attempt to do so, the Townsend movement of the 1930s, achieved great visibility and power for a time, but eventually collapsed due to membership turnover, partial success (the creation of Social Security), an overreliance on purposive incentives, and an inability to replace a charismatic leader (Dr. Francis Townsend). It was not until the late 1950s and early 1960s that there were successful attempts to organize the elderly: the AARP and the National Council of Senior Citizens (NCSC). Pratt (1983) argues that a 1950 expansion of Social Security to cover more white-collar workers helped spur the formation of seniors' organizations. It created a new clientele that was easier to organize. It also led to wider acceptance of sixty-five as the retirement age. The percentage of men over sixty-five who were not in the workforce soared during the 1950s.

While membership turnover plagues most organizations, it poses particular problems for seniors' groups. Every year, many of their members will die. Most members will probably die within fifteen or twenty years of joining. Others will drop out due to poor health or widowhood.[3] After peaking when a person is between the ages of sixty-five and seventy-five, political activity declines after age seventy-five precisely because so many people become impaired or widowed. The over-eighty-five population is particularly hard to organize, due to their short life expectancy, poor health, low income, social isolation, widowhood, and skewed sex ratio (women outnumber men over eighty-five by about two to one). In order to keep functioning, senior groups must constantly add new members. These new members will likely belong to another generation, with different values and experiences (Day 1990; Peterson and Somit 1994).

Senior groups also confront the special nature of elder identity. Many older Americans do not think of themselves as being "old"; those who do often have a weak attachment to their agedness (Pratt 1983). Other identities often take precedence. People tend to form their identities in adolescence and young adulthood, decades before they become eligible to join the AARP. To put it another way, no one grows up as an old person. People are socialized as men, veterans, Republicans, Mormons, or pharmacists long before they are socialized as senior citizens. This means that senior groups can call upon a much weaker sense of identity than many other organizations. In addition, older Americans who identify strongly as "old" tend to be sicker, poorer, and more female than average—and are therefore less likely to politically participate (Peterson and Somit 1994).[4]

Senior organizations must also confront the challenge of heterogeneity. Celebrating one's sixty-fifty (or fifty-fifth or fiftieth) birthday does not magically make a person's other identities magically disappear (Peterson and Somit 1994; MacManus 1996). Surveys show that seniors do not differ strongly from other Americans on most issues; there is more division within the senior population than between it and younger Americans (Day 1990; MacManus 1996). Broadly speaking, the senior population is politically heterogeneous; it exhibits the same differences along party, class, and racial lines as other generations.[5]

The elderly are also split along lines of age. Experts on aging divide seniors into three categories: the "young old" (65–75), the "old old" (75–85), and the "oldest old" (85-plus). They also refer to the "near old" (55–65), who have many of the same concerns as the 65-plus population. To this, we may add the "not old yet" (50–55), who are eligible to join the AARP even though many have children in college or high school. The "young old" are the most likely to participate in politics; in fact, they are probably the most participatory age group in the entire population. The "oldest old" are least likely to participate of all seniors: they are the poorest, the sickest, most widowed, and most female (Day 1990; Peterson and Somit 1994).

Gray Power?

But there are also many advantages to organizing seniors. Today's seniors are wealthier, healthier, and better educated than their predecessors (Day 1990). Seniors now have a lower poverty rate than the nonaged population, although many live near poverty (Pratt 1993). Senior identity has increased thanks to the expansion in retirement, the growth of adults-only retirement communities, the growth in services for the aged, and the decline of multi-generational households. All of these trends may increase in coming decades, as baby boomers retire, given their sheer numbers, their strong generational identity, and their good fortune of spending their peak earning years during the prosperous 1980s and 1990s.

While some early studies of political behavior found that political partici-pation decreased after age sixty-five, this trend vanished once researchers ac-counted for the influence of seniors' poorer health and education (Nie and Verba 1972; Rosenstone and Wolfinger 1980). If anything, senior citizens par-ticipate more than their younger counterparts. They certainly vote at the high-est rate of any age group, although the "young old" vote more than the "old old" or the "oldest old" (Peterson and Somit 1994; MacManus 1996; A. L. Campbell 2003).

Getting the Goods

The AARP bestows a wide variety of material benefits on its members. These include *AARP Magazine,* which is now the nation's most popular mag-azine; discounts on prescription drugs; travel programs and discounts; lower-cost auto, life, and homeowners' insurance; and a lower-cost credit card. These fit Mancur Olson's definition of selective benefits in that they can be denied to nonmembers. This has allowed the AARP to build its huge membership. It also confers stability on the organization, since overall demand for these ben-efits is not likely to change drastically (Day 1990). Light (1985) cites an AARP survey that found the most popular benefits were the group's publications, its insurance and drug discounts, and its travel clubs.

But the AARP's material benefits are ones that people can, if they wish, do without. It is much easier for one to give up a discounted auto insurance pol-icy if one dislikes the AARP's policy views than it is to quit one's job if one dis-likes a union's policy views. This places the AARP at special risk of losing its members if it embarks on a controversial course. This may account for its cau-tion. The AARP also confers solidary benefits upon its members through its network of over 3,000 state and local chapters. The AARP initially built from the top down, with members joining the national organization to obtain ma-terial benefits. But it has steadily nurtured its grass roots. Still, only about 10 percent of its members belong to an AARP chapter.

The AARP does not appear to rely much on purposive incentives. Light (1985) cites an AARP survey that showed only 17 percent of members joined the organization because of its reputation for defending the interests of the elderly. This is an asset in some ways: Moe (1980) finds that a reliance solely on purposive incentives can lead to instability. But it also constrains AARP. Staff cannot assume that their members hold homogeneous preferences on all issues that face older Americans.

A Brief History of the AARP

The AARP was founded in 1958 in California by Ethel Percy Andrus, president and founder of the National Retired Teachers Association. The NRTA marketed life insurance to its members, later spinning off this operation as Colonial Penn Insurance. At the time, the elderly had a very difficult time buying life insurance. The popularity of the NRTA's program led many nonmembers to express interest; Andrus created the AARP to include these people. While Andrus was concerned about the status and self-esteem of older Americans, the AARP has always relied heavily on material incentives (Pratt 1983; Pratt 1993).

In its early days, the AARP had a reputation for being a relatively conservative organization with a membership skewed toward the affluent. Its first Washington lobbyist was a Republican with strong ties to then House minority leader Gerald Ford. It avoided social-welfare issues, such as Social Security and Medicare. Instead, the AARP's primary interest was in ending mandatory retirement. Many of its members were well-educated professionals who enjoyed their work and resented being forced to quit at sixty-five. But the AARP's fight against mandatory retirement went nowhere in the 1960s; business groups disliked federal regulation in general, while unions were more concerned with gaining earlier retirement for their members, many of whom worked at unpleasant jobs and looked forward to getting a pension as soon as possible (Day 1990; Pratt 1983, 1993).

Andrus died in 1967. Thanks to its insurance and mail-order pharmaceutical programs, the AARP had grown to 1 million members. But its time of greatest change was still ahead of it. Cyril Brickfield, an old Washington hand, replaced Andrus as president; the AARP soon moved its national headquarters to Washington from Long Beach, California. Under Brickfield's leadership, the AARP experienced the most rapid growth in its history, expanding to 28 million members by 1987, when he retired. Brickfield expanded its government-relations staff from two employees in 1969 to between 150 and 160 in 1986 (Holmes 2001; Pratt 1993).

The AARP became more of a legislative power in the 1970s and 1980s. After it cut its ties to Colonial Penn in the late 1970s, the AARP lost its conservative reputation and became known as a "moderate-to-liberal" group. As its membership expanded, it became more diverse, with blue-collar Democrats joining affluent Republicans. Generational replacement also changed the AARP, as New Dealers with warm memories of Franklin Roosevelt replaced World War I-era seniors who idolized Calvin Coolidge (Day 1990; Pratt 1993). The AARP finally achieved its most cherished policy goal, ending mandatory retirement, working closely with Rep. Claude Pepper (D-FL) to pass legislation that, in

1978, forbade mandatory retirement until the age of seventy, and in 1986, banned it entirely (Pratt 1993).

But social-welfare issues remained difficult for the AARP because of the diversity of its membership. Light (1985) finds that policymakers saw the AARP as having been ineffective and indecisive during the 1983 debate on Social Security reform. The AARP's membership diversity crippled its ability to act. The NCSC, whose members were mostly union retirees, had a much more homogenous membership that gave it clear priorities.

Dealing With Diversity

The AARP experienced the problem of membership diversity in a particularly brutal way during the battle over catastrophic health insurance. Congress had added this provision to Medicare to cover senior citizens beset by sky-high medical bills for serious illnesses. The AARP had lobbied hard for this legislation and helped persuade President Ronald Reagan not to veto it (Pratt 1993). But affluent seniors resented the plan's $60 annual increase in Medicare premiums and its annual surtax that ran as high as $800. After being swamped by protests from high-income retirees, Congress repealed the program in 1989. About 12,000 to 14,000 members resigned from the AARP to protest its support for catastrophic care. The AARP was forced to discipline some of its state and local activists (Pratt 1993; Holmes 2001). While this was a tiny percentage of the AARP's membership, it did show that losing touch with the grass roots could have serious consequences.[6]

More importantly, the episode showed that issues that split seniors could devastate the AARP. Since its membership is based on material incentives, the AARP has a membership that is heterogeneous in its issue preferences. Indeed some of the AARP's material benefits (such as travel discounts and investment plans) and its solidary incentives (participation in local and state chapters) should appeal more to higher-income and healthier seniors (Verba, Schlozman, and Brady 1995; Peterson and Somit 1994). Indeed, AARP's members are disproportionately affluent, educated, male, and white (A. L. Campbell 2003). On a program that redistributed income from higher-income, healthier seniors to lower-income, sicker ones, participation in the AARP is likely to be biased toward the opponents. (However, Verba, Schlozman, and Brady [1995] note that participation is much more biased on demographic factors than on attitudinal ones.)

As a response to the catastrophic-care debacle, the AARP opened many more state and local offices. But they also learned to avoid identification with either party or with controversial policies. The AARP has since stuck close to the political center, fearful of alienating its membership. As William Novelli, then associate executive director of the AARP, explained:

AARP has developed a certain lobbying position. What it boils down to is, don't get way out in front of your membership. We're not Planned Parenthood. Try to work with both sides, bring them together, keep raising the bar in terms of what you want. When you represent 34 million people, the majority of whom vote, you don't have to smack people in the head with a stick. (Holmes 2001)

The AARP found itself at odds again with many of its members during the health care debate of 1994. After temporizing for months, the AARP board of directors endorsed the Mitchell-Gephardt health care bill in August 1994 (Grimes 1994; Weisskopf 1994). But almost instantly, AARP members "flooded the organization's switchboards," denouncing the group's decision (Shogren 1994).

New Century, New Leadership

William Novelli, a veteran of the public relations world, became AARP's CEO in 2001. While Novelli had built his reputation conducting "social marketing" efforts for groups such as the Campaign for Tobacco-Free Kids, he had worked for Richard Nixon's 1972 reelection campaign and enjoyed warm relationships with many top Republicans. Novelli seems to have brought to the job a desire for the AARP to take a higher profile in Washington policy debate and a willingness to work more closely with Republicans (Serafini 2002). But Novelli has found this route often fraught with controversy.

While the AARP did not immediately embrace the Bush administration's Medicare drug benefit, Novelli met with Speaker of the House Dennis Hastert (R-IL) in early 2003 and agreed to work together on this issue. When a House-Senate conference committee was considering the bill, Novelli joined deliberations between Hastert, House Majority Leader Tom DeLay (R-TX), and Senate Majority Leader Bill Frist (R-TN) to hammer out a compromise. This particularly enraged congressional Democrats, since no members of their party participated in this conclave (Vaida 2004).

Angry reactions were not limited to Capitol Hill; AARP's online message board soon filled with statements denouncing the organization, while seniors demonstrated outside the group's headquarters (Serafini 2003). At an AARP forum in New Hampshire, Democratic presidential candidates vied with one another in denouncing the group's perfidy. When AARP presented a commercial supporting the benefit, the crowd erupted in hisses and boos (Connolly 2003). Many AARP volunteers complained that they had not been consulted about the endorsement or even informed in advance. Some longtime AARP activists ascribed this neglect to Novelli's centralizing power in the Washington headquarters. For example, the AARP convention no longer chooses the group's leadership; now a self-selecting nominating committee of ten volunteers chooses new board members (Vaida 2004).

Novelli later admitted that AARP lost 60,000 members because of its support for the Medicare benefit. Many members apparently saw the benefit as overly generous to the pharmaceutical industry or as a partisan victory for the Bush administration. Novelli sought to ameliorate members' concerns by calling for reimportation of pharmaceuticals and by urging drugmakers to voluntarily lower drug prices (Riskind 2004; Vaida 2004).

A Different Shade of Gray

The AARP's caution and nonpartisanship stand in vivid contrast to the activities of another major seniors' group, the National Council of Senior Citizens. The NCSC grew out of Senior Citizens for Kennedy, a labor-backed Democratic organization created for the 1960 election. The next year, the group was transformed into the National Council of Senior Citizens for Health Care Through Social Security (it shortened its name after the passage of Medicare). Most of the NCSC's members were union retirees; organized labor provided much of the organization's funding, and it enjoyed a close relationship with the Democratic National Committee. The NCSC reflected labor's liberal politics and its tendency to mobilize its members for political activity. Unlike the AARP, the NCSC strongly supported the adoption of Medicare (Day 1990; Pratt 1993).

But, in recent years, the NCSC was unable to recruit enough members to be a truly effective alternative to the AARP. In January 2001, the AFL-CIO disbanded the NCSC and created a new organization called the Alliance for Retired Americans (ARA). All AFL-CIO retirees and NCSC members automatically belonged to the new group, although others could join as well (Serafini 2000b). As expected, the ARA has served as an ally of organized labor and of the Democratic Party; its 4 million members are mostly retired union members (Berry 2004; Halbfinger 2004; Serafini 2004a; Vaida 2004).

Notes

1 California, New York, Illinois, Michigan, Ohio, and Pennsylvania.

2. AARP-VOTE, "Election Rules and Regulations That Impact AARP Election Activities."

3. The unmarried are less likely to participate than the married, and unmarried women (the vast majority of the widowed are women) are especially less likely to participate. Older widowed women face a wide array of problems that are likely to reduce their political participation: low income, social isolation, or poor health. They also are

likely to have been socialized into gender norms that consider politics to be a "male" activity. See Peterson and Somit (1994).

4. One possible exception to this rule is seniors living in retirement communities. Since they are surrounded by their contemporaries (and isolated from their families), they are socialized into being "old." But they are also healthier and wealthier than average. It is no surprise that transplanted retirees have long been recognized as a political force, from the California retirees who built the "Townsend movement" to today's Florida "condo commandos."

5. Both presidential candidates targeted senior voters in 2000. Seniors had trended Republican in the 1990s, perhaps because of personal dislike for Bill Clinton, perhaps because of generational replacement as New Dealers die off and members of the "Silent Generation" enter their golden years. Gore proposed a Medicare prescription drug benefit and warned of the dangers posed by Bush's plan to partially privatize Social Security. Bush defended his proposals and warned of the cost of Gore's drug plan. Bush also sought to capitalize on the distaste that many seniors felt for the moral climate of the Clinton years. See Glenn R. Simpson and Jacob M. Schlesinger, "Benefits of Doubt: For the Last Big Push, Social Security Offers Both Sides a Weapon." *Wall Street Journal.* October 31, 2000. Gore won 51 percent among voters over sixty—his best showing among any age group. But that was only three points higher than his showing among the overall population. The gaps by age were small compared to those by race, sex, or religiosity. But in 2004, Bush scored his greatest gains among voters over sixty, winning them by a 54-to-46 percent margin over Senator John Kerry, according to the National Election Pool exit poll. Once again, moral issues (especially gay marriage) may have driven older voters toward the GOP; generational replacement may also have played a role.

6. Ironically, the catastrophic-care debacle actually enhanced the AARP's clout on Capitol Hill, since it confirmed many congressmen's respect for the political clout of senior citizens. Since many of the seniors protesting the plan were AARP members, some officeholders may have concluded that the AARP actually opposed the benefit. See Kondracke 2001.

4

Purposive Power: The NRA, Sierra Club, EMILY's List, NARAL, and the National Right to Life Committee

RELIANCE ON PURPOSIVE INCENTIVES CAN SHAPE ORGANIZATIONS in several important ways. Such groups often face significant volatility in membership; both the NARAL Pro-Choice America and the National Rifle Association (NRA) have seen their membership swing wildly as their issues pass in and out of fashion. Purposive incentives appeal to higher-status, politically aware citizens who hold intense views on issues—people who are highly likely to vote and otherwise participate in politics. These groups often seek to turn some of their members into activists; they also try to use their "brand name" to speak out to the public, sometimes to clearly defined segments of the public.

The National Rifle Association

The National Rifle Association is the United States' primary association of gun owners. After declining for several years, its membership rose during the 2000 election to just over 4 million, but declined afterwards (Eilperin 2000b; Birnbaum 2001). It allegedly spent $20 million on political activity during that year's campaign (MacPherson 2000; Miller and Miller 2000). *Fortune*, in the 2001 edition of its annual survey of Washington insiders, rated the NRA as the single most effective lobby in the nation's capital (Birnbaum 2001). The NRA is run by a seventy-six-member board of directors; the executive vice president (currently Wayne LaPierre) holds most power over day-to-day operations (Patterson 1999; Davidson 1993). Patterson and Singer (2002) find that, over the past two decades, the NRA has shifted from material to purposive incentives, raising membership dues and reducing the tangible benefits of belonging to the group. NRA members generally agree with the organization's positions on issues; for example, a 1998 poll found that 44 percent of NRA members opposed all restrictions on gun ownership; only 11 percent of non-members felt this way. Like most organizations that rely on purposive incentives, the NRA has experienced substantial membership volatility (Patterson and Singer 2002; Moe 1980; Hansen 1985).

The Institute for Legislative Action (ILA) conducts most political activity, including the NRA's PAC, the Political Victory Fund. The NRA makes direct contributions to candidates, conducts independent expenditures (usually aimed at gun owners), and communicates with its members (Patterson 1999). In recent years, it has increased the proportion of its PAC contributions that go to Republicans from 64 percent in 1992 to 86 percent in 2004.

The NRA was founded in 1871 by Union Army veterans to promote marksmanship in the wake of the Civil War, but it collapsed within a decade when New York State withdrew its subsidy (Spitzer 1995; Davidson 1993). It was revived in 1901, after the Spanish-American War showed the continued need for training in marksmanship. Federal support helped the new NRA to thrive during the early twentieth century: the government authorized the sale of military surplus to NRA shooting clubs, funded shooting matches, and sent military personnel to assist at NRA events (Spitzer 1995; Davidson 1993). The NRA grew rapidly after World War II, when many returning servicemen brought back a new interest in firearms; the NRA changed its focus from marksmanship to hunting to accommodate its new members' primary focus. By the mid-1950s, its membership had reached about 300,000 (Spitzer 1995; Davidson 1993).

The NRA Fires Back at Gun Control

But it was the 1960s and 1970s that brought revolutionary change to the NRA. A series of assassinations and a crime wave increased interest in gun control. In the 1930s, Congress had passed some restrictions on interstate gun sales and the sale of machine guns; these laws passed with the NRA's support. But the passage of the 1968 Gun Control Act (which banned the interstate shipment of firearms and ammunition, increased penalties for using guns in federal crimes, restricted gun imports, and banned the sale of guns to convicted felons, minors, and drug addicts) began the transformation of the NRA from a quasi-official shooting club to a powerful political lobby. In the aftermath of the legislation, the NRA claimed credit for the defeats of Senators Joseph Clark (D-PA) and Joseph Tydings (D-MD), two strong supporters of gun control. In 1975, the NRA created the Institute for Legislative Action to run its political activities; a year later, it created the Political Victory Fund.

Conflict between the NRA's pragmatic and ideological factions eventually led to a revolt at the organization's 1977 national convention. Harlon Carter, former director of the ILA, took control of the NRA and set it on a more aggressive course. This began a period of rapid growth for the NRA. Its membership grew from 1 million in 1977 to 2.9 million in 1984. For the first time, the NRA endorsed a presidential candidate, backing Ronald Reagan in 1980. This period of growth climaxed with the passage of the Firearms Owner Protection Act of 1986 (usually known as "McClure-Volkmer" for the names of its sponsors), which overturned some of the provisions of the Gun Control Act of 1968 (Davidson 1993; Spitzer 1995; Patterson and Singer 2002).

Out of Ammunition?

But the NRA went through a difficult period during the late 1980s and early 1990s. Without a clear threat, its membership dropped from 2.9 million in 1984 to 2.3 million in 1991. The NRA experienced internal division and leadership turnover. It endured friction with the Bush administration, particularly with drug czar William Bennett, and refused to endorse George H. W. Bush for reelection in 1992. It was subjected to bad publicity for the extremist statements made by some NRA leaders (Davidson 1993; Spitzer 1995; Patterson and Singer 2002).

With the NRA's influence waning, handgun control advocates achieved a number of successes: enactment of a ban on import of assault weapons in 1989, passage of the Brady law in 1993, and a ban on assault weapons in 1994. This series of setbacks and the ascent of a presidential administration openly hostile to the NRA revived interest in the organization. The NRA gained 1 million members between 1991 and 1994, reaching a new high of 3.5 million; the organization played a key role in electing a Republican Congress in 1994 (Patterson and Singer 2002).

But continuing leadership turmoil and charges of extremism hurt the NRA during the late 1990s. In 1995, NRA executive vice president Wayne LaPierre was forced to fight off a challenge from a more hard-line rival (Patterson and Singer 2002). (As a purposive organization, the NRA is more likely to experience demands from its activists for ideological purity. See Moe 1980.) Its membership fell from 3.5 million to 2.8 million and its reputation for effectiveness diminished (Eilperin 2000c). Many Democrats saw gun control as a potent "wedge issue" that would win over suburban women who usually voted Republican. The Columbine High School shootings in

April 1999 increased popular support for gun control (Broder 1999b; Fineman 1999).

Reloaded for Action

But the NRA revitalized itself during the 2000 elections, as the threat of further gun control legislation helped the NRA mobilize gun owners. Bill Clinton called for new gun licensing requirements while Al Gore and Bill Bradley, competing for the Democratic presidential nomination, both called for gun registration (Eilperin 2000b). By election eve, the NRA's membership had reportedly hit a new high of 4.1 million. The NRA reportedly spent a total of $20 million on political activity in 2000 (Eilperin 2000b; MacPherson 2000; Miller and Miller 2000). The NRA gave $1.5 million in soft money to the Republican Party (it gave nothing to the Democrats), making it the fourth-biggest donor organization to the GOP.[1] The NRA's PAC gave $1.5 million to candidates, with 86 percent going to Republicans.[2] Federal Election Commission (FEC) data show that the NRA spent just under $2.2 million on independent expenditures supporting Bush and attacking Gore.

Despite the NRA's efforts, Gore did carry several states that the organization targeted, including Michigan, Pennsylvania, and Wisconsin. But Bush won in Arkansas, Tennessee, and West Virginia; the NRA claimed credit for these victories, which were all essential for Bush's election to the presidency ("Tobacco, Abortion, Gun Groups" 2000). The NRA was also involved in House and Senate races. The Center for the Study of Elections and Democracy found the NRA to be the single most active group in the study's sample of competitive House and Senate races (Magleby 2001b). The NRA's activities included direct mail, broadcast ads, billboards, and yard signs. The NRA aimed its efforts at gun owners, both NRA members and nonmembers. But in Senate races, seven of the top ten beneficiaries of NRA independent expenditures lost, including the number-one such candidate, Senator Spencer Abraham (R-MI). Similarly, seven of the top ten House beneficiaries of NRA independent expenditures, once again including the number-one such candidate, Derek Smith (R-UT).[3] Nevertheless, the NRA was able to claim credit for some Republican victories, including the defeats of Senator Charles Robb (D-VA) and Rep. David Minge (D-MN).

After the 2000 election, the threat of gun control dissipated. NRA allies controlled the White House and Capitol Hill, and many Democrats avoided the issue of gun control, blaming it for Gore's defeat. In 2004, the assault weapons ban, which had so angered gun owners a decade before, expired without much effort to preserve it. In 2002 and 2004, several Democratic Senate candidates loudly proclaimed their devotion to the Second Amendment. Senator John Kerry (D-MA), the 2004 Democratic presidential nominee, had a long history of supporting gun control, but avoided discussing the issue and sought to reassure hunters that he posed no danger to their right to bear arms. Not surprisingly, the NRA lost members (falling from over 4 million in 2000 to 3.4 million three years later), experienced some financial difficulties, and found it difficult to find issues to motivate gun owners. While the NRA was generally satisfied with George W. Bush's performance (and strongly supported him for reelection), there was some friction with the administration over its antiterrorism policies (Allen 2004; Strom 2003).

Still Carrying a Full Barrel

The NRA spent $1.31 million on independent expenditures in the 2002 congressional elections (Magleby and Tanner 2004). Biersack and Viray (2005) say that the NRA focused on grassroots mobilization, conducting more than sixty grassroots workshops that trained 5,000 NRA members. Monson (2004) finds the NRA was among the top players in a successful Republican ground war, organizing training programs in 331 congressional districts and recruiting 311 election volunteer coordinators. The NRA sent extensive mail to gun owners in a wide variety of races, including the unsuccessful attempt to oust Senator Tim Johnson (D-SD) and the successful drive to elect a Republican to a newly created House seat in Colorado (Bart and Meader 2004; D. A. Smith 2004).

In 2004, the NRA was active in a number of Senate races in the South, supporting such candidates as Richard Burr (R-NC), Jim DeMint (R-SC), and Johnny Isakson (R-GA). It also supported John Thune's successful challenge to Senate Minority Leader Tom Daschle (D-SD), sending a mailer depicting Daschle as a puppet with Senators Edward Kennedy (D-MA) and Hillary Rodham Clinton (D-NY) pulling his strings (Justice 2004). While most of its favored candidates won, the NRA did see Peter Coors (R-CO) go down to defeat. It did intervene in one House Democratic primary, supporting Missouri's Third District candidate Steve Stoll, who lost to a more liberal candidate. Unlike some conservative groups, the NRA backed Senator Arlen Specter (R-PA) for reelection against a primary challenge from Rep. Pat Toomey.

In the presidential race, the NRA ferociously attacked John Kerry as an enemy of the right to bear arms, mocking his claims of being a lifelong hunter. The NRA produced billboards and flyers showing a French poodle wearing a Kerry-Edwards button with the label "That Dog Won't Hunt," warning gun owners not to believe Kerry's claims to support private firearms ownership. The NRA's website featured a list of seventeen points supporting the organization's claim that "John Kerry Wants to Ban Guns in America." Surfers could also access TV ads attacking Kerry. One spot, aired on the Outdoor Life Network, concluded with Chris Cox, head of the ILA, declaring, "Remember, John Kerry is not a hunter. He just plays one on TV." Overall, the NRA claimed to have spent $20 million to defeat Kerry, with only about $1 million going to TV ads, which included a thirty-minute infomercial (Anderson 2004; Kelly 2004). The NRA spent $2.88 million on independent expenditures either for Bush or against Kerry.

The NRA is governed by a seventy-six-member board of directors, chosen by NRA members. The board selects the president, executive vice president, and vice president. Beneath the vice president is the ILA, currently headed by Chris Cox. Endorsements are made by the board of the Political Victory Fund, the NRA's PAC. The board also grades candidates on a scale of A to F (Patterson 1999).

TABLE 3
The NRA's Top Independent Expenditures in 2004

Bold indicates winner. Amount includes both spending supporting the candidate and opposing his or her opponent. * indicates incumbent.

Senate

Name	Amount ($)
Richard Burr (R-NC)	172,770
John Thune (R-SD)	130,847
Jim DeMint (R-SC)	92,124
Johnny Isakson (R-GA)	73,251
Arlen Specter (R-PA)*	62,803
Peter Coors (R-CO)	59,469
Mel Martinez (R-FL)	44,946
Bill McCollum (R-FL)	12,410
Lisa Murkowski (R-AK)*	3,474

House

Name	Amount ($)
Pete Sessions (R-TX)*	52,000
Steve Stoll (D-MO)	15,066
Heather Wilson (R-NM)*	13,817
Dan Boren (D-OK)	4,395
Rico Oller (R-CA)	3,758

Source: Center for Responsive Politics.

TABLE 4
The NRA's Top Independent Expenditures in 2002

Bold indicates winner. Amount includes both spending supporting the candidate and opposing his or her opponent. * indicates incumbent.

Senate

Name	Amount ($)
Jim Talent (R-MO)	245,529
Wayne Allard (R-CO)*	119,074
Norm Coleman (R-MN)	116,496
Tim Hutchinson (R-AR)*	87,420
John Sununu (R-NH)	71,594
John Thune (R-SD)	69,748
Saxby Chambliss (R-GA)	68,118
Suzanne Terrell (R-LA)	52,472
Gordon Smith (R-OR)*	3,120
Elizabeth Dole (R-NC)	1,934

House

Name	Amount ($)
John Dingell (D-MI)*	75,797
Rick Clayburgh (R-ND)	43,770
Randy Forbes (R-VA)	27,385
Jeb Bradley (R-NH)	21,223
Bill Janklow (R-SD)	20,371
Robin Hayes (R-NC)*	16,795
Tom Feeney (R-FL)	14,026
Chris Chocola (R-IN)	13,420
Brose McVey (R-IN)	13,401
Rick Renzi (R-AZ)	13,185
Ernie Fletcher (R-KY)*	12,741

Source : Center for Responsive Politics.

The Sierra Club

The Sierra Club is one of the nation's leading environmental organizations. Along with the League of Conservation Voters, it is one of the two principal environmental organizations active in elections. It has over 700,000 members. Naturalist John Muir founded the Sierra Club in 1892 in California. For the first sixty years of the Sierra Club's existence, its membership was limited mostly to California and its activities limited mostly to encouraging outdoor activity. David Brower, who took over as director in 1952, made the club much more aggressively political. Its membership grew dramatically and became national in scope

(Mundo 1992). In 1966, the club ran newspaper ads opposed to the building of dams on the Colorado River. As a result, three years later the club lost its status as a 501 (R) 3 charity, thereby losing its right to collect tax-deductible contributions. The club set up the Sierra Club Foundation as its charitable affiliate (Foskett 1998). Although Brower quit as director in 1969 to head the newly created Friends of the Earth, the Sierra Club's prominence grew as the environmental movement came of age during the 1970s and 1980s. Increasingly, people joined the club in order to support its environmental policies, rather than to enjoy its outdoor programs; this marked a shift from material and solidary incentives to purposive incentives. The Sierra Club created a PAC in 1976. While the Sierra Club has its headquarters in San Francisco, it has a large Washington staff as well as a field staff (Mundo 1992).

The nature of this membership has caused the Sierra Club to develop relatively open decision-making procedures. It also has led to challenges to the club's leadership; in the spring of 2000, more ideological environmentalists sought unsuccessfully to take control of its board of directors (Carlton 2000). In 2004, former Colorado governor Dick Lamm led a slate that wanted the club to officially support more restrictions on immigration (a position the club had held before 1996). The club, conscious of the need to cultivate Hispanic voters, opposed Lamm. While Lamm's slate received much publicity (in part for the support it received from some racist and nativist groups), it fell far short of victory (Woellert 2004; Steers 2004; Eilperin 2004a; Barringer 2004a). The Sierra Club's activist membership also participates in the club's endorsement process. Local chapters make endorsements, which are usually approved by the national committee. The club has a policy of always supporting proenvironmental incumbents for reelection (Cantor 1999).

After a period of complacency, the Sierra Club has increased its political activity since the 1994 Republican takeover, which devastated the club's influence on the congressional agenda. Indeed, some Republican leaders took pride in their disdain for the environmental movement (Cantor 1999). In response to the GOP takeover, the Sierra Club boosted its political activity, increasing its fund-raising, and became far more aggressive and partisan. The Sierra Club's $150,000 expenditure on behalf of Oregon Senate candidate Ron Wyden (D) was seen as key to Wyden's defeat of Republican Gordon Smith in a highly visible special election in January 1996 (Cantor 1999). Smith, who was elected to Oregon's other Senate seat ten months later, said that the Sierra Club "busted my chops pretty good. It's an organization with a warm and fuzzy name that engages in real brass knuckle tactics" (Foskett 1998). Daniel J. Weiss, who served as the club's political director between 1993 and 2000, said that the Oregon special election "made an environment a much more political, dangerous issue for people in Congress to mess with" (Kriz 2000). In

1996, 1998, and 2000, the Sierra Club distributed voter guides and produced issue ads attacking the policies of the Republican Congress. While it continued its activities in 2002, the club's spending fell, as 9/11 pushed environmental issues from the public agenda (Magleby and Tanner 2004). In 2004, the club moved away from broadcast advertising and instead emphasized grassroots mobilization. A variety of reasons were given for the club's switch: restrictions by the Bipartisan Campaign Reform Act (BCRA), restrictions on broadcast advertising, lack of interest by most voters in the environment, and dissatisfaction with some club campaigns in 2002 (Stanton 2003; Carney, Stone, and Barnes 2003; Eilperin 2004b).

The club's activities in some House and Senate races went beyond simply running broadcast ads. One study found that the club was the leading pro-Democratic group on the ground in the 2000 Michigan Senate race, sending four unique pieces of mail (Traugott 2001). The Sierra Club was also a pioneer in using so-called Section 527 organizations to collect anonymous donations before federal regulations were extended to them during the summer of 2000 (Foskett 2000).

EMILY's List

EMILY's List (EMILY stands for "Early Money is Like Yeast"—it makes the dough rise) was founded in 1985 to help elect pro-choice Democratic women to Congress and governorships. Its primary activity has been "bundling" the checks written by its members to endorsed candidates. EMILY's List relies primarily on purposive incentives; its close ties to Democratic committees make it a quintessential member of a party network. The Campaign Media Analysis Group estimated that EMILY's List spent $3.4 million on TV ads. This included $2.2 million in House races; this made EMILY's List the fourth-most active group in these contests (Brennan Center for Justice 2000). EMILY's List asserts that its 65,000 members contributed a total of $9.2 million during the 1999–2000 cycle.[4] By 2004, its membership had risen to over 100,000, contributing about $10.6 million to candidates (EMILY's List 2004). EMILY's List also transfers some of its funds to party committees and other PACs. It also operates a nonfederal Section 527 committee that can accept unlimited contributions that can then be used to reimburse the federal PAC. In 2000, the nonfederal committee also transferred more than $1.2 million to the Democratic National Committee's (DNC) federal operating fund.

EMILY's List personnel are deeply involved in Democratic politics; long-time president Ellen Malcolm serves on the DNC's Executive Committee,

Mary Beth Cahill left her job as EMILY's List executive director to head John Kerry's presidential campaign, and Ellen Moran left another position at EMILY's List to head the DNC's independent expenditure campaign supporting Kerry.

Since 1995, EMILY's List has conducted the Women Vote! project, which it describes as a "long-term program to mobilize women voters to go the polls." In 2000, EMILY's List reportedly spent $10.8 million on Women Vote!, which included broadcast ads, phone banks, direct mail, and door-to-door canvassing. Women Vote! also included the EMILY's List Women's Monitor poll, which helped the organization determine women voters' priority issues and which demographic groups of women are the best targets for Democrats. This helped EMILY's List to design mail pieces and telephone scripts. Under the Women Vote! project, EMILY's List also trained activists in grassroots mobilization.[5] Women Vote! and its various state affiliates also serve as joint fundraising committees.

Like many liberal groups, in 2002, EMILY's List strongly backed Senator Jean Carnahan (D-MO) and Senate candidate Jeanne Shaheen (D-NH); both lost in close races. But it preferred to support Senator Mary Landrieu (D-LA) for reelection after she voted to ban "partial-birth" abortions (Alpert 2002). EMILY's List asserts that its 97,000 members contributed a total of about $9 million during the 2001–2002 cycle.[6]

In 2004, EMILY's List supported losing Senate candidates Inez Tenenbaum (D-SC), Nancy Farmer (D-MO), and Betty Castor (D-FL). Two other EMILY's List favorites, Diane Farrell (D-CT) and Lois Murphy (D-PA), narrowly lost challenges to incumbent Republican congressmen. EMILY's List supported some successful candidates. Stephanie Herseth (D-SD), elected in a special election to fill a vacant seat, won a full term. Melissa Bean (D-IL) scored one of the sweetest Democratic victories of 2004, knocking off Phil Crane, a onetime presidential candidate and the most senior Republican in the U.S. House of Representatives. Gwen Moore (D-WI) was the first African American elected to Congress from Wisconsin. EMILY's List provided more than $767,000 for Allyson Schwartz's (D-PA) successful House campaign, both through bundling and through an independent expenditure ("Biographies of the New Members" 2004). EMILY's List also helped reelect three longtime favorites, Senators Barbara Mikulski (D-MD), Barbara Boxer (D-CA), and Patty Murray (D-WA).

NARAL Pro-Choice America

With about 400,000 members, NARAL Pro-Choice America is one of the nation's most prominent organizations opposing restrictions on abortion.

(Previously known only as the National Abortion and Reproductive Rights Action League, it adopted its current name in 2003.)[7] NARAL's history supports Moe's (1980) observation that a reliance on purposive incentives can lead to volatility in membership. NARAL offers impressive evidence to support this. In 1989, before the Supreme Court's *Webster v. Reproductive Health Services* decision increasing states' ability to regulate abortions, NARAL had 250,000 members. Within three years, its membership had more than doubled (Thomas 1994). But with the election of a pro-choice U.S. president, NARAL's membership dropped rapidly. (Thomas 1999). After the election of the unabashedly antiabortion George W. Bush, NARAL's membership rebounded to 400,000 (Rosenberg 2003). NARAL has often faced a problem in mobilizing support when the threat to abortion rights has not been clear. By contrast, its opponents have faced a constant threat: abortion has been basically legal since 1973. They also have enjoyed two other advantages: the relative constancy of religious practice (which is the best predictor of opposition to abortion) and the consistent support offered by religious institutions (particularly the Roman Catholic Church).

In contrast to its opponents' power at the grass roots, NARAL's strength has "always been [its] professionally staffed central organization" (Craig and O'Brien 1993). It was founded in February 1969 as the National Association for the Repeal of Abortion Laws. NARAL played a prominent role in the drive to repeal state abortion laws during the early 1970s. The organization changed its name after *Roe v. Wade* legalized abortion nationwide in January 1973. NARAL's leadership was surprised by the strength of the pro-life movement during the mid-1970s, which led to passage of the Hyde Amendment in 1976 that banned federal funding for abortion. As a response, NARAL established a PAC the following year after the National Women's Conference (O'Connor 1996). NARAL had difficulty establishing itself as a political actor. A string of pro-life victories in 1978 and 1980 made the downside of supporting abortion rights all too apparent. By contrast, pro-choice voters assumed that *Roe* guaranteed that abortion would remain legal, so they did not see the issue as important (Thomas 1994).

Joining the Fold

During the Reagan years, NARAL gradually became a mainstream member of the Democratic coalition, helping lead opposition to the nomination of Robert Bork to the Supreme Court, and showing that it could help Democratic candidates win. But a series of events during the George H. W. Bush administration led to a huge increase in NARAL's membership and funding. Two

Supreme Court decisions (*Webster v. Reproductive Health Services* [1989] and *Planned Parenthood of Southeastern Pennsylvania v. Casey* [1992]) significantly expanded states' ability to regulate abortion. A few months after *Webster*, victories by pro-choice Democrats over pro-life Republicans in gubernatorial races in New Jersey and Virginia sparked discussion among politicos that an antiabortion stance could be a serious liability. Candidates began soliciting NARAL's support. NARAL expanded its electoral activity in 1990, including mass media campaigns in seven states, 2 million pieces of mail, and 500,000 pieces of door-to-door literature drops. NARAL claims to have contacted 1.5 million voters. Abortion-rights forces made across-the-board gains in the 1990 elections (Thomas 1994, 1999).

The nomination of Judge Clarence Thomas to the Supreme Court in 1991 activated many pro-choice women, especially after it was charged that Thomas had sexually harassed a subordinate. Outrage over the Thomas hearings helped spark several Democratic women to run for Congress, making 1992 the "Year of the Woman." *Webster* and the Thomas nomination convinced many pro-choice advocates that the 1992 election could determine whether the Supreme Court would maintain a pro-choice majority. Many observers expected that the Supreme Court would use *Casey* to overrule *Roe.* In this atmosphere, NARAL launched its most extensive membership drive ever; its membership grew and record contributions poured into its PAC. When the Supreme Court ruled on *Casey* on June 29, it only narrowed *Roe* rather than overturning it. Fund-raising quickly trailed off (Thomas 1999).

In 1992, NARAL conducted coordinated campaigns with Senate candidates Carol Moseley-Braun (IL), Barbara Boxer (CA), and Dianne Feinstein (CA), among others. NARAL spent $850,000 on independent expenditures, with much of its spending going to broadcast ads. In later campaigns, NARAL would switch its emphasis to direct voter contact. NARAL conducted a grassroots program to contact more than 1 million pro-choice voters in key districts and states. All told, NARAL PAC spent about $3 million in 1992. Pro-choice forces gained eleven seats in the House of Representatives and one in the Senate (O'Connor 1996; Craig and O'Brien 1993; Thomas 1994, 1999).

The Perils of Success

But the election of Bill Clinton, the first unambiguously pro-choice president, ended this period of growth, as abortion-rights advocates became complacent. Clinton named two *Roe* supporters to the Supreme Court, staving off the threat to legal abortion. As one would expect for a group reliant on purposive incentives, NARAL's fund-raising fell and some state affiliates closed.

The 1994 elections were not only a big defeat for Democrats, but also a disaster for pro-choice activists. They lost five seats in the Senate and thirty-nine in the House; wiping out all their gains in 1990–1992. Pro-choicers still have not recouped these losses. While Republicans had not mentioned abortion in their Contract with America, they soon passed a series of restrictions on abortion, particularly on federal funding. This defeat was a wake-up call for NARAL, leading it to revamp its political operations, but it was unable to increase its fund-raising. Many of the abortion restrictions passed by the Republican Congress were complex and difficult to understand; they did not easily translate into fund-raising appeals. NARAL adapted to the new environment by channeling its PAC funds to challengers and open-seat candidates; it also decreased its overall PAC giving in favor of increased spending on voter education (Thomas 1999).

In 1996, NARAL targeted seven Senate and twenty-four House races, including fifteen Republican freshmen. It conducted phone and mail campaigns targeted at Republican and independent women. It also conducted a voter turnout campaign (Clines 1996; "Insider Commentary" 1996). Two of their more visible victories were the defeats of Reps. Randy Tate (R-WA), who went on to head the Christian Coalition, and Peter Blute (R-MA), whose district had never elected a pro-choice representative before (Connelly 1996; Nangle 1996; Murakami 1996). But NARAL had difficulty responding to the "partial-birth" abortion issue, which was brought up in several races. There was little change in the balance on the issue in Congress ("Spotlight Story" 1996; "Partial Birth Abortion Debate" 1996).

In the 1998 congressional elections, NARAL scored some important victories, helping to defeat Senator Al D'Amato (R-NY) and Rep. Jon Fox (R-PA). In those races, NARAL ran phone banks and sent mailings to pro-choice voters; it also ran TV ads specifically attacking D'Amato (Kolodny, Suarez, and Rodrigues 1999; O'Donnell 1998). Despite these high-profile victories, 1998 saw only a slight change in the balance of power on the abortion issue: pro-choicers gained five seats in the House but lost one in the Senate (Harwood 1998).

In 2000, NARAL reportedly spent $7.5 million on direct voter contact and advertising. NARAL claims that its effort included making 3.4 million phone calls, mailing 4.6 million pieces of election mail, running more than $1.5 million of television advertising, and organizing "thousands" of volunteers to conduct grassroots activities (Dao 2000). NARAL's turnout campaign also included taped phone messages from celebrities urging pro-choice women to turn out to vote: women twenty-five to thirty-five heard from Sarah Jessica Parker, star of HBO's *Sex and the City*, women over thirty-five heard from NARAL president Kate Michelman describing her experience with an illegal abortion (Mintz 2000; Von Drehle 2000). In 2004, NARAL used taped messages from another *Sex and the City* star, Cynthia Nixon (Lightman 2004).

NARAL reportedly targeted over 2 million women, many of them independents or Republicans, in sixteen key states. Eleven of those states voted for Gore; two others elected pro-choice Democratic senators to replace pro-life Republicans (Mintz 2000; Balz 2000). Among its biggest victories were helping to oust Republican senators Rod Grams (MN), Spencer Abraham (MI), John Ashcroft (MO), and Slade Gorton (WA). NARAL also conducted independent expenditures in House races, although the three leading beneficiaries all lost: Lauren Beth Gash (D-IL), Nancy Keenan (D-MT), and Dianne Byrum (D-MI). NARAL-backed candidates who won included Rick Larsen (D-WA), Mike Honda (D-CA), and Reps. Joe Hoeffel (D-PA) and Mark Udall (D-CO). There was a slight net gain for pro-choice forces in Congress, picking up three seats in the House and two in the Senate ("Tobacco, Abortion, Gun Groups See Gains and Losses" 2000). In 2002, NARAL put special emphasis on electing to the U.S. Senate Democrats Tom Strickland of Colorado and Jeanne Shaheen of New Hampshire; both of these states have a history of supporting abortion rights. But both candidates lost in narrow races. Indeed, few of NARAL's top candidates fared well in 2001–2002.

NARAL focused on voter turnout in 2004, particularly among unmarried women under forty. It targeted New Hampshire, Oregon, Pennsylvania, Washington, D.C., and Wisconsin (Starr 2004; Lightman 2004). It remained neutral in one of the most hotly contested Senate races of the year, declining to endorse Ken Salazar (D-CO) because he supports parental notification and the partial-birth abortion ban. But NARAL still made sure to denounce Republican nominee Peter Coors for his unswerving opposition to abortion. Beth Ganz, director of Colorado NARAL, declared:

> Pete Coors is an extremist on the issue. Given his views, if he has the opportunity to outlaw abortion he will do so. He just will. I think that's true whether it's a piece of legislation restricting access to abortion or contraceptive services or voting on the nomination of a Supreme Court justice. (Bartels 2004)

NARAL also sought to highlight the importance of the abortion issue by holding a rally in Washington that attracted between 500,000 and over 1 million participants in April 2004. It was the first such pro-choice event since 1992. Speakers including Senators Hillary Rodham Clinton (D-NY) and Dianne Feinstein (D-CA) and House Minority Leader Nancy Pelosi (D-CA) declared their fervent support for abortion rights (Phelps 2004; Marinucci 2004).

TABLE 5
NARAL's Top Independent Expenditures in 2002

Bold indicates winner. * indicates incumbent.

Senate

Name	Amount ($)
Tom Strickland (D-CO)	539,548
Jeanne Shaheen (D-NH)	515,775
Bob Torricelli* / **Frank Lautenberg** (D-NJ)	313,524
Ron Kirk (D-TX)	203,449
Paul Wellstone* / Walter Mondale (D-MN)	188,419
Jean Carnahan (D-MO)*	120,267
Erskine Bowles (D-NC)	77,697
Alex Sanders (D-SC)	65,165
Max Cleland (D-GA)*	31,971
Bill Bradbury (D-OR)	26,696

House

Name	Amount ($)
Cheryl Jacques (D-MA)	181,689
Louise Lucas (D-VA)	18,858
Bill Luther (D-MN)*	9,302
Ann Hutchinson (D-IA)	5,966
Julie Thomas (D-IA)	5,924

Source: Center for Responsive Politics.

The National Right to Life Committee

The National Right to Life Committee (NRLC)—which has about 400,000 members—and its fifty state affiliates are among the most politically active groups working to restrict access to abortion. One estimate claims that the NRLC has 3,000 chapters in fifty states (Lightman 2004). Verba, Schlozman, and Brady (1995), like many others, have found that church attendance is a strong predictor of opposition to abortion. They also have found that church attendance helps many lower-status individuals (who are generally more religious) develop civic skills that they would not have acquired on the job. Public opinion polls generally show more people taking the extreme pro-choice position ("abortion should be legal in all cases") than the extreme pro-life position ("abortion should be illegal in all cases"). Pro-choicers are generally more educated, which is a strong predictor of civic activism. But Verba, Schlozman, and Brady (1995) find that pro-lifers' religious involvement and the skills they have thereby developed—as well as their greater intensity of belief—lead their activity to surpass that of the more numerous pro-choicers. Indeed, Protestant and Catholic clergy have been at the forefront of opposition to abortion and their churches have often been centers of pro-life activity. Through the support it gains from organized religion, the pro-life movement can benefit from solidary as well as purposive incentives.

The National Right to Life Committee was created in 1970 at the behest of Father James McHugh of the U.S. Catholic Conference's Family Life Division. At that time, abortion was still illegal in most states but a nationwide drive was already on to overturn those laws. California, Colorado, and North Carolina had liberalized their abortion laws in 1967; Georgia joined them in 1968; five states followed in 1969. Alaska, Hawaii, New York, and Washington State repealed their antiabortion laws in 1970 (Garrow 1994). The NRLC was particularly active in opposing efforts to overturn abortion laws in the courts and contributed an amicus brief in *Roe v. Wade*.

After *Roe* overturned state abortion bans in 1973, the NRLC and its state affiliates became increasingly active in electoral politics and lobbying. This effort led to a series of victories in the late 1970s. The Hyde Amendment, passed in 1976, forbade Medicaid funding of abortions. The NRLC established a PAC in 1980. Previously, the NRLC had maintained a close relationship with the Life Amendment Political Action Committee (Gunn 1994). In 1978 and 1980, a number of prominent pro-choice politicians were defeated in races where abortion played a major role, including Senators Dick Clark (D-IA), Wendell Anderson (D-MN), John Culver (D-IA), George McGovern (D-SD), and Birch Bayh (D-IN). And in 1980, the Republican Party adopted an unambiguously antiabortion platform and nominated and elected Ronald Reagan, an avowed opponent of abortion. The strength of the pro-life movement surprised many of its opponents, who thought that *Roe* marked an end to the conflict over abortion.

Less Than They Had Wished

But the NRLC found that having a pro-life presidential administration would not mean victory for its cause. Efforts to pass a right-to-life constitutional amendment failed with little backing from the White House. When the NRLC supported a more modest version that would have simply sent the issue back to the states, other pro-life organizations accused them of selling out. In 1981, the Reagan administration nominated Sandra Day O'Connor, an Arizona state judge whose record gave little reason to suppose that she would overturn *Roe*. (Indeed, she has repeatedly upheld *Roe*.) The NRLC opposed the O'Connor nomination, angering the White House. When the Senate overwhelmingly approved O'Connor, the NRLC lost much of its political clout. In general, the Reagan administration avoided making abortion a priority issue. Symbolically, President Reagan would address pro-life events only by phone, never in person (Craig and O'Brien 1993).

A New Strategy

When *Webster* and *Casey* expanded states' rights to regulate abortion, while also revitalizing the pro-choice movement, the NRLC decided to follow an incrementalist strategy. This included backing candidates who did not support it on every issue (Gunn 1994). The NRLC and its state affiliates succeeded in lobbying many state legislatures to pass measures requiring parental consent or notification for minors having abortions, waiting periods for abortions, and requirements that abortion providers inform patients of the status of their fetuses. Many of these laws have been struck down by the courts, however (Craig and O'Brien 1993).

More recently, the NRLC has spearheaded the drive for bans on a late-term abortion procedure, so-called partial-birth abortion. Congress passed such a ban in 1996, only for it to be vetoed by President Clinton. In November 2003, President George W. Bush signed the Partial-Birth Abortion Act into law. Bush has also signed two other bills backed by pro-life activists: the Born-Alive Infants Protection Act and the Unborn Victims of Violence Act. Bush has also ordered that the unborn be included in the Children's Health Insurance Program. Bush has also helped pro-life activists on many international issues, reinstating the so-called Mexico City policy, which bans funding of family-planning groups that perform or encourage abortions overseas, and cutting off funding to the U.N. Population Fund after it was accused of condoning forced abortions and sterilization in China. While Bush has not explicitly sought to overturn *Roe v. Wade*, the NRLC nevertheless called him the "most solidly pro-life president" since that decision (Carney 2004; Munro 2004; Toner 2004; Sangillo 2003).

The NRLC spends most of its PAC funds on independent expenditures, mostly going to phone and mail campaigns targeting identified pro-life voters. In both 2002 and 2004, the NRLC was especially active in several key Senate races in the South, helping to elect John Cornyn (R-TX), Saxby Chambliss (R-GA), Elizabeth Dole (R-NC), Mel Martinez (R-FL), Richard Burr (R-NC), Tom Coburn (R-OK), and Jim DeMint (R-SC). The NRLC also played a prominent role in the traditional antiabortion stronghold of South Dakota, assisting in defeating Senate Minority Leader Tom Daschle but failing to elect Republican Larry Diedrich to the at-large House seat. In a statement released after the 2004 election, NRLC political director Carol Long Tobias hailed the election of seven new pro-life senators (Martinez, Burr, Coburn, DeMint,

John Thune [R-SD], David Vitter [R-LA], and Johnny Isakson [R-GA]) and declared that 57 percent of House members were pro-life. She asserted that antiabortion voters reelected Bush (Tobias 2004).

The NRLC had a mixed record of success in high-profile Senate primaries, successfully helping Martinez to defeat former Rep. Bill McCollum in Florida but failing to block the nomination of Rep. Johnny Isakson in Georgia, who defeated two more adamantly antiabortion opponents. It also failed to unseat longtime foe Senator Arlen Specter (R-PA) when he was challenged by Rep. Pat Toomey in the Republican primary.

The NRLC did play a significant role in a Democratic primary in the Third District of Missouri, vacated by Rep. Richard Gephardt when he sought the presidency. Although this is a socially conservative district with a strong an-

TABLE 6
The NRLC's Top Independent Expenditures in 2004

Senate

Bold indicates winner. * indicates incumbent.

Name	Amount ($)
Mel Martinez (R-FL)	212,452
Richard Burr (R-NC)	94,993
Tom Coburn (R-OK)	64,717
Christopher Bond (R-MO)*	56,177
Peter Coors (R-CO)	55,748
Tim Michels (R-WI)	52,159
John Thune (R-SD)	50,682
Jim Bunning (R-KY)*	42,664
Jim DeMint (R-SC)	34,583
George Nethercutt (R-WA)	14,203

House

Name	Amount ($)
Larry Diedrich (R-SD)	71,739
Steve Stoll (D-MO)	41,969
Alice Forgy Kerr (R-KY)	23,981
Kris Kobach (R-KS)	18,974
Joseph Pascuzzo (R-PA)	17,520
Jim Gerlach (R-PA)*	14,172
Heather Wilson (R-NM)*	10,539
Stan Thompson (R-IA)	10,244
Steve LaTourette (R-OH)*	9,584
Max Burns (R-GA)*	8,274

Source: Center for Responsive Politics.

tiabortion constituency, Right to Life's chosen candidate, state senator Steve Stoll, finished third behind two pro-choice Democrats. But Missouri Right to Life activists still took credit for the state voting for President Bush and electing Republican Matt Blunt as governor (Mannies 2003; Mannies 2004a; Mannies 2004c; Franck 2004).

In 2000, the NRLC's largest single independent expenditure was on behalf of Rep. Bill McCollum (R), who sought to be elected to the U.S. Senate from Florida. The NRLC spent $111,859 supporting McCollum, who described himself as "pro-life, 100 percent" and backed a constitutional amendment banning abortion except in case of a danger to the mother's life[8] (Crowley 2000; A. C. Smith 2000; Nelson 2000). McCollum lost 52 percent to 47 percent to Bill Nelson, the state Insurance Commissioner and a pro-choice Democrat.

TABLE 7
The NRLC's Top Independent Expenditures in 2002

Bold indicates winner. * indicates incumbent.

Senate

Name	Amount ($)
John Cornyn (R-TX)	204,879
Jim Talent (R-MO)	191,241
Wayne Allard (R-CO)*	124,301
Saxby Chambliss (R-GA)	123,154
Elizabeth Dole (R-NC)	104,950
Suzanne Terrell (R-LA)	97,768
John Thune (R-SD)	92,650
Tim Hutchinson (R-AR)*	66,511
Greg Ganske (R-IA)	53,198
Lamar Alexander (R-TN)	52,582

House

Name	Amount ($)
Scott Garrett (R-NJ)	29,817
Bill Janklow (R-SD)	28,473
Randy Forbes (R-VA)	25,308
Lincoln Davis (D-TN)	23,119
Jim Gerlach (R-PA)	22,161
Rick Renzi (R-AZ)	18,499
Helen Bentley (R-MD)	18,087
Marilyn Musgrave (R-CO)	17,093
Anne Northup (R-KY)*	16,731
Bob Beauprez (R-CO)	15,645

Source: Center for Responsive Politics.

Other leading beneficiaries of NRLC independent expenditures lost, including Senators John Ashcroft (R-MO) and Spencer Abraham (R-MI) and House candidates Mark Baker (R-IL) and Charles Starr (R-OR). But Senate candidate George Allen (R-VA) and Senators Rick Santorum (R-PA) and Mike DeWine (R-OH) won. In Virginia, postelection analyses suggested that abortion was one of the issues that helped Allen run strongly in rural areas and hence oust Senator Charles Robb (D-VA) (Whitley 2000). A study of House and Senate races found that Right to Life activities comprised mostly mailings, phone banks, and voter guides (Magleby 2001b).

Notes

1. Center for Responsive Politics. www.crp.org.
2. Center for Responsive Politics. www.crp.org.
3. Federal Election Commission. www.fec.org.
4. www.emilyslist.com.
5. www.emilyslist.com.
6. www.emilyslist.com.
7. NARAL, long known as the National Abortion Rights Action League, changed its name in 1993 to reflect its avowed concern with broader issues of reproductive health. See Thomas (1999).
8. Federal Election Commission.

5

Professional Politics:
The NFIB, ATLA, and AMA

P ROFESSIONAL ASSOCIATIONS OFTEN RELY ON A COMBINATION OF MATERIAL, purposive, and solidary incentives. With their relatively elite memberships,
groups like the National Federation of Independent Business (NFIB), Association of Trial Lawyers of America (ATLA), and American Medical Association
(AMA) often encourage their supporters to donate money or otherwise assist
candidates. The NFIB and ATLA have extremely strong ties to the Republican
and Democratic parties, respectively; the AMA has traditionally supported
Republicans, but has cooperated with Democrats on some issues.

The National Federation of Independent Business

With 640,000 members, the National Federation of Independent Business is
the nation's largest organization of small-business owners (Birnbaum 2001).
The NFIB is a peak business association that has many of the characteristics
of a purposive or ideological organization. Most corporations and trade associations confine their political activities to setting up political action committees that donate to candidates, and to contributing soft money to the political
parties. (Boatright et al. 2003 find that many of these corporations felt relieved
by the BCRA's abolition of federal money; they had given primarily at the in-
stigation of party leaders.) The NFIB, by contrast, focuses its efforts on mobilizing its members for political activity.

Many corporations and trade associations, fearful of offending members of
Congress, primarily back safe incumbents for reelection and avoid helping

challengers. While most prefer Republicans, they seek allies in both parties. Even under Republican control, about one-third of corporate PAC contributions go to Democrats. The NFIB, however, supports almost exclusively Republicans, including many challengers. Its PAC contributed about $1 million to candidates in the 2003–2004 cycle; 98 percent that sum went to Republicans, high even for a business PAC.[1]

Most corporations and trade associations focus on a narrow set of issues that directly affect their interests. For example, Godwin and Selden (2002) find that corporate lobbyists seek mostly "private goods," benefits that accrue solely to the corporations themselves, rather than to an entire sector or to business as a whole. Such private goods include government contracts, regulatory waivers, and patent extensions. These issues do not usually break along party lines; lobbyists for these groups usually contact members of both parties who represent affected districts. By contrast, the NFIB is interested in a wide variety of issues and takes a sharply ideological and partisan tack. The NFIB shares these characteristics with some other peak business associations such as the U.S. Chamber of Commerce and the National Association of Manufacturers.

Always on the Prowl for New Members

With its diverse membership and reliance on purposive incentives, the NFIB must deal with a high degree of membership volatility. Shaiko and Wallace (1999) report that 20 percent of NFIB members leave the group every year. Since its very nature is that of a small-business organization, the NFIB cannot rely on a handful of large members to provide a stable core of support, as do other peak business associations. So the NFIB must constantly search for new members. The bulk of its staff consists of hundreds of sales personnel (Shaiko and Wallace 1999). While the NFIB does offer some material incentives, it must also supply a steady stream of purposive incentives: die-hard support for economic conservatism and Republican politicians.

The NFIB sets its policy agenda, which generally reflects Republican orthodoxy, by member ballot. Surveys show that its members hold homogenous, intensely conservative views on economic issues (Schier 2000). Its network of members is probably the NFIB's greatest political asset. The organization encourages them to volunteer for probusiness candidates, helps them hold fundraisers, and distributes candidate-related "foldouts" that they can display in their shop windows. The foldouts are considered internal communications, so they do not have to be paid for with PAC money (Shaiko and Wallace 1999).

The NFIB's membership is composed primarily of retail and service companies, but construction and manufacturing businesses also have a strong presence. The majority of NFIB member companies have fewer than ten employees and generate annual revenues of less than $1 million. This sets it apart from many trade associations, which often represent a small number of large firms. The NFIB maintains links to its members in a variety of ways. It offers selective material benefits, including publications and travel and insurance discount packages. It holds periodic conferences of its members. The NFIB also allows its members to participate in its internal decision making. While only a small proportion of NFIB members take part in the organization's political activity, they are still able to have a considerable impact in both campaigning and lobbying (Shaiko and Wallace 1999).

N.F.I.B. Stands for G.O.P?

The NFIB was founded in 1943. Under the leadership of Jack Faris, who became president in 1992, the NFIB greatly increased its political activism. It built strong ties to the congressional Republican leadership; the NFIB was also one of the leading opponents of the Clinton health care plan. Indeed, some observers gave the NFIB's grassroots network credit (or blame) for the plan's demise. Unlike representatives of big business, who were initially sympathetic to health care reform, the NFIB was adamantly opposed from the start. Many of its members feared that a health insurance mandate might drive them out of business. As a group dependent on purposive incentives for survival, the NFIB had a vested interest in convincing small-business owners that their economic interests were under attack. The NFIB's campaign against the Clinton plan solidified its ties to the GOP and helped build its grassroots network (Shaiko and Wallace 1999).

Under the direction of top officials Marc Nuttle and Jeff Butzke, the NFIB increased its staff eightfold and used its PAC more aggressively during the 1993–1994 cycle. The NFIB conducted opposition research, provided advice to candidates, and sent mailings to its members (Drew 1997). Balz and Brownstein (1996) call the NFIB part of the "leave us alone" coalition that also included the NRA and the Christian Coalition and that helped elect a Republican Congress in 1994. The NFIB spent $3.5 million on the 1994 congressional elections (Shaiko and Wallace 1999).

After the Republican takeover, the NFIB was able to gain influence over the congressional agenda. But despite its power, it was unable to prevent Congress from raising the minimum wage in the summer of 1996 (Drew 1997). The NFIB was active in defending the Republican majority in the 1996 congressional elections. It helped form the business-based "Coalition" that ran issue ads to counter the AFL-CIO's campaign; it also used its grassroots network to provide intelligence on House and Senate races. It mailed nearly 200,000 letters to NFIB members in 103 districts; it also sent nearly 240,000 foldouts, which were not considered to be campaign posters even though they fulfilled the same function as them. The NFIB's PAC gave about half of its funds to nonincumbents—an unusually high percentage for all but the most ideological groups. The NFIB's involvement included monetary contributions, in-kind media ads, fund-raisers, press conferences, volunteer recruitment, voter turnout, and member contact (Herrnson 1998; Shaiko and Wallace 1999). NFIB officials later took credit for the Republicans' holding on to control of Congress (Drew 1997).

The NFIB reportedly spent $8 million on congressional races in 2000, supporting thirty candidates in the House and Senate (all Republican), of whom half won (Fields 2000). One study found that, in a sample of House and Senate races, the NFIB was the most active Republican group in conducting ground operations, such as running phone banks and sending mail. The NFIB claimed to have spent $8 million on the 2000 elections, focusing primarily on communicating with its members (Baker and Magleby 2003). In 2002, the NFIB was among the several business groups that increased their efforts to elect Republicans to Congress (Magleby and Tanner 2004). In both 2002 and 2004, the NFIB took part in the Prosperity Project, an effort led by the Business Industry Political Action Committee that was aimed at helping businesses communicate about politics with their employees.

The Association of Trial Lawyers of America

The Association of Trial Lawyers of America represents 56,000 members of the trial bar. It began in 1946 as the National Association of Claimants' Compensation Attorneys; it evolved into ATLA, which was incorporated in 1972. In 1977, ATLA's headquarters moved from Boston to Washington, D.C. ATLA operates one of the most generous PACs, donating $2.1 million to candidates in 2003–2004, with 93 percent going to Democrats. It ranked seventh among all PACs in contributions to candidates; it ranked fourth in giving to Democrats. (ATLA also contributed to pro-Democratic 527s such as America Votes and America Coming Together.) ATLA far outstrips any other nonlabor PAC in contributions to congressional Democrats.[2] But ATLA's PAC giving is dwarfed by the political donations of individual trial lawyers and firms. Partners in Williams & Bailey, a Houston personal injury firm that has been involved in tobacco litigation, gave $1.4 million in soft money to the Democrats in 1999–2000. The firm of Peter Angelos, a Baltimore trial lawyer and owner of the Baltimore Orioles, gave $1.2 million. ATLA itself gave $965,000, virtually all of it to the Democrats. The Center for Responsive Politics reports that lawyers and law firms gave more than $84 million to candidates and parties in 2003–2004; only one of the top ten donor firms gave more to the GOP than to the Democrats. Overall, lawyers and law firms gave 80 percent of their contributions to Democrats.[3]

According to the *Washington Post*, ATLA "serves as a kind of rapid financial response team for Democratic candidates in need," letting lawyers around the country know that they need to lend their support (Morgan 2000). The settlement of a variety of class action lawsuits on subjects ranging from tobacco to asbestos has increased trial lawyers' coffers, allowing them to give even more to the Democrats (Cohen 2000). Trial lawyers strongly supported the presidential candidacy of Al Gore, who had opposed tort reform and backed allowing patients to sue their health maintenance organizations (HMOs). By contrast, George W. Bush had passed tort reform in Texas, traditionally a trial lawyer stronghold.

As expected, President Bush turned out to be a fierce opponent of the trial bar. He backed limits on awards in malpractice suits; such bills passed the House in 2003 and 2004, but were filibustered in the Senate both years. Bush also fought to restrict class action lawsuits and finally won in early 2005. On these issues, ATLA battled a coalition that included the U.S. Chamber of Commerce, the Business Roundtable, the American Insurance Association, and the American Medical Association. ATLA worked with consumer, environmental, and civil rights groups (Serafini 2004b; Zeller 2003; Stone 2003b).

ATLA conducts a program called ATLA's List, "a network that communicates with 3,000 members, identifying candidates, causes and organizations sympathetic to ATLA's views" (Morgan 2000). In 1998, millionaire trial lawyer John Edwards (D-NC) ousted Senator Lauch Faircloth (R); in 2000, three other wealthy trial lawyers sought to be elected to the House and Senate. All lost. When Edwards ran for president in 2004, trial lawyers provided the bulk of his funding; they proceeded to strongly support John Kerry's campaign, especially after Kerry named Edwards as his running mate.

The American Medical Association

The American Medical Association, founded in 1847, is the nation's leading organization of doctors, with 290,000 members. It has a federated structure composed of state medical societies. It is presided over by a board of trustees, who are chosen by the House of Delegates, the AMA's governing body. Members may join to participate in AMA activities and to support its political activities, but the AMA offers a variety of material incentives to members, most notably a subscription to the prestigious *Journal of the*

American Medical Association. The AMA came to dominate American medicine during the nineteenth century, when it successfully established standards for medical education (DiBacco 1998). By the early twentieth century, doctors could not practice without belonging to their state medical societies, which in turn belonged to the AMA (Goldstein 1998).

The AMA reached its peak of influence during the 1940s and 1950s, when 90 percent of American physicians belonged. The AMA and state medical societies controlled entry into the profession, effectively limiting the number of doctors. But the AMA lost credibility when, after fighting against Medicare for years, the program actually increased many doctors' income. Medicare and Medicaid led to increased demand for health care, so the AMA lost its control over the education of doctors, whose proportion to the population doubled from 1970 to 1998. As more doctors were educated as specialists, they joined specialty societies but not the AMA. As the AMA's ability to deliver material incentives declined, so did its dominance of the medical profession. Today, 70 percent of doctors belong to specialty societies. In 1975, 50 percent of physicians belonged to the AMA; by 2001, only 32 percent did. These specialty societies, now organized into the Alliance of Medical Societies, are competing with the AMA on Capitol Hill ("Declining Professions" 1998; Goldstein 1998; Tye 1999b; Wolinsky 1999; Zuger 1997; Zeller 2003; Dreyfuss 1998; Romano 2001).

The changing nature of the medical profession has also hurt the AMA. The number of female and minority physicians has soared in recent years, but most have not joined the AMA, which has retained a reputation as a conservative organization dominated by older white men. In the AMA's heyday, most doctors owned their own practices or worked in hospitals that they controlled; today, most doctors are salaried employees. The federal government and private corporations have pushed to control costs, limiting doctors' autonomy to practice medicine. The AMA, so long the dominant lobby in the health care world, has lost prominence to specialty societies, managed care organizations, and public and private purchasers. This decline has contributed to a decline in the AMA's once-vaunted political clout. Internal squabbles and what has been described as a "dysfunctional" Washington staff have convinced many policymakers that the AMA no longer speaks effectively for American medicine (Zuger 1997; "Declining Professions" 1998; Dreyfuss 1998; Goldstein 1998; Gusmano 1999; Zeller 2003).

Potent Political Medicine?

The AMA has been a leading user of independent expenditures since 1986. AMPAC spent $1.8 million on independent expenditures in 2000. Its beneficiaries included Senator Lincoln Chafee (R-RI), Senate candidate John Ensign

(R-NV), House candidates Paul Perry (D-IN) and Bill Sublette (R-FL), and Reps. Clay Shaw (R-FL), Marge Roukema (R-NJ), Saxby Chambliss (R-GA), and Jim Maloney (D-CT). AMPAC spent almost $2 million on independent expenditures in 2002, with 85 percent of its spending supporting Republicans. Top beneficiaries included Iowa Senate candidate Greg Ganske (R), House candidate Phil Gingrey (R-GA), Senator Wayne Allard (R-CO), and House candidate Dennis Cardoza (D-CA). Ganske, Gingrey, and Allard are all physicians. Two years later, the AMA spent just over $1 million on independent expenditures, virtually all of it supporting Republicans. Its top beneficiary was Senate candidate Richard Burr (R-NC); the AMA spent $719,992 supporting his candidacy. The AMA spent $199,067 supporting the House candidacy of Tom Price (R-GA), a physician. Both Burr and Price won. Other beneficiaries of AMA independent expenditures included Senator Lisa Murkowski (R-AK), Senate candidate Jim DeMint (R-SC), Rep. Earl Pomeroy (D-ND), and House candidate Melissa Brown (R-PA). Only Brown, an ophthalmologist, lost.

AMPAC was created in 1961 and is the oldest trade association PAC.[4] Its board is chosen by the AMA's Board of Trustees. The board in turn chooses the executive director. AMPAC makes its decisions about contributions through its Congressional Review Committee. Besides donating to candidates, AMPAC also makes in-kind contributions. These include training candidates and supplying them with polling data. The AMA also benefits from the grassroots political activity of its members. The AMA runs an academy that trains doctors to be effective campaign volunteers; the AMA also encourages doctors to run for political office. Doctors have long been active in raising money for members of Congress; in recent years, the AMA has tried to coordinate this activity in support of favored candidates (Gusmano 1999).

Notes

1. Center for Responsive Politics. www.crp.org.
2. Center for Responsive Politics. www.crp.org.
3. Center for Responsive Politics. www.crp.org.
4. The proximate cause for the creation of AMPAC was the election of John F. Kennedy, who supported the creation of Medicare. But the AMA had been politically active for decades, opposing proposals for national health insurance and supporting the election of conservative candidates. See Gusmano 1999.

III
THE RESOURCES

6

Money

GROUPS HAVE THREE FUNDAMENTAL RESOURCES that they can use to affect elections: money, membership, and expertise.[1] These resources, of course, influence one another: a money-rich group can develop expertise that would be beyond the means of a poorer group. A group with a membership in the millions can ordinarily raise funds that would dwarf those of many smaller groups, although a few relatively small groups, such as the Association of Trial Lawyers of America (ATLA) or the Club for Growth, have been able to raise impressive sums from their wealthy members. Groups can combine these resources in pursuit of their goals: groups that have developed credibility on particular issues can exploit this by using money to air broadcast ads.

Obviously, not every group has the same amount of money available for political spending. Some locally based grassroots groups have been able to affect elections by focusing on directly contacting voters by mail or by otherwise distributing literature. For example, some right-to-life groups leaflet church parking lots just before election day in order to reach churchgoing voters, who are more likely to support their cause. But, in general, political activity requires thousands or even millions of dollars.

The most common means of spending money in elections is sponsoring a political action committee (PAC). But PACs have their limitations. PACs can give only $10,000 per candidate per campaign per cycle—hardly enough to affect the outcome of a race. While groups may use their treasury funds to pay for overhead, these funds may not be used for contributions. Contributions may be paid for only with "hard money" donations, which are limited to $5,000 per individual. A PAC contribution also does little for a group that is interested in drawing attention to its issue, whether to highlight its importance, show its salience to voters, or defend its side against opponents. The political environment of the late 1990s, with narrow margins of control in Congress, with the two parties increasingly polarized on issues (at least on Capitol Hill), and with a limited number of competitive races would seem tailor made for groups to find ways around the limitations of PACs.

Negative Factors

Despite the advantages offered through spending money outside the PAC system, most politically active groups shy away from direct action in congressional elections. Corporations that are seeking access almost always confine their activities to sponsoring a PAC (Sabato 1984). More interested in currying favor with incumbents than in unseating them, they fear angering members who could retaliate against them. Such corporations also lack the incentive to get around restrictions on PAC giving, since they often prefer to spread their money around to influence the largest possible number of members rather than concentrate their resources in a few close races (Eismeier and Pollock 1988; Handler and Mulkern 1992). Access-oriented corporations are often concerned with technical issues of taxes or regulation that have little saliency with the general public. And while they tend to favor Republicans, these corporations seldom adopt the kind of strong partisanship that would lead them to increase their political activity (see Mutch 1994 and 1999 for an example of a corporation that has taken avoidance of controversy to an extreme).

Before the Bipartisan Campaign Reform Act of 2002 (BCRA), corporations that wished to affect elections but had no resource other than money could spend that money on broadcast ads. Since these corporations rarely have a positive image (or much of an image at all) and may fear retaliation from angered politicians, they tend to donate to groups that will sponsor ads rather than sponsoring ads themselves. In 2000 and 2002, pharmaceutical companies, seeking to shape a potential Medicare prescription drug benefit, gave heavily to an existing group (the U.S. Chamber of Commerce), a newly created "front group" (Citizens for Better Medicare), and a long-standing "front group" (the United Seniors Association) run by a longtime Republican consultant. All three groups ran ads on the prescription drug benefit that were targeted to more competitive races. In a study conducted by the Center for the Study of Elections and Democracy, 58 percent of respondents had a negative impression of the pharmaceutical industry; only 5 percent viewed the United Seniors Association negatively (Magleby 2004).

Another probusiness group, Americans for Job Security (AJS), spent millions on issue ads covering a variety of topics, including attacking Washington Senate nominee Maria Cantwell (D) for her views on salmon preservation, and defending Senator Spencer Abraham (R) for backing expanded immigration. AJS claims to have spent between $10 and $12 million on issue ads in 2000 (March and Fechter 2000). The Brennan Center for Justice tracked almost $2 million in spending by AJS on TV ads in the months leading up to the election (Brennan Center for Justice 2000). Unlike Citizens for Better Medicare, which published a list of its members, Americans for Job Security has not released its donors. It was founded in 1997 with a $1 million gift by the American Insurance Association (AIA); the AIA, however, claims that it no longer supports AJS.[2]

Before BCRA, corporations could also, of course, give soft money to the political parties. In the 1999–2000 cycle, corporations gave 88 percent of soft money contributions; Democratic committees received 80 percent of their soft money from corporations, while the GOP received 94 percent.[3] Corporate funds split 57 percent to 43 percent in favor of the GOP. Federal soft money was banned under BCRA. According to Boatright et al. (2003), most corporations gave to the parties because the corporations were solicited by politicians. While some corporations may give to new independent groups loosely associated with the parties, most will simply withhold the funds. Even before BCRA, some corporate lobbyists expressed wariness about soft money, and looked forward to its eventual abolition.

The Business Industry Political Action Committee (BIPAC), a longtime lead PAC in the business/conservative community, began in 2000 a program to help corporations speak to their employees about elections.[4] Greg Casey, president of BIPAC, explained that his group had found that business's traditional means of participation—contributing money to candidates and parties, which then use the funds to pay for commercials—was losing effectiveness because broadcast ads do not sway voters as well as they used to. He came to believe that businesses would do better if they used the credibility that they have with their employees to shape their political views.[5] (This is discussed further in chapter 5.) But as one business lobbyist commented, "Business traditionally doesn't like politics. I mean, it's just easier to write a check, it's easier to contribute to a candidate, a party. There is discomfort in many businesses about talking to employees generally about policy issues."[6]

Money can also allow a group that had previously stayed out of the electoral arena to enter it in a major fashion—to exploit its expertise. In 2000, thanks to a large undisclosed gift, the National Association for the Advancement of Colored People (NAACP) was able to create a 501 (c) (4) affiliate, the NAACP National Voter Fund (NVF) (Eversley 2000; Fletcher 2000). This fund spent about

$11 million on broadcast issue advocacy and on a voter turnout effort, allowing the NAACP to turn decades of "issue credibility" into political power (Lawrence 2000). Kweisi Mfume, president of the NAACP, estimated that the group registered more than 2.5 million African Americans to vote (Mintz 2000). The NVF reportedly spent $2 million on broadcast ads. These included two television commercials criticizing George W. Bush for vetoing a hate crimes bill. Both featured Renee Mullins, daughter of James Byrd, an African American man dragged to his death in Jasper, Texas (J. Broder 2000; Freeman 2000). According to an NAACP official, the fund also aired commercials on black talk radio.[7]

Another group that shies away from non-PAC activity is AARP, which also does not sponsor a PAC. Martin Burns, a lobbyist for AARP, explained that his organization avoids any activity that could support parties or candidates:

> Burns: [O]ur membership is very varied and diverse. They see us as being an advocate for them as opposed to being an advocate for any party, person, political philosophy. . . . One of the key things for understanding AARP, unlike any organization, for better or for worse that you will ever come upon, we have 33 million members. It's almost impossible to kind of get a consensus on anything. So it's hard for us to move on a particular issue because our membership is so varied and diverse.
>
> Skinner: Have you ever considered setting up a political action committee?
>
> Burns: No, for the same reasons. Our members kind of want us to be involved in the political process in the sense of being involved in issues, but they don't want us to endorse candidates, they don't want us to give people any money.[8]

AARP does distribute voter guides, but they simply feature statements by major candidates on the organization's key issues, which include Medicare, Social Security, long-term care, and managed care. It also conducts advertising campaigns on these issues, but these campaigns generally do not refer to candidates. The AARP's reliance on material incentives, combined with its inability to prevent exit by its members, and the sheer heterogeneity of its membership force it to remain cautious in its political activity.

Legal issues also restrict interest groups' use of money. If groups are conducting independent expenditures, they may not coordinate their efforts with the candidates they are supporting or with groups aiding those candidates. One political activist said in an interview that during the regular meetings of interest group leaders he attended, representatives of groups conducting independent expenditures would have to leave the room during discussions of relevant races. Mary Crawford, communications director for the National Federation of Independent Business (NFIB), explained that her group shies away from independent expenditures because

[i]f you're going to do an independent expenditure, you really have to keep a fire-wall between your organization and the campaign, to make sure what you're doing is truly independent. And we talk to campaigns, our political people talk to campaigns on a pretty regular basis, at least ones that matter. So it's pretty hard to meet that test.[9]

Yet another restriction on groups' use of money is that groups can conduct independent expenditures only by setting up a PAC and by raising "hard money"—contributions of limited size donated by individuals and other PACs. Groups may not use their treasury funds. In the wake of a series of court decisions reaffirming the "magic words" standard, this limitation may have encouraged groups to engage in issue advocacy instead.

Positive Factors

Groups that have a strong partisan preference and whose issues are highly salient to voters have powerful incentives to get involved beyond PAC contributions. Groups whose agendas are affected greatly by partisan control, such as organized labor, may feel the need to sway the balance of power. Groups interested in visible and salient issues, such as abortion and the environment, may believe that they can move public opinion, or at least mobilize their supporters, in a fashion that would produce a favorable legislative result.

Another key factor is simply having enough money to have an impact. The AFL-CIO and the National Rifle Association (NRA), for example, regularly spend tens of millions of dollars nationwide, while many smaller groups might spend a hundred thousand or less. These smaller groups might be able to conduct some get-out-the-vote activity, but conducting a major broadcast campaign is well beyond their capacity.

Besides simply swaying elections, groups may engage in direct communication in order to raise the visibility of their issues. Groups need to show that voters care about their issues enough to affect their votes. Much as politicians "claim credit" for legislation (see Mayhew 1974), groups "claim credit" for the election or defeat of candidates.[10] Simply making a PAC contribution or giving soft money cannot communicate such a message. Nor can such contributions build a longer-term base of support for the group or contribute to organizational maintenance. Gloria Totten, former political director of NARAL, explained:

[A]ll of our electoral choices have to be made and considered how it's going to promote the issue. Are people going to think it's more salient? Are they going to understand, are we going to be able to use the election to make sure people understand what is happening legislatively, you know, this year what the court could do with the issue, and our driving, and doing things that instill in them a stronger sense of activism on the issue, a stronger sense of wanting to demonstrate it by voting for this candidate but it has a longer term goal. We are going to go back to those people to do the constituent work and the lobbying work.[11]

Totten gave the 1998 U.S. Senate race in New York as an example of NARAL's efforts to make the abortion issue salient. Senator Al D'Amato, an antiabortion Republican representing a mostly pro-choice state, faced a challenge from Rep. Charles Schumer (D), a staunch supporter of abortion rights. D'Amato had long downplayed his views on abortion in order to win support from pro-choice voters. NARAL got involved in this race in part because Schumer was willing to use the abortion issue against D'Amato:

I mean, when you've looked at the Senate races and you looked at how much faith we had that Schumer could do this and that he could actually take D'Amato out, then we started looking at the polling and we realized that seven out of ten pro-choice New Yorkers did not know D'Amato's position on the issue, which is huge if we could turn it around, then we would be contributing to the margin of victory in a significant way.... D'Amato's a classic target candidate for us who voted against the Freedom of Clinic Entrances Act, he's cosponsor of the Human Life Amendment. He's somebody we could really raise the issue over. ... [B]ecause he was such a great target, because Schumer also used the issue even though we were independent, it made it a lot better.[12]

Groups can also capitalize on the visibility of their issue created by the actions of politicians. Chuck Cunningham, director of federal affairs for the National Rifle Association, said that his organization found it much easier to motivate gun owners for the 2000 election because Bill Clinton and Al Gore had both spoken out in favor of gun control. Also, in the wake of the mass shooting at Columbine High School in 1999, congressional Democrats had pushed greater restrictions on gun shows. The Million Mom March rallied in Washington in favor of gun control. The Million Moms were addressed by talk show host Rosie O'Donnell; a tape of this address later was incorporated into an NRA infomercial. The NRA mailed gun owners information that included quotes from Gore and from the Clinton Justice Department. The prominence of the gun issue thus allowed the NRA to mobilize gun owners to a greater extent than would have been the case if Clinton, Gore, and O'Donnell had remained silent.

In 2004, NARAL attempted to turn an issue that had harmed it—partial-birth abortion (PBA)—into an asset. In November 2003, when Bush signed into law the PBA ban, he was surrounded by the bill's sponsors: six white men. Afterward, the leadership of both Planned Parenthood and NARAL mocked Bush, with NARAL's Kate Michelman declaring, "It's an enduring image and we're going to make sure it's an enduring image" (Carney 2004; Stolberg 2003). During the 2004 campaign, NARAL sent a mailing depicting the signing ceremony with the accompanying text: "Raise your hand if you ever had a gynecological exam" (Candisky 2004).

Options for the Use of Money

Before the passage of BCRA, one obvious option for the use of money was to donate soft money to one or both of the political parties. Giving soft money has the advantage of being unlimited; groups can give millions of their treasury funds, and they regularly do so. Not surprisingly, many corporations made soft money their principal form of extra-PAC involvement. But of the groups included in this study, only two gave soft money in any significant amount: the AFL-CIO and the NRA. Chuck Cunningham of the NRA explained that his group gave PAC money so that its lobbyists could attend fundraisers, where they can meet with elected officials. The AFL-CIO and its member unions, which have access to huge treasury funds, were among the Democratic Party's principal soft-money donors. But their soft-money giving remained constant between 2000 and 2002 at about $30 million. Even as unions poured millions into the Democrats' coffers, they did not significantly increase their PAC giving, which remained at about $50 million from 1997–1998 through 2001–2002 (Boatright et al. 2003; Center for Responsive Politics). While ATLA did not give soft money, its members gave millions of dollars in soft money to the Democrats.

But most issue groups did not give soft money, perhaps because they saw it as an inefficient use of their resources. Giving soft money does not build an organization nor does it raise the profile of an issue. Many group representatives believed that a given increment of money was more effectively spent by them than by parties because they had more credibility with certain audiences. Carol Long Tobias, political director for the National Right to Life Committee (NRLC), argued that her group's independent expenditures moved pro-life voters in a way that party or candidate communications could not:

> If we contribute money to a candidate, the candidate can go out and talk about education or crime, or you know, whatever issue is important to them. But that generally doesn't encourage pro-lifers to cross party lines, which we think we can—well, we know we can get people to cross party lines to vote for pro-life

candidates. We find it more effective to go directly to pro-life voters and say, this is the great candidate, you know, vote for him or her. And we think coming in as a third party rather than a candidate herself, we can also being some more credibility to the candidate's position.[13]

One important decision for groups is whether to engage in express advocacy, that is, whether to do independent expenditure or issue advocacy. Both allow groups to have a much bigger impact than they would have by just making PAC contributions. Tobias explained this advantage of going independent:

And also part of it is that the contribution limit being $5,000, especially if you're talking about a statewide senate race, you can't do anything for $5,000. You know, radio ads, you could blow that in, you know, one day. And then you, you know . . . independent expenditures allow you to do a lot of extras . . . the campaign has absolutely no knowledge of what you're doing.[14]

Similarly, Totten explained that independent expenditures allow NARAL to spend hundreds of thousands of dollars on a race.

As tables 3, 4, and 5 (see chapter 4) show, a relatively few number of groups dominate spending on independent expenditures, most of them highly ideological or partisan. These groups—such as the NRA or the NRLC—usually favor one party virtually exclusively in their independent spending. They also usually have hundreds of thousands—or even millions—of members who can contribute to the group's PAC, which is the only means by which they can fund an independent expenditure.

But independent expenditures and issue advocacy operate under different rules and offer different opportunities. Independent expenditures must be funded with scarce "hard money"; issue advocacy can be funded from any source (since it falls outside the campaign finance system). Independent expenditures may not be coordinated with candidates; issue advocacy falls into a grayer area. Independent expenditures may explicitly endorse a candidate; issue advocacy may not. The NRA and NRLC frequently engage in independent expenditures; the AFL-CIO and the Sierra Club have been pioneers in issue advocacy; NARAL has done both.

Issue advocacy also allows groups to draw on sources of money normally off limits. Businesses, trade associations, and membership groups can use their treasury funds. Labor unions can use membership dues. Groups of all kinds can use very large donations from wealthy individuals—which Planned Parenthood and the NAACP have done.

Issue advocacy has its disadvantages, though. A staffer for one of the most politically active labor unions explained that his group prefers independent expenditures to issue advocacy because it prefers to keep the distinction clear between elections and lobbying.

The Sierra Club has conducted one of the most visible issue advocacy programs, the Environmental Voter Education Campaign (EVEC), which has used local issues to highlight the voting records of members of Congress. EVEC has included broadcast ads, which have mostly run in closely contested races. Deanna White, deputy political director for the Sierra Club, described EVEC:

> Part of what education is about is exposing a targeted segmented of the population to something that polling shows they care about and letting them know what their candidate in a race is doing or not doing on their behalf. Part of what we know is that people are woefully ignorant about what goes on in Washington. They have no idea how their member is voting. They have no idea if the member is voting on things that affect exactly what's going on in their backyard, either drinking water or the quality of the air their kids breathe, and so what we want to do is reach them in a way that's not political. It's not like sending them a direct mail piece. It is about trying to latch into something local that they care about. And television is very good at that. It's very evocative, obviously, it's a visual medium. And it says, here's your Candlewood Lake in Connecticut. Jim Maloney has been great about making sure it isn't developed. . . . I can show people swimming, and water skiing on Candlewood Lake. And it evokes all their childhood memories and the memories they hope to give their own children. So, why not use the most powerful tool available?[15]

White said the Sierra Club selects issues for EVEC through public opinion research; EVEC ads tend to be aimed at women with children because they supposedly tend to be the voters most concerned about environmental issues. White said that local issues—whether hog farms in North Carolina or the Great Lakes in Michigan—tend to be more effective at swaying voters, because the voters can grasp them more easily. Kim Haddow, media consultant for the Sierra Club, admitted that the club concentrates its ads in close races, but only because "that means that the elected official or candidate whose attention we're trying to get is paying attention to what people are saying, and our voter education program is designed to create demand for environmental protection."[16]

Both Haddow and White insisted that EVEC is meant primarily to lobby members of Congress to back environmental protection. White admitted that she had no evidence that EVEC led members to change their votes, but she asserted that its ads "shine a spotlight" on particular issues. Haddow recalled that Sierra Club ads aired during the 1998 Senate race in Nevada resulted in the candidates' paying more attention to clean-water and clean-air issues. However, environmental issues "work best in a negative context," according to White, because "people are shocked . . . when a member does something stupid like vote against the Clean Water Act or toughening clean water standards."[17]

Another example of issue advocacy in the 2000 election was the campaign of Montanans for Common Sense Mining Laws (MCSML). Senator Conrad Burns (R-MT) was a major target for trial lawyers in 2000. Trial lawyers contributed $400,000 to Montanans for Common Sense Mining Laws, which ran TV ads in January attacking Burns for his sponsorship of a bill limiting corporate responsibility for asbestos-caused illnesses. Business groups later responded with their own ads, but Burns eventually withdrew his support for the legislation (D. Carney 2000; Wilson 2001; Hitt and Cooper 2000). Trial lawyers strongly supported Burns's Democratic opponent, Brian Schweitzer (D. Carney 2000). Indeed, *Business Week* credited trial lawyers with "making a race out of what was a snoozer" (D. Carney 2000). Burns, who had been favored for reelection, narrowly defeated Schweitzer, even as Bush carried the state by a huge margin. An official with ATLA said that while his group did not create MCSML, the two organizations held the same position on asbestos litigation, and it was likely that many ATLA supporters backed the Montana group.[18]

In 2000 and 2002, business dominated issue advocacy, with the pharmaceutical industry backing such "shell groups" as Citizens for Better Medicare and the United Seniors Association, and also funding advertising sponsored by the U.S. Chamber of Commerce (Magleby and Tanner 2004; Baker and Magleby 2003).

Two abortion-rights groups engaged in issue advocacy in 2000, mostly focusing on the presidential race. By comparison, antiabortion groups mostly stayed off the airwaves, although there have been campaigns aimed at changing long-term attitudes about abortion. Both NARAL and Planned Parenthood ran broadcast ads; NARAL also conducted a voter turnout campaign. Before the election, Totten explained NARAL's presidential-issue advocacy:

> [W]e're doing issue advocacy because people do not know that George W. Bush is antichoice. . . . And so in March 1999, we started doing issue advocacy in the presidential campaign with television ads. We've done four ads that focus on George W. Bush's antichoice position and the powers of the president to select Supreme Court justices.[19]

A top official with Planned Parenthood criticized NARAL's focus on the Supreme Court, because many voters know little about the Court and its effect on their lives. Instead Planned Parenthood featured in its issue ads Republican women discussing George W. Bush's views on abortion, family planning, and sex education.

Totten explained that NARAL does independent expenditures in key races in constituencies where it has identified many pro-choice voters or where it has a strong state affiliate. In states where NARAL is weak—for example, most of the Deep South—it will simply contribute to a candidate's campaign. But NARAL will give top-tier treatment to states where its organization is strong and where there are multiple key races: presidential, Senate, House. NARAL staff will visit the state and compose a campaign plan that may include broadcast ads, phone banks, literature mailings, and volunteer recruitment. NARAL may also send organizers to assist candidates in mobilizing pro-choice voters.[20]

One of NARAL's most prominent independent expenditures was conducted against Senator Al D'Amato (R-NY). In the New York Senate contest, NARAL's effort was assisted by the widely publicized murder of an abortion provider a few weeks before the election. It also ran TV ads specifically attacking D'Amato (Kolodny, Suarez, and Rodrigues 1999; O'Donnell 1998). One ad that was widely viewed as effective featured a woman who had been badly injured in the bombing of an Alabama abortion clinic. She attacked D'Amato for opposing legislation protecting access to abortion facilities. The ad appeared shortly after the widely publicized murder only a few days before the election of an upstate doctor who had performed abortions. Polls then showed D'Amato and Rep. Charles Schumer (D) neck and neck (McCarthy 1998; Waldman 1998). Schumer won by eleven points, ousting an eighteen-year incumbent. Postelection analyses concluded that the abortion issue had hurt D'Amato, particularly in the aftermath of the shooting. D'Amato lost women to Schumer 60 percent to 40 percent; he also fared poorly in some traditionally Republican suburban counties (Flynn 1998; Turner 1998).

In 2000, NARAL reportedly spent $2.2 million on independent expenditures in congressional elections (Magleby and Beal 2003). In Senate races, NARAL conducted four independent expenditures that exceeded $100,000. In Michigan, NARAL spent $368,974 backing Rep. Debbie Stabenow (D) in her successful challenge to Senator Spencer Abraham. One study found that NARAL assigned two paid staffers to help Stabenow and recruited over 500 volunteers for literature drops and writing letters to key newspapers. NARAL reported that its staffers contacted more than 150,000 pro-choice voters through persuasion and get-out-the-vote phone calls and mail (Traugott 2001). The *Detroit News* attributed Gore's and Stabenow's victories in Michigan, in part, to their strength in the Detroit suburbs, where many middle-class women reportedly disliked Bush's and Abraham's views on abortion (Trowbridge 2000).

In Missouri, NARAL spent $343,892 supporting Gov. Mel Carnahan (D) in his race against Senator John Ashcroft (R). Despite Carnahan's death in a plane crash in October, he defeated Ashcroft and his wife, Jean, was appointed to fill the Senate seat. NARAL claimed to have compiled a list of 170,000 pro-choice Missouri voters (Dao 2000). Before the election, NARAL announced plans to distribute 125,000 flyers in Missouri supporting Gore, Carnahan, and gubernatorial candidate Bob Holden (Von Drehle 2000). NARAL also reportedly ran a phone bank jointly with Planned Parenthood of the St. Louis Region that contacted at least 15,000 people (Kropf et al. 2001).

In Minnesota, NARAL spent $235,422 supporting former state auditor Mark Dayton in his successful challenge to Senator Rod Grams (R). It reportedly planned to call about 90,000 pro-choice voters in the state on behalf of Gore and Dayton ("Happenings Monday in the 2000 Campaign" 2000). NARAL's fourth-largest independent expenditure in a Senate race was in Washington State, where it spent $209,889 supporting former representative Maria Cantwell, who ousted two-term Senator Slade Gorton (R) by just over 2,000 votes. Before the election, NARAL announced plans to contact 150,000 voters by mail and telephone to urge them to turn out to back Gore and Cantwell (Connelly 2000).

In 2002, NARAL was the second-largest user of independent expenditures in congressional races, spending $2.37 million (Magleby and Tanner 2004). It continued its focus on using mail and telephone to reach targeted voters. In its unsuccessful drive to reelect Senator Jean Carnahan (D-MO), NARAL sent 332,000 pieces of mail and made 184,000 phone calls (Kropf et al. 2004). But NARAL saw Carnahan and several other favorites go down to defeat. In 2004, NARAL sponsored ads attacking George W. Bush for cutting family-planning funds, restricting stem cell research, and appointing officials who have opposed the "morning-after pill" (Kinnard 2004; Lightman 2004). NARAL spent $1.6 million on independent expenditures in the 2004 presidential race.[21]

According to Totten, NARAL is more likely to get involved in a race where there is a clear distinction between the candidates on the issue of abortion. She admitted that since pro-choicers tend to be more "multi-issue" than their opponents, NARAL has to work to make the issue "more salient" to voters.

Over the Air or On the Ground?

Another major decision a group must make about its political involvement is whether to reach voters through broadcast ads or through phone and mail contact. These decisions are shaped partially by the incentives that groups offer to members. Groups that offer purposive incentives, especially those that focus on issues with a narrow appeal, often avoid broadcast ads. The National Federation of Independent Business avoids broadcast ads because it prefers to concentrate its resources on communicating with its members. The National Right to Life Committee sponsors a small number of radio ads but it does not run television ads. Carol Long Tobias, political director for the NRLC, claimed that television stations had refused to air her group's ads.[22] The committee did sponsor a few radio ads in 2000, though.[23] Even its radio ads tend to be highly targeted; in the 2002 Missouri Senate race, Right to Life ran spots on Christian radio stations, whose listeners are likely to be highly sympathetic to the antiabortion cause (Kropf et al. 2004). But since Right to Life organizations tend to focus on turning out identified supporters of their cause, rather than speaking to the general public, it makes sense that they tend to avoid broadcast ads. Sponsoring broadcast ads would also raise the profile of the abortion issue and so stimulate the opposition.

The National Rifle Association, although it generally focuses on contacting gun owners through phone and mail, has sponsored some broadcast ads. Its most visible (and successful) campaign consisted of television infomercials that aired in 1999 and 2000 and encouraged gun owners to join the NRA. One infomercial explained the effect of gun restrictions passed in Great Britain, Australia, and Canada; gun owners from those countries urged Americans to join the NRA in order to defend their right to bear arms. Another featured talk show host Rosie O'Donnell addressing the Million Mom March; Chuck Cunningham, federal affairs director of the NRA, called O'Donnell a "frothing gun prohibitionist" who advocates gun control in such strident terms that she acts as a red flag to gun owners.[24] Cunningham said that Wayne LaPierre, executive vice president of the NRA, told him in early 2000 that the association had to increase its membership in key swing states. Cunningham and LaPierre decided to focus the ads on these states; much like NARAL, the NRA targeted states that were competitive in the presidential race and that had competitive House and Senate races. According to Cunningham, the ads' "primary reason . . . was membership solicitation," and they are so successful that "they bring in as much revenue as they cost to run them." In addition, they "energize[d]" members who viewed the ads.[25] By increasing the NRA's membership (which topped 4 million by election day), the infomercial campaign gave the association a large number of potential voters and supporters to mobilize in the campaign.

The NRA had occasionally produced broadcast ads in previous campaigns. Not all of those ads focused on gun rights. For example, in 1992, the NRA sponsored radio ads that criticized Reps. Dan Glickman (D-KS) and Mike Synar (D-OK) for taking foreign "junkets" and bouncing checks drawn on the House bank.[26] In 2004, the NRA began producing a news/talk program that airs on the Sirius satellite radio service.

The NRA's principal opponent on firearms issues, Handgun Control (now known as the Brady Campaign to Prevent Gun Violence), entered the issue advocacy fray in 2000 with a broadcast television campaign. Two onetime officials with Handgun Control explained that their group took to the airwaves because it had a relatively weak grassroots organization.[27] By contrast, Greg Casey of BIPAC has been encouraging the business community to grow its grassroots operations in order to take advantage of employers' relationships with employees. He argued that while broadcast ads may make donors feel good, they rarely have the impact of a strong ground campaign.[28] An official with the NAACP National Voter Fund argued that her group's broadcast ads, while well publicized, were far less effective than its program of contacting by phone African Americans who vote infrequently. She claimed only $2 million of the group's $11 million budget went to broadcast media.[29]

While it has shifted its focus to ground operations, the AFL-CIO remains one of the most important sponsors of broadcast ads. According to data from the Campaign Media Analysis Group, the AFL-CIO spent $21.1 million on issue ads in the 1999–2000 cycle; $9.5 million worth of ads appeared after Super Tuesday. The AFL-CIO spots made up 15 percent of all nonparty ads after Super Tuesday—14 percent of those that appeared after September 1 (Brennan Center for Justice 2000). Magleby and Tanner (2004) report that in its sample of 2002 House and Senate races, the AFL-CIO was the second-largest group for broadcast advertising; in a comparable study for 2000, Baker and Magleby find the AFL-CIO ranking fourth. According to AFL-CIO political director Steve Rosenthal, the federation advertises primarily in areas where there are few union members (Boatright et al. 2003). While many press accounts declared that the AFL-CIO dramatically changed its strategy after the 1996 elections, Mike Podhorzer, assistant political director for the labor federation, argued that it was simply adapting to changing conditions:

'96 . . . was a unique circumstance, because it was our feeling, and I think it was justified both by everything from our polling to what actually has happened in American politics since then, that the Gingrich Revolution was extremely threatening to working people, and that that had to become part of the national debate. And the principal purpose of the advertising, general advertising we did in '95, '96, was to protect Medicare, fight for minimum wage, take on what was then a very live debate about issues that mattered enormously to all working people. And that made sense in our context. Many people have characterized for us that it was about electioneering politicking, and certainly we wanted to hold members of Congress who disagree with us accountable. There's no question about that. But again, the context was the government shut down $270 billion from Medicare, just a complete assault on labor unions as an institution. And we had to fight back. And I think we did. In '98, there wasn't the same charged national issue environment.[30]

Podhorzer argued that in 2000, the AFL-CIO ran broadcast advertisements that were more focused on particular issues, as opposed to the more sweeping approach taken in 1996. While some of these issues came from debates on Capitol Hill, others came from surveys of members taken by volunteers in union locals. The AFL-CIO also conducts regular polls and focus groups of union members.[31] (The NRA also regularly polls its membership.) Some of the AFL-CIO's broadcast campaigns, such as the 1996 drive for an increase in the minimum wage, appear to have had multiple purposes: seeking the defeat of an unfriendly member, lobbying for a particular legislative result, and shaping public opinion on an issue. A report by a Campaign Finance Institute task force on disclosure (Campaign Finance Institute 2001) concluded that these three purposes are not easily disentangled. The authors of the report compare the three purposes to overlapping circles in a Venn diagram: "Any communication can have any one, any two or all three effects at once. It is intrinsic to this form of communication that you cannot surgically separate the three circles. The question is whether you can capture the part of the circle that overlaps with other circles" (Campaign Finance Institute 2001, sec. 3).

Getting Involved

Most of the groups included in this study use the same criteria for determining involvement in particular races and for determining the priority given those races. Generally, a group will back any incumbent who consistently supports its agenda.[32] Most groups rate members and candidates in some fashion; NARAL rates them from zero to one hundred; the NRA grades them from A to F. Groups use those ratings in different ways: NARAL will endorse only candidates who get a 100 rating, while the National Right to Life Committee does not have such a policy. The NFIB will not oppose the reelection of any incumbent who receives at least a 70 rating. Generally, incumbents get rated on their voting record; non-incumbents must answer a questionnaire or be interviewed, although those who have held public office will also be evaluated on their records. Some groups go further: the NRA also collects news clippings and broadcast transcripts.

Some organizations have highly centralized procedures for making endorsements. Chuck Cunningham of the NRA said that he makes the final decision on ratings and endorsements in federal races based on the recommendations of lobbyists. He also decides on the level of involvement, in conjunction with the trustees of the Political Victory Fund.[33] By contrast, the national AFL-CIO follows the lead of its state affiliates.[34]

Most groups in this study designate some races for priority involvement beyond simply making an endorsement. Generally, competitiveness and contrast are the most important factors in determining the level of involvement. Groups are more likely to step up their involvement in close races where they can make a difference, whether in protecting an ally or defeating an opponent (more than one interviewee admitted that groups can rarely move more then 5 percent of the electorate). They are also more likely to get involved where there is a clear difference between the candidates on the relevant issue, especially when one of the candidates takes a particularly visible stand. As Chuck Cunningham of the NRA explained:

> We will support a pro-gun incumbent who is being challenged by a pro-gun challenger. But we'll invest most of our resources in races where there's clearly a constrast between opposing candidates on gun control issues. We protect a good incumbent if they're being challenged by pro-gun candidate, but at the same time, we'll not gonna pull out the stops with radio and posters and stickers and all the rest. We'll communicate with our members and endorse them and send them a contribution.[35]

Similarly, the NFIB expands its involvement in key races to include contacting its activist members through the Value Added Voter Program.[36] Mike Podhorzer of the AFL-CIO said that the federation has enough resources to target every race that is seriously contested and that includes a pro-labor candidate. Both Podhorzer and Cunningham added that they reevaluate races as the campaign proceeds and add and subtract them from their priority list. For example, in the fall of 2000, Cunningham de-emphasized two House races in Oregon where the highly touted Republican nominees turned out to be lackluster campaigners, instead shifting their resources to defeating Reps. Sam Gejdenson (D-CT) and David Minge (D-MN), whose challengers showed surprising strength. Both Gejdenson and Minge lost.[37]

But many organizations have learned that their most important asset is not money. While corporations may sometimes have to rely only on giving money, labor unions and issue groups have memberships, sometimes in the hundreds of thousands, sometimes in the millions, that can be mobilized to vote or otherwise participate in politics. Most notably, the AFL-CIO has shifted its focus away from broadcast ads to turning out its members to vote. In the words of one union official, labor has shifted away from "buying the way"; instead, they are talking to their members.

Corporations and trade associations dominate soft-money and PAC giving, but most steer away from direct communication. Many corporations prefer to avoid public controversy or are interested primarily in narrow, technical issues with little partisan edge. Their PACs (unlike their labor equivalent) rarely contribute the maximum to candidates, so they have no need to get around the limits on donations.

There are a few notable exceptions to the political caution of business. "Peak business associations"—those organizations that strive to speak for the business community as a whole—are highly ideological and politically active. They include the NFIB, the National Association of Manufacturers, and the U.S. Chamber of Commerce. The pharmaceutical industry was the primary business sponsor of issue advocacy during the 2000 and 2002 elections, mostly through "shell groups" such as Citizens for Better Medicare and the United Seniors Association. Unlike most business interests, the pharmaceutical industry has been concerned with highly visible issues that break strongly along partisan lines, most notably the structure of a Medicare prescription drug benefit and the protection of patent rights for their products.

Some "shell groups" appear to be simply masks for their patrons. The Pharmaceutical Research and Manufacturers Association has admitted that it was the primary funder of Citizens for Better Medicare; the American Federation of State, County and Municipal Employees (AFSCME) has acknowledged that it set up American Family Voices (which ran advertisements attacking George W. Bush in 2000), although it was actually run by a Democratic consulting firm. Other "shell groups" such as Americans for Job Security may be better understood as service providers, much like political consultants. Instead of polling or fund-raising advice, AJS sells anonymity to corporations and trade associations that wish to fund advertising without risking adverse consequences.

Money is a resource probably best used in conjunction with membership and expertise. Whether it is the AFL-CIO communicating with its members, the Sierra Club exploiting its credibility on the environment, or the NRLC using its ability to speak to antiabortion voters, groups seem to function best when they use money to capitalize on other advantages. Having a ground organization also seems to help groups use money more effectively; for example, NARAL concentrates its efforts in constituencies where it has a significant state affiliate.

Notes

1. The following four chapters are based on two series of interviews with interest-group representatives in the Washington area. The first series was conducted during May and June 2000, the second—meant to review the 2000 election—was conducted during February and March 2001. These two batches of interviews are supplemented by work done by the author and others for the Campaign Finance Institute (CFI). Two roundtables were held by CFI during the spring of 2001 and included representatives from leading interest groups. The author was partially responsible for selecting participants for these events. The roundtables were followed by a series of interviews that

summer; the author conducted all the interviews, either on his own or in cooperation with Mark Rozell and Clyde Wilcox. The author thanks CFI, Rozell, and Wilcox for giving him permission to use these interviews.

2. Interview with AIA official, June 11, 2001.

3. Center for Responsive Politics, www.opensecrets.org/overview/blio.asp? Cycle=2000&display=Soft. These figures perhaps exaggerate the importance of corporate giving, since they include individual gifts from corporate executives. Some of what is labeled as "corporate" soft money is in fact large individual donations. Before BCRA, the Democratic Party was especially dependent on large individual donors. Nine of the ten top individual donors in 1999–2000 gave 97 percent or more of their gifts to Democrats, according to the Center for Responsive Politics (www.opensecrets.org/overview/topindivs.asp?cycle=2000). These included Hollywood tycoon Haim Saban and Loral Spacecom head Bernard Schwartz, whose million-plus donations to Democratic committees were classified as "corporate."

4. A *lead PAC* is one that makes its contributions early in the cycle and so sends a signal to allied PACs about which candidates are supportive and viable. For four decades, BIPAC has conducted research on probusiness congressional contenders.

5. Greg Casey, BIPAC, CFI Business/Conservative Roundtable, April 18, 2001.

6. Interview, June 6, 2001.

7. Participant, CFI Labor/Liberal Roundtable, April 11, 2001.

8. Interview with Martin Burns, AARP, June 13, 2000.

9. Interview with Mary Crawford, NFIB, May 24, 2000.

10. In 1978, the right-to-life movement "claimed credit" for the defeat of Senator Dick Clark (D-IA), showing that antiabortion Democrats would cross party lines on the issue. In 1989, National Abortion and Reproductive Rights Action League (NARAL) "claimed credit" for the election of Democratic governors in Virginia and New Jersey, showing that the issue of abortion rights could sway suburbanites away from pro-life Republicans. Most recently, the NRA has "claimed credit" for the election of George W. Bush, arguing that their efforts to get gun owners to vote for Bush made the difference in Arkansas, Tennessee, and West Virginia.

11. Interview with Gloria Totten, NARAL, May 26, 2000. Her comments were echoed by representatives of several other groups, including the National Education Association, Handgun Control, and the Service Employees International Union.

12. Interview with Gloria Totten, NARAL, May 26, 2000. Her comments were echoed by representatives of several other groups, including the National Education Association, Handgun Control, and the Service Employees International Union.

13. Interview with Carol Long Tobias, National Right to Life Committee, May 22, 2000.

14. Interview with Carol Long Tobias, National Right to Life Committee, May 22, 2000.

15. Interview with Deanna White, Sierra Club, June 15, 2000.

16. Interview with Kim Haddow, Sierra Club, June 15, 2000.

17. Interview with Deanna White, Sierra Club, June 15, 2000.

18. Interview with ATLA official, February 28, 2001.

19. Interview with Gloria Totten, NARAL, May 26, 2000.

20. Interview with Gloria Totten, NARAL, May 26, 2000.

21. Center for Responsive Politics. www.crp.org.

22. Interview with Carol Long Tobias, National Right to Life Committee, May 22, 2000.

23. Interview with Carol Long Tobias, National Right to Life Committee, April 30, 2001.

24. Interview with Chuck Cunningham, National Rifle Association, February 7, 2001.

25. Interview with Chuck Cunningham, National Rifle Association, February 7, 2001.

26. Interview with Chuck Cunningham, National Rifle Association, May 26, 2000.

27. Participant, CFI Labor/Liberal Roundtable, April 11, 2001; interview with Handgun Control Official, July 17, 2001.

28. Interview with Greg Casey, BIPAC, June 11, 2001.

29. Participant, CFI Labor/Liberal Roundtable, April 11, 2001.

30. Interview with Mike Podhorzer, AFL-CIO, March 1, 2001.

31. Interview with Mike Podhorzer, AFL-CIO, March 1, 2001.

32. This can create problems, especially in a purposive organization whose members may have other concerns. Chuck Cunningham of the NRA said that he receives the most complaints over an endorsement when the NRA supports an incumbent who takes liberal positions on other issues, such as abortion or taxes. In 1998, the Human Rights Campaign, the nation's leading gay and lesbian lobby, endorsed Senator Al D'Amato (R-NY) for reelection. The organization received much criticism from its members for this decision, in part because D'Amato opposed abortion rights.

33. Interview with Chuck Cunningham, National Rifle Association, May 26, 2000.

34. Interview with Mike Podhorzer, AFL-CIO, March 1, 2001.

35. Interview with Chuck Cunningham, National Rifle Association, May 26, 2000.

36. Interview with Mary Crawford, NFIB, February 8, 2001.

37. Interview with Chuck Cunningham, National Rifle Association, February 7, 2001.

7

Membership

<hr>

THE NATURE OF A GROUP'S MEMBERSHIP SHAPES ITS POLITICAL ACTIVITY. Four characteristics play particularly important roles. One is the type of *incentive* that is offered to members to join: purposive, material, or solidary (see Wilson 1973). Another is a group's *size*: a group with a membership in the millions has options that are not available to smaller groups. Yet another is the ease of *exit*, which affects the freedom of action possessed by a group's staff. Finally, a group's *grassroots organization* influences its ability to use its members as activists. A group that has active local affiliates can use its members more effectively than one whose members are simply names on a mailing list—or one whose only "members" are a handful of wealthy benefactors.

According to Rosenstone and Hansen (1993), "Citizen participation is a resource that political leaders use selectively in their battles for political advantage." Perhaps nowhere is that more important than in the electoral arena. Verba, Schlozman, and Brady (1995) note that one of the most common reasons that people give for engaging in political activity is that someone asked them. The groups included in this study have become expert at asking their members to become politically active. But they do not all ask members to do the same things. Most purposive groups, with their relatively small, highly politicized memberships, do not waste much time asking their members to vote. The members are too few to sway elections by themselves, and, by the very act of joining such groups, they have shown themselves to be very likely voters. Instead, purposive groups focus on recruiting their members to become activists, who will help sympathetic candidates by giving their time, or donors, who will help them by giving their money.

By contrast, labor unions make turning out their members to vote their top priority. There are 13 million Americans who belong to AFL-CIO affiliate unions, dwarfing most purposive groups. And unlike people who join purposive groups, union members are not *necessarily* highly politicized since they did not join their unions for political reasons. Nor are union members as high status as the individuals who join purposive groups—although union members today are concentrated in the top three socioeconomic quintiles (see Brady et al. 2002). So unions possess the numbers to affect elections, but they have to mobilize their members to vote and to vote for their endorsed candidate. (In 2000, a year when organized labor strenuously supported Democrat Al Gore for president, 37 percent of union-household voters backed George W. Bush; in 2004, 40 percent did.) Unlike some (but not all) purposive groups, unions have real grass roots: their members work together and know one another. This allows unions to talk to their members in a way that other groups cannot replicate.

Labor: From One Member to Another

Organized labor has long been a potent force in elections. Unions build their membership through material incentives and coercion, creating a large "captive audience" that can be mobilized for political activity. Unlike many other politically active groups, unions can also draw on the solidary bonds between workers. Unions also have staff that are highly experienced and politicized, often holding views that are far more liberal than those of rank-and-file members. This gap encourages unions to expend significant resources on educating their members and turning them out to vote. This has been a major function of organized labor since at least the 1930s.

But the AFL-CIO has significantly increased its efforts since John Sweeney, former president of the Service Employees International Union (SEIU), took command of the labor federation in October 1995 (the AFL-CIO was also responding to the new threat of a Republican-controlled House of Representatives). While the AFL-CIO's broadcast ads received the bulk of publicity in 1996, unions also expanded their efforts to talk to their members. There were several postmortems on the AFL-CIO's 1996 effort. Most suggested that large expenditures on broadcast advertising were no substitute for strong, well-funded candidates (Business Industry Political Action Committee 1997, 1998; Gerber 1999). G. C. Jacobson (1999), however, finds that the AFL-CIO's campaign was responsible for defeating seven of the twelve Republican freshmen who lost in 1998. The AFL-CIO conducted studies that reportedly showed that personal contact was the most effective way to persuade members to back union-endorsed candidates (Edsall 2000).

Organized labor had another reason for changing its strategy. After the 1996 election, many Republicans vowed revenge for the AFL-CIO's attacks on them. Although their efforts to limit union power on the federal level failed, Republicans succeeded in placing on the California ballot Proposition 226, a referendum on "paycheck protection." This would require labor leaders to get the consent of their members in order to deduct money from their paychecks for political purposes. While this proposition failed (in large part, thanks to a huge turnout by union members), labor strategists realized that they needed to find ways to achieve political victory without unduly alienating potential Republican allies. Their success in mobilizing union members in California against Proposition 226 also convinced them that they had a resource their opponents generally lacked: an apparatus capable of turning out thousands of supportive voters (Dark 1999).

Finally, labor leaders knew that 1998 was likely to be a low-turnout election in which only about one-third of eligible Americans would vote; turnout in 1998 was actually 36 percent, the lowest ever (Abramson, Aldrich, and Rohde 1999). Midterm elections always see lower voter turnout than presidential years; union leaders also knew that peace and prosperity had produced an apathetic electorate. Under such circumstances, money spent on broadcast advertisements might well be wasted since most viewers would not vote. It would be more efficient for unions to expend resources on making sure that their members and other likely Democratic voters (especially African Americans) got to the polls. In the months before the election, many observers predicted that the Monica Lewinsky scandal would depress Democratic turnout, producing a GOP sweep that might increase support for Bill Clinton's impeachment. Given Clinton's support for organized labor's agenda (except on trade), the prospect of his removal gave turnout efforts a special urgency.

The AFL-CIO ended up spending $15 million on the "ground war" during the 1998 election, reportedly sending more than 9 million pieces of mail and placing 5.5 million phone calls. Labor's efforts were aimed mainly at encouraging voter turnout among union members. These efforts succeeded; exit polls indicated that union members composed a higher percentage of the electorate than in recent elections (Abramson, Aldrich, and Rohde 1999). Magleby (1999) credits organized labor's get-out-the-vote efforts with the reelection (by 401 votes) of Senator Harry Reid (D-NV). A huge mobilization campaign contributed significantly to a Democratic sweep in California. Union activity also helped defeat incumbent Republican senators Al D'Amato (NY) and Lauch Faircloth (NC).

Many observers credited organized labor for the surprisingly strong Democratic showing in the 1998 congressional elections. Most attention focused on unions' success in voter mobilization (Greenhouse 1998). But their issue advocacy efforts, whether through broadcast advertisements or direct mail, played a significant role in defeating Reps. Bill Redmond (R-NM), Jon Fox (R-PA), and Vince Snowbarger (R-KS), and in reelecting Reps. Leonard Boswell (D-IA) and Lane Evans (D-IL) (Stone 1997; Edsall 1998; Marcus 1998a; Magleby 1999).

The AFL-CIO planned to spend $46 million for its 1999–2000 political activities, targeting seventy-one congressional districts for special attention (Lawrence 2000; Swoboda 1999). It endorsed Vice President Al Gore for president in October 1999; two affiliate unions, the Teamsters and the United Automobile Workers (UAW), did not back Gore until the general-election season. Other labor unions, including SEIU and American Federation of State, County and Municipal Employees (AFSCME), backed Gore strongly during the primaries; one study found that the AFL-CIO was the most active interest group in the presidential primaries (Magleby 2000).

In the general election, the AFL-CIO reportedly targeted twelve states: Florida, Iowa, Michigan, Minnesota, Missouri, New Mexico, Ohio, Oregon, Pennsylvania, Washington, West Virginia, and Wisconsin (Dine 2000). Steve Rosenthal, political director of the AFL-CIO, said the federation had 1,300 full-time organizers working in the field (Dine 2000). One report claimed that unions had 100,000 campaign workers on election day driving people to the polls, making phone calls, and distributing leaflets (Dao 2000). While the AFL-CIO concentrated on the "ground war," it also conducted an "air war," reportedly spending $9.5 million on TV ads after Super Tuesday (Annenberg Public Policy Center 2001). The ads supported a "patient's bill of rights" and a Medicare prescription drug benefit. Unions did not increase their PAC contributions: between 1997–1998 and 2001–2002; overall labor PAC giving remained stable at around $50 million (Boatright et al. 2003).

Organized labor proved successful at turning out its members. Union voters cast 26 percent of the ballots in 2000, up from 23 percent in 1996 and 19 percent in 1992 (Dreazen 2000). This effort was credited with Gore's surprisingly wide victories in such strong union states as Michigan, Pennsylvania, and Washington. Gore also eked out victories in Oregon, Wisconsin, and Minnesota. Of the targeted states, only West Virginia, Ohio, and Missouri voted for Bush.

Democrats' net gain of five seats in the Senate also owed much to organized labor. Winning candidates Tom Carper (DE), Mel Carnahan (MO), Hillary Rodham Clinton (NY), Jon Corzine (NJ), Mark Dayton (MN), and Maria

Cantwell (WA) all received abundant labor support. In New York, the AFL-CIO reportedly distributed 1 million pieces of literature at 10,000 work sites (Levy 2000). Perhaps the most visible example of labor's campaign was the election of Rep. Debbie Stabenow over Senator Spencer Abraham in Michigan. Stabenow benefited from the UAW's winning of election day as a paid holiday in contract negotiations. She also was helped by the successful campaign conducted by the state's teachers' unions against a ballot proposition that would have provided vouchers for parents to pay for private or parochial schools. One study found the AFL-CIO to be the leading interest-group advertiser that supported Stabenow. Each union member reportedly received four to seven pieces of literature. Members of union households comprised 43 percent of voters and voted 63 percent for Stabenow (Traugott 2001). Two unsuccessful Senate candidates who received strong labor support were Ron Klink (D-PA) and Brian Schweitzer (D-MT).

The AFL-CIO further improved and expanded its "ground war" in the 1998 and 2000 elections. Francia (2000) finds that unions greatly increased their spending on grassroots communications in 1998 as compared to 1994. Spending on phone banks more than doubled in that time period, from $77,064 to $188,366, while spending on direct mail nearly quadrupled from $397,965 to $2.2 million. Francia (2000) also finds that members of union households were 1.6 times more likely to vote than other Americans. Members of union households accounted for 23 percent of voters in 1998 (26 percent in 2000), despite making up only 17 percent of the voting-age population. In 1994, only 14 percent of voters came from union households. In 1998, membership in a union household was a significant predictor of voter turnout; it was not in 1994 (Francia 2000). According to a high union official, from 1992 to 2000, nonunion turnout fell by 15.5 million voters while union turnout rose by 4.8 million voters.[1]

This increase in turnout appears to have been due to the unions' increased efforts to communicate with their members. According to an exit poll conducted by Hart Research Associates, 70 percent of union members reported that their unions contacted them about the 1998 elections (Francia 2000). Members of union households were twice as likely as nonmembers to attend a rally or meeting in 1998; this was not true in 1994. Members of unions that conducted the most grassroots activity were more likely to vote in 1998; once again, this was not true in 1994 (Francia 2000). Democratic House members who received grassroots help from unions fared better than those who did not; union assistance was more effective and better targeted than in 1994 (Francia 2000).

In 2002, unions continued to be politically active. Steve Rosenthal, political director of the AFL-CIO, estimated that there were 225,000 union members involved in turning out the vote (Kiely 2002). In 2002, the AFL-CIO employed

4,000 local coordinators in forty-seven House and sixteen Senate races, over-seeing the distribution of 17 million flyers at work sites and 15 million pieces of direct mail, as well as the placing of 5 million phone calls to union house-holds (Herrnson 2005). The AFL-CIO spent at least $3.6 million on TV ad-vertising ("One Billion Dollars Spent" 2002). Labor continued to enjoy suc-cess in its efforts to turn out voters, but was confronted in 2002 by an improved Republican "ground war" (Monson 2004). An AFL-CIO survey found that 93 percent of member households received information from a union source. The most common means of contacting voters were by mail, by phone, and by a flyer at a workplace. Members of union households voted more than two-to-one Democratic in House and Senate races and composed 23 percent of voters (Monson 2004).

Labor played a major role in numerous congressional races, including the reelection efforts of Senators Paul Wellstone (D-MN), Jean Carnahan (D-MO), and Tim Johnson (D-SD) (Flanigan et al. 2004; Kropf et al. 2004; Bart and Meader 2004). Medvic and Schorson (2004) give the AFL-CIO's ground war much of the credit for the victory of Rep. Tim Holden (D) over Rep. George Gekas (R) when the two incumbents were drawn into the same Penn-sylvania district. Each of the more than 40,000 AFL-CIO members in the dis-trict was contacted between seven and eleven times. In the Missouri Senate race, the AFL-CIO sent twenty-one unique mailers to unionists, including seven distinct statewide mailers. Individual unions also sent their own litera-ture, including a Teamsters mailing that showed a picture of Carnahan skeet shooting—the mailing was meant to persuade workers that she posed no threat to their right to bear arms.

Using Workplace Ties

The AFL-CIO's political staff ascribes their movement's "ground war" strength, in part, to the ties built between workers on the job. One top politi-cal adviser explained that he had found that when unions communicate with their members, they win. The most effective way to communicate is one mem-ber talking to another at work or at home.[2] Another AFL-CIO official ex-plained that when "somebody you know and respect gives you information, it's going to be enormously more powerful and convincing to you than if you get a flyer in your mailbox."[3] This approach is supported by Green and Ger-ber (2004), who find that personal contact is more effective at stimulating voter turnout than are phone calls or direct mail.

According to one high union official, phone banking has proven to be an effective way to reach workers, especially when union members talk directly to other members. This gives unions another advantage over other groups, many of whom are finding it difficult to get past voters' telemarketing fatigue. They lack the grassroots infrastructure that would allow them to communicate from member to member. In fact, this official envisioned unions' political operations replacing long-withered local party organizations.[4] The SEIU now operates trucks that serve as portable phone banks and so can be sent around the country. Inside the trucks, SEIU members can call their colleagues through a computerized phone system that automatically calls the next number on the list. This makes phone banking much more efficient and gives volunteers a greater sense of accomplishment. It also allows coordinators to better evaluate the effectiveness of their campaign.[5] To get around members' dislike of getting calls at home, the National Education Association now sends recorded messages from local leaders during the day so they end up on answering machines or voice mail, rather than disturbing people during the evenings. An NEA official praised these calls for not intruding in people's lives. Union members come home, press a button, and listen to a message from their local president. This is less annoying than having someone call in the middle of dinner to read a message to them.[6]

A "ground war" requires not just generals and foot soldiers, but junior officers as well. David Bounby, a member of the AFL-CIO's political staff, said that one of the AFL-CIO's main goals was to develop a more permanent grassroots infrastructure. This requires a more effective means of recruiting activists. After sending in national staff during the 1996 election, the federation consulted more with local leaders in 1998, getting them to recruit their members as district coordinators. In 2000, the AFL-CIO asked each union local to provide its own person, who could then contact its members. The representatives would meet periodically to coordinate their efforts.[7] The AFL-CIO coordinator would then work with the local activists to conduct the mobilization program. Despite this change, a top union official still expressed regret that unions had not succeeded in establishing a lasting organization, since participants returned to their regular jobs after the election.[8] Former AFL-CIO political director Steve Rosenthal later led the way in creating America Coming Together as a means of building such a long-term structure.

Providing information to members appears to work better than simply telling them how to vote. Karen Ackerman, deputy political director of the AFL-CIO, said that workers do not want a letter from a local union president ordering them to vote for a candidate. Union members want information about issues important to them and expect their union to provide them with it. They then can make up their own minds.[9] These issues include ones that appeal to workers in general, such as Social Security and Medicare, and ones that appeal to particular segments, such as education for teachers or Davis-Bacon for the building trades.[10] Another AFL-CIO staffer explained that unions now tell their members, "We know you're intelligent people, and we're telling you that on the issues that you pay us to represent you, here's where the candidate stands." Workers appreciate being treated as adults who can make up their own minds, while union leaders find that issues sway their members better than dictates from above.[11] The SEIU, the AFL-CIO's largest affiliate union, now holds town hall meetings with candidates. This makes members feel they have played a role in endorsement decisions.[12]

Bounby said that the affiliates' network of locals helps them contact voters in a more personal fashion. Workers know their local in a way that they do not know a huge national organization. Yet the AFL-CIO has the resources of a huge national organization. So the federation has assembled a database of its members organized by local. This allows them to target locals based on demographic information: for example, locals that are heavily African American or that have many women members. National headquarters can then send customized material to targeted locals.[13]

Unions enjoy credibility with their members because of their record of delivering material benefits for the members. This allows unions to speak to members about issues concerning their work. Mike Podhorzer, a member of the AFL-CIO's political staff, explained that unions have learned that

> if you explain to working Americans what's actually at stake in the election, and you go in and you say, "We're your union, we represent your grievances, we represent you in your contract negotiation, and we'll tell you that there are these five issues that Congress is going to deal with in the next two years."[14]

Unions are able to speak more effectively on "bread-and-butter" issues like Social Security and the minimum wage because they have a track record of delivering for their members. Few other groups active in American politics can say that they have improved their members' standard of living.

But unions can confront particular problems with their membership on nonmaterial issues such as gun control. (Obviously, there are many union members who also differ with their leadership on material issues such as taxes or national health insurance.) In 2000, the National Rifle Association (NRA) made a special effort to target union members in such states as Michigan, Pennsylvania, Wisconsin, and West Virginia, mostly by warning them that Al Gore opposed private gun ownership. According to Podhorzer, the NRA also claimed that there was no difference between Gore and George W. Bush on union issues; there was a flyer asserting that "George Bush doesn't want to take away your union, but Al Gore wants to take away your gun." The AFL-CIO responded with material claiming that "Al Gore doesn't want to take away your gun, but George Bush wants to take away your union." In this fashion, unions countered an appeal to values with an appeal to material interests.

In 2002 and 2004, unions continued their struggle to hold on to the loyalties of their gun-owning members. In an unsuccessful effort to reelect Senator Jean Carnahan (D-MO) in 2002, the Teamsters distributed a mailing that showed a picture of Carnahan skeet shooting, with the state's hunting schedule on the other side (Kropf et al. 2004). Two years later, United Mine Workers president Cecil Roberts presented John Kerry with a 12-gauge shotgun at a Labor Day rally; Roberts explained, "We wanted to send the message that this is somebody who believes in protecting hunters' rights to guns" (Davis 2004). One poll showed that 54 percent of union households owned a gun (Stolberg 2004). Activists in the UMWA, the UAW, the United Steelworkers of America, and the Carpenters Union all mentioned gun control as a major factor keeping many of their members from supporting Kerry (Williams 2004; Mannies 2004b). The AFL-CIO distributed a flyer showing Kerry shooting a rifle and proclaiming that "John Kerry won't take your gun away. He likes his own too much" (Justice 2004).

Podhorzer believes that unions generally beat the NRA in this battle in 2000, with the exception of West Virginia. Bush carried West Virginia—only the third Republican presidential candidate to do so in forty years—in large part because he ran about even among union members. (Bush performed about as well in 2004.) According to Podhorzer, the unions' usual pro-Gore argument—that Gore was better for workers' jobs—persuaded fewer voters in West Virginia because the NRA and the Bush campaign had highlighted comments Gore had made opposing the use of coal, a bulwark of the state's economy.[15] This allowed Republicans to challenge unions' main appeal to their workers—the ability to improve or at least maintain their living standards.

The National Rifle Association: Aiming for Victory

Most purposive groups simply do not have enough members to affect elections by turning the members out to vote. One exception is the National Rifle Association, whose membership hit a new high in late 2000 at over 4 million. The NRA mails extensively to its members, both to encourage them to vote and to encourage them to volunteer. Chuck Cunningham, director of federal affairs for the NRA, said these mailings are most effective when they

> make clear the positions of the partisan opponents. That's why the information that we can get about someone taking an antigun position, not just saying they're antigun, but proving it through their voting records or their statements, anything documentable, is very important because that will maintain our credibility with

members who will not just get involved for one reason or another, whatever reason they might think, but there's actually a significant difference between candidates.[16]

Perhaps the most visible mailing is the NRA bumper sticker endorsing a candidate. In 2000, these stickers often read, "Vote Freedom First. Elect (candidate's name)." This sticker not only reinforces the NRA member's support for this candidate; it advertises it to others, including the candidate's campaign. This is another way of "claiming credit."[17] NRA members and other gun owners also receive the NRA's trademark orange postcards and get-out-the-vote calls on election eve, reminding them to vote for the organization's endorsed candidates.[18]

The NRA's membership has waxed and waned with the prominence of gun control as an issue. During 1999–2000, the threat of further gun control legislation helped the NRA win new members. Bill Clinton called for new gun licensing requirements while Al Gore and Bill Bradley, competing for the Democratic presidential nomination, both called for gun registration. The "Million Moms" marched on Washington to demand tougher gun controls; video clips of talk show host Rosie O'Donnell's address at this rally later appeared in an NRA infomercial. These thirty-minute television advertisements were part of an impressive effort to increase NRA membership (Eilperin 2000b). By election eve, the NRA's membership had reportedly hit a new high of 4.1 million. The NRA reportedly spent a total of $20 million on political activity in 2000 (Eilperin 2000b; MacPherson 2000; Miller and Miller 2000).

In the fall of 2000, the NRA held a series of rallies around the country in order to motivate members to vote and volunteer in the upcoming election. Speakers included NRA president Charlton Heston and country singer Hank Williams Jr. Rallies were held in such key states as Michigan, Arkansas, Tennessee, and West Virginia. The rallies attracted tens of thousands of people and received much media attention.[19]

One area where the NRA faced a surprising challenge was in registering its members to vote. In 2000, the NRA began a new program in selected states that compared registration lists with its membership lists. Those members who were not registered received an application in the mail. But some members (and other gun owners) expressed the concern that registering would lead them to be called for jury duty. Perhaps the same suspicion of government that makes them defenders of their right to bear arms also makes them fearful of their name appearing on a government list.[20]

No Turnout Help Needed

Other purposive groups place less of an emphasis on turning their members out to vote. They rarely have more than a few hundred thousand members, too few to make an impact. Since their members have taken the trouble to join an expressly political organization, they generally are unusually interested in politics and so are likely to vote. While these groups frequently remind their members which candidates they have endorsed, they focus their resources elsewhere. For example, the National Abortion and Reproductive Rights Action League (NARAL Pro-Choice America) does do turnout mailings to its membership, but Gloria Totten, its former political director, admits that most of the organization's members are registered and highly likely to vote.[21]

Much like organized labor, AARP has millions of members who joined to gain material benefits. But unlike unions, which can be confident that their members will not quit to protest political endorsements, AARP is constantly in danger of losing its members if it takes a stand that alienates them. It does encourage its members to vote through its publications (most notably *AARP Magazine*), a website, and the AARP-VOTE program. Each congressional district has an AARP-VOTE coordinator who runs candidate forums, distributes literature, and recruits volunteers. But the AARP does nothing that is aimed at the election of specific candidates.[22]

Businesses are not generally considered membership organizations, but people do in a sense "join" in order to gain a material benefit: a paycheck. While businesses have often steered away from political involvement, in 2000, the Business Industry Political Action Committee (BIPAC), a longtime leader in the business community, worked to help companies turn their relationships with employees to political advantage. It launched Project 2000, which assisted companies in communicating with workers about politics (after the election, it was renamed The Prosperity Project). This included an Internet program in which BIPAC developed a database on issues before Congress that included members' votes on legislation. BIPAC would then work with business executives to select issues that were salient to their corporations. BIPAC could then compose a scorecard or information packet that the corporation could mount on its website. The information would come from BIPAC, but it would look like the corporation, with its logo and other design elements.[23] BIPAC continued its efforts in 2002 and 2004, as part of a broader effort by business to contribute to the GOP ground war (Magleby 2004; Monson 2004).

In 2002, business dominated interest-group activity. BIPAC continued its efforts to help corporations communicate with their workers about politics; one official claimed the effort reached 11 million voters. Several business organizations, including the Business Roundtable, contracted with BIPAC to develop materials for their members. The pharmaceutical industry was the most active of all business interests, giving $14 million to candidates, three-quarters of them Republicans, and mobilizing volunteers for voter turnout drives (Weisman 2002). The United Seniors Association, largely funded by the pharmaceutical industry, spent at least $8.7 million on TV ads in 2002. Americans for Job Security, another business-funded group, spent $1.5 million ("One Billion Dollars Spent" 2002). On election eve, the U.S. Chamber of Commerce planned to send out over 2 million pieces of mail and make 1 million get-out-the-vote phone calls (Kirchhoff and Kornblut 2002).

In terms of mobilizing workers, corporations have many characteristics similar to those possessed by unions. Neither has to worry much about exit since few workers will quit their jobs because of their union's or their employer's political views. Stockholders may sell, but someone else will buy. With their reliance on material incentives, both unions and corporations have politically heterogeneous constituencies that must be mobilized to participate. Corporations can also take advantage of solidary ties between workers, just as unions can. But the differences between corporations and unions are probably greater than the similarities. Many unions have been highly political since their beginnings, while most corporations are skittish about electoral involvement (beyond simply writing a check). Corporations must also worry about alienating consumers, who could boycott their products, and officeholders, who could punish them for their opposition.

Using Members as Volunteers

Groups whose memberships are smaller and more elite than those of the AARP, the NRA, or the AFL-CIO (which would include most purposive organizations) focus more on mobilizing their members as volunteers rather than as voters. Purposive incentives attract a highly politically aware membership that is almost certain to vote; they also usually attract a smaller number of members than material incentives do. But the characteristics that make people join a political organization—high political interest and efficacy, relatively high education levels, strong civic and verbal skills, early political socialization, recruitment through an organization (e.g., a church or a union), strong beliefs on an issue (or set of issues)—can make them good volunteers for their cause (see Verba, Schlozman, and Brady 1995). Thus many purposive groups seek to recruit their members as activists who will devote their time to promoting their cause or an endorsed candidate. Indeed, Moe (1980) argues that volunteering can be a benefit in itself.

One of the advantages of recruiting volunteers is that their work can be highly visible, especially to the candidates. (Of course, volunteers can also keep a low profile if that is required.) This can allow groups to "claim credit" for a candidate's victory. This can be especially important for such controversial issues as abortion and gun control. Carol Long Tobias of the National

Right to Life Committee (NRLC) explained the effect that pro-life volunteers had on one candidate:

> I had one candidate in here who had run for Congress and came very close, but didn't quite make it. So two years later, you know, he was going to try it again. And he came in the second time . . . just to kind of say, "Hi, I'm running again, I'd like you to help me if you can." And then he told me that he had ten women from the local chapter that volunteered on his campaign. He said [he] would take those ten women over 200 volunteers anytime. You know, he said it didn't matter what he needed done, whether it was setting up chairs for a meeting, or calling supporters, or licking stamps on envelopes and getting something out in the mail. He said, "I could count on them for anything."[24]

Similarly, the NRA provides its members with bumper stickers and yard signs that tout its support for candidates. This constitutes a highly visible means of both assisting candidates and showing the NRA's clout. In addition, volunteers stimulated by NRA mailings may pour into campaign headquarters. Chuck Cunningham, director of federal affairs for the NRA, explained the effect of a preelection mailing urging NRA members to help the campaign of Chris Chocola, a Republican seeking a House seat in Indiana: "The Chocola campaign . . . sent out an e-mail message within forty-eight hours of our mailing hitting, saying that if you've got any yard signs in your trunk or in your garage, to bring them into headquarters because they have had more requests than they have supplies; more demand than supply for yard signs."[25] (After a strong but unsuccessful campaign in 2000, Chocola was elected in 2002.)

The NRA also uses volunteers to reach gun owners who do not belong to the organization:

> Here was a guy and a gal in Virginia who went through five congressional districts and visited every gun store, dropped off bumper stickers, got [the stores'] customer lists . . . so we could put them in our database, so they had the people who were buying guns who weren't necessarily NRA members or licensed hunters or concealed carry permit holders.[26]

Holsworth and others (2003) note the success the NRA had in operating a volunteer network in support of former Virginia governor George Allen in his victorious 2000 challenge to Senator Charles Robb (D). Primarily targeting rural voters, volunteers manned phone banks, distributed literature, placed yard signs, and sent e-mail in support of Allen. The NRA's campaign was assisted by the presence on the ballot of a constitutional amendment guaranteeing Virginians' right to hunt and fish. Robb found it difficult to counter the NRA's message because most of it was distributed "under the radar." The NRA's success at mobilizing gun owners allowed Allen to focus on courting suburban moderates, even suggesting that he might support a renewal of the assault weapon ban.

The prowess that the NRA and the NRLC have shown in stimulating volunteer efforts gives these organizations greater leverage over candidates: even if the general public is apathetic or hostile, pro-life and pro-gun volunteers can show that their issue is still a net plus. Organized labor also has a long history of turning out volunteers to contact both members and nonmembers. Shop stewards recruit members to work on behalf of union-endorsed candidates.[27]

Perhaps the organization in this study that depends most on mobilizing its members as activists is the National Federation of Independent Business (NFIB). As a business association with purposive characteristics, the NFIB has a membership that is not only highly likely to vote, but well suited for other political activity. The NFIB's members are strewn across the country, involved in the lives of their communities and in contact with other voters day after day. So the NFIB helps them contact people on behalf of pro-small-business candidates. The NFIB has identified 20,000 members as activists. These people have volunteered in previous elections, contributed to NFIB's PAC, hosted fund-raisers, or simply asked to become more involved. The NFIB recruits these activists for the Value Added Voter Program. Each member participating in this program agrees to contact thirteen other small-business people to become politically active. The NFIB supplies them with a grassroots-training manual, which, among other things, gives them guidance on what they can say to their employees on behalf of a candidate. The NFIB also trains its activists regarding hosting fund-raisers and contributing to candidates.[28] The NFIB also sends to all its members mailings about elections, including a letter referring them to the volunteer coordinator of the endorsed candidate in their constituency.[29]

In 2000, one of the NFIB's top candidates was Dick Zimmer (R-NJ), a former congressman trying to regain the seat he had vacated four years before. The NFIB conducted its Value Added Voter Program, sending ten different mailings to its members, encouraging its members to contact other businesspeople, and urging them to place pro-Zimmer material in their shops. Despite this effort, Zimmer lost to Rep. Rush Holt (D-NJ) by just over a thousand votes (Berinsky and Lederman 2003).

Mary Crawford, onetime communications director for the NFIB, argues that her organization benefits from its members' unity on issues of taxes and regulation:

> I think that you would find—not that small business owners are all affiliated with the Republican party—or any other party, but that they're—the priorities and the issues that matter to them when they go into the voting booth are very much the same. I think there is more homogeneity there than there is among union members.[30]

She believes that while unions have many more members than the NFIB, they face a "bigger hurdle" when it comes to mobilizing members for political action.[31]

Crawford said the NFIB's focus was now on "really cultivating" its member activists. The organization is planning programs to motivate and train them. These may include electronic newsletters and town halls especially for them.[32] The NFIB has conducted research into methods of better mobilizing its members and other business owners. In a 2001 special election in Virginia, the NFIB spent $100,000 on research; it discovered that personal contact was far more effective than broadcast advertisements (Monson and Tanner 2004). In both 2002 and 2004, the NFIB continued to emphasize contacting its members, encouraging them to vote early and talk with their employees and fellow business owners (Vaida and Stone 2004).

Groups that rely on purposive incentives can expect that their members are already highly politicized and are therefore likely to vote. Mobilizing members for activism may be more productive than pulling them to the polls. As a purposive organization with a membership in the hundreds of thousands, NARAL puts a premium on reaching sympathetic nonmembers, whether through broadcast media, phone, or mail. But it does cultivate a number of its members as activists. Gloria Totten, former political director for NARAL, argues that "one of the things that's unique" about her organization is that "we have the bodies"—the volunteers necessary to run a grassroots operation. She says that NARAL has an "expectation" of their affiliates that 15 percent of their membership will be volunteers and that the organization will compile databases in order to contact these volunteers. In the spring and summer of an election year, NARAL conducts workshops for volunteers in targeted states. Totten says that NARAL members are "going to be asked periodically to volunteer. When you come in and agree to stuff envelopes, we're going to start cultivating you to become the mail supervisor." Two major tasks for volunteers are "visibility" and "earned media," according to Totten. "Visibility" includes standing outside supermarkets, setting up tables at parades and festivals, and otherwise boosting the cause of the pro-choice candidate and NARAL. "Earned media" includes writing letters to the editors of targeted newspapers, a natural task for the articulate, educated people who tend to be attracted to purposive groups.[33]

One campaign where NARAL was especially visible in 2000 was the Senate race in Michigan, where pro-choice Rep. Debbie Stabenow (D) ousted pro-life incumbent Republican Spencer Abraham. According to one account, NARAL recruited over five hundred volunteers for literature drops and for a letter-writing campaign (Traugott 2001). Totten explained:

> We looked at Michigan [and] we said, how many communities do we have that we need to focus on? Ten. That means we need to have two cochairs in each

community for each activity. So we have two cochairs for the visibility, so [we] organized what parades we're going to be at, where we're going to table, and what supermarkets we're going to stand outside of. And two for the earned media targeting what papers we're going to send letters to the editor, getting people recruiting people to sign letters, writing sample letters, helping people write letters, whatever.[34]

The Sierra Club also relies on its members to distribute its literature and otherwise contact voters: "Our strength is not in being able to write a $5,000 check; our strength is being able to talk to our 5,000 members in that district and say, you need to support this person, you need to go out and work for this person."[35]

Enhancing Member Participation

Those groups that seek to mobilize their members as activists try to make that participation as effective as possible. They seek to apply one resource— expertise—to better exploit another—membership. One method of accomplishing this is to train volunteers. The American Medical Association (AMA), the NRA, the NFIB, NARAL, and the affiliate unions of the AFL-CIO all have formal programs to train volunteers in campaign techniques. Another means is to send staffers into the field to coordinate volunteer work and other "ground war" activity. NARAL, the Sierra Club, the NRA, and the AFL-CIO all dispatch coordinators to targeted constituencies during the months preceding an election. The AARP actually has field coordinators in every House district responsible for distributing voter guides and conducting candidate forums.

Members Giving Money

Some groups have become adept at encouraging their members to give money to favored candidates. The most common means of mobilizing member money is "bundling," that is, having members write checks to approved candidates and mail them to the bundler, which then sends them to the candidate's committee. "Bundling" is probably best suited to relatively small groups with highly politicized, high-status members. This technique was pioneered by the Council for a Livable World in 1962, but it was EMILY's List that made the concept famous (S. W. Thomas 1980). EMILY's List, founded in 1985, bundles contributions to pro-choice female Democratic candidates. EMILY's List now has 97,000 members. It reported that it bundled about $9 million in

2001–2002.[36] Besides bundling, EMILY's List conducts polling, runs TV ads, staffs campaigns, and provides strategic advice (Edsall 2002).

Other groups have followed EMILY's List's lead. Most notable is the Club for Growth, which supports free-market candidates, and which was explicitly modeled after EMILY's List. In 2003–2004, the club claimed to have bundled over $3.3 million for thirty House and Senate candidates (all Republicans). These included Senate candidates John Thune (R-SD), Mel Martinez (R-FL), Richard Burr (R-NC), Jim DeMint (R-SC), Tom Coburn (R-OK), and David Vitter (R-LA) (Novak 2004). Coburn received over $1 million from club members; DeMint received $762,860.[37] The club has also supported primary challengers to moderate Republicans, most notably, Assemblyman Scott Garrett against Rep. Marge Roukema (R-NJ) and Rep. Patrick Toomey against Senator Arlen Specter (R-PA). Both Garrett and Toomey lost, although Garrett was later elected to the House after Roukema retired. During the 2000 campaign, the club had only 1,500 members.[38]

More established groups also facilitate member giving. The Association of Trial Lawyers of America (ATLA) encourages its members to give and has developed some formal mechanisms for doing so. It has created ATLA's List, "a network that communicates with 3,000 members, identifying candidates, causes and organizations sympathetic to ATLA's views" (Morgan 2000). An ATLA official explained that candidates get on ATLA's List for supporting "civil justice," being in competitive races, and needing money. Candidates are placed on the list by a committee of members after being recommended by staff. The list is then mailed or faxed to participating members. About thirty House and Senate candidates made the list in 2000.[39] The list includes information on polling and demographic information pertaining to each race. Donors pledge to give a particular amount to ATLA's List candidates during the election cycle; they can choose which endorsed candidates they will support, and their contributions count against their pledge. Candidates who have benefited from ATLA's List support include Senators Maria Cantwell (D-WA) and Debbie Stabenow (D-MI) (Association of Trial Lawyers of America, undated).

In addition, several trial lawyers have sought public office in recent years—most notably, Senator John Edwards (D-NC)—and ATLA does provide them with advice on their campaigns.[40] Senator in 2000, Conrad Burns (R-MT) was a major target for trial lawyers, who strongly supported Burns's Democratic opponent, Brian Schweitzer (D. Carney 2000). Lawyers and lobbyists contributed $291,212 to Schweitzer, about one-seventh of his total receipts.

Trial lawyers also gave heavily to other Democratic Senate candidates, including Hillary Rodham Clinton (D-NY), the recipient of almost $1.5 million from lawyers and law firms; Bill Nelson (D-FL), who received $944,283; Mel

Carnahan (D-MO), who received $874,668; Charles Robb (D-VA), who received $692,464; and Ron Klink (D-PA), who received $650,081. The only Republican Senate candidates to receive more than half a million dollars from lawyers and law firms were two New Yorkers: Rick Lazio ($1,022,343), Rudy Giuliani ($643,940), and Spencer Abraham ($648,521). (Abraham helped found the Federalist Society, an organization of conservative lawyers.)[41] In 2002, lawyers were once again generous to Democrats, giving over $1 million to Democratic Senate candidate Ron Kirk (D-TX) and Senator Jean Carnahan (D-MO). All of the top ten Senate candidates for receipt of contributions from lawyers were Democrats; six of them were southerners. Trial lawyers are especially important to southern Democrats, since the other two primary sources of Democratic funds—labor unions and culturally liberal voters—are weak in the region. Trial lawyers also helped support John Edwards's presidential campaign, giving $11.6 million, more than ten times the amount given by the second-ranking occupational groups (Victor 2004). After Edwards quit the race, many trial lawyers joined John Kerry's campaign; by the summer, one in ten of Kerry's top fund-raisers was a trial lawyer (Edsall, Grimaldi, and Crites 2004).

Facilitating member giving generally works best for relatively small groups with elite memberships. Contributing money to political campaigns is an activity strongly biased toward the wealthy and well educated (Verba, Schlozman, and Brady 1995). For example, surveys of "significant contributors" (those who gave more than $200) to congressional and presidential campaigns found that most earn more than $100,000 a year and have at least some graduate education (Wilcox et al. 2003; Francia et al. 2003). But at least one larger group has begun to encourage its members to contribute to candidates. In some races, the NRA encouraged gun owners to send checks to pro-gun candidates with "Second Amendment" written in the subject line. This served the dual purpose of funding favorable candidates and bringing attention to the influence of gun owners.[42]

Membership and Political Activity

Do groups seek members in order to use them in political activity? Or do they attract them for other purposes, and then use the existing membership as a political resource? Some groups clearly fall on one side or the other. The Roman Catholic Church created the National Right to Life Committee and its state affiliates, in part, in order to mobilize the activity of antiabortion voters. On the other hand, Ethel Percy Andrus created the AARP primarily to give older people access to the insurance policies offered by the National Retired Teachers Association. While Andrus was interested in raising the status of senior citizens, the AARP's lobbying efforts did not begin until several years after its creation. The AARP did not become a major political player until the 1970s and 1980s, and its electoral activity remains limited (see Day 1990, Pratt 1993).

For other groups, the picture is more mixed. Today, no interest group mobilizes more members to vote than organized labor. But the unions of the American Federation of Labor generally avoided politics before the New Deal era, instead focusing on immediate material gains for their workers. More radical groups such as the Knights of Labor and the Industrial Workers of the World failed to establish the AFL's permanency and clout. While union leaders included a few leftists and anarchists, Samuel Gompers of the AFL and John Mitchell of the United Mine Workers opposed socialism and the creation of an independent political party. Although the AFL did support legislation regulating wages and hours and prohibiting child labor, political activism always came second to Gompers's agenda of "more and more" for his members. The AFL did increase its political activity during the 1930s and 1940s, but its leaders preferred to exercise their influence informally, behind the scenes; the AFL did not endorse a presidential candidate until Adlai Stevenson in 1952 (Taft 1964; Wilson 1973). The unions of the AFL did not build their memberships in order to use them for political activity.

By contrast, the founders of the CIO had more complex motivations. Certainly, they wished to improve material conditions for workers (although those in the auto and steel industries, where the CIO experienced its greatest success, already enjoyed above-average wages). But most leaders of the CIO also saw organizing workers as a means to some broader political end. For John L. Lewis, longtime leader of the UMW and first head of the CIO, it may have been establishing himself as a political boss with national clout (a dream that died when his endorsement of Wendell Willkie for president in 1940 failed to move workers or other labor leaders). For the Communists who played prominent roles in many labor unions in both the AFL and CIO, it may have been building the infrastructure for world revolution. For Walter Reuther and the other radicals who built the UAW, it may have been transforming America into a social democratic utopia. For Philip Murray, Lewis's successor as leader of the CIO, and for Sidney Hillman, head of the Amalgamated Clothing Workers and founder of the CIO-PAC, it may have been supporting President Franklin Roosevelt and other liberal politicians friendly to organized labor. Whatever these men wanted, it was more than just "more and more." They clearly saw their unions' membership as a tool to be used for political power and social change (Taft 1964; Wilson 1973).

Organized labor is also an example of an organization that may have not been maximizing its use of its resources. By most accounts, unions had allowed their ability to mobilize their members to decline during the 1970s and 1980s. There are a variety of explanations for this underperformance. Union leaders may have grown complacent: Democrats controlled the House of Representatives for forty years, liberal Democrats set the agenda for the House after the reforms of the early and mid-1970s, and Speakers Thomas O'Neill, Jim Wright, and Thomas Foley all enjoyed warm relationships with organized labor. While union leaders faced a series of hostile presidents, they could trust the House leadership to kill unfavorable legislation. This may have encouraged union leaders to de-emphasize grassroots mobilization in favor of lobbying and PAC contributions. The leadership of organized labor gained an image as elderly white men out of touch with the rank and file, secure in their privileges while workers saw their own living standards stagnate (of course, many of the white men in the rank and file were voting for Richard Nixon and Ronald Reagan; [Dark 1998; Asher et al. 2001; Francia 2000]).

In the 1970s, conflict between conservative AFL-CIO president George Meany and more liberal leaders such as Jerry Wurf of AFSCME reduced the federation's effectiveness and alienated many potential allies. Meany's opposition to procedural reform, his adamant anticommunism, and his cultural conservatism all stuck in the craw of liberals inside and outside organized labor. Meany's successor, Lane Kirkland, healed many ideological wounds and built new ties to liberal activists and Democratic leaders. But he also pursued an interest in foreign policy, particularly supporting anti-Communists in Eastern Europe, that may have been commendable but did little to restore the AFL-CIO's political effectiveness (Dark 1998; Francia 2000). Kirkland also proved ineffective in coordinating the member unions of the AFL-CIO in pursuit of common political goals (Asher et al. 2001).

All of these factors changed in 1994–1995. Democrats lost control of Congress to militantly antiunion Republicans, who posed a threat to labor not seen since the days of Taft-Hartley. Kirkland was replaced by John Sweeney of the SEIU, marking the total victory of the liberal/activist wing of the labor movement. Not only was Sweeney a member of the Democratic Socialists of America, but two of his top lieutenants, political director Steve Rosenthal and Andrew Stern, who replaced Sweeney as head of the SEIU, were both former student radicals. Sweeney reoriented the AFL-CIO's priorities to emphasize grassroots political activity (Dark 1998). Ironically, Sweeney sought to emulate the tactics used by such groups as the NFIB to defeat the Clinton health care plan (Asher et al. 2001). The track record of organized labor in recent elections suggests that Sweeney's changes have been effective (See Francia 2000).

Mobilizing Members for Political Victory

A group's membership can be an important resource for winning elections. Members can vote, they can volunteer, they can donate money. Organized labor benefits from having such a large membership, formed through material incentives and coercion. But because workers do not join unions to support a political program, staffers must educate them to support pro-labor objectives and must encourage them to vote. Because exit from a union is relatively expensive, staff need not worry that their political activity will alienate members. By contrast, the AARP is highly vulnerable to exit, and must proceed with caution. Encouraging its highly diverse membership to vote is fine, but open partisanship could lead to flight from the organization.

Groups based on purposive incentives usually do not waste their time encouraging their members to vote (the NRA is an exception). Their members are already highly likely to vote, and their numbers usually are not great enough to swing an election. Instead, such groups focus on exploiting their members' additional political resources, for example, money, free time, ideological zeal, and verbal skills. Not only are members not alienated by these requests, they may see the opportunity to volunteer as an important reason to remain within the organization. While purposive groups must be constantly prospecting for new members, they usually need not fear that encouraging political activism will dissuade people from joining.

Grassroots organization also plays a critical role in the mobilization of members for political activity. Strong networks of locals have been key to organized labor's political might. Similarly, powerful state organizations lie at the political power of the right-to-life movement. On the other hand, groups that exist mainly as mailing lists or bank accounts do not have the same ability to mobilize their members on the ground.

Notes

1. Participant. AFL-CIO, CFI Labor/Liberal Roundtable, April 11, 2001.
2. Participant. AFL-CIO, CFI Labor/Liberal Roundtable, April 11, 2001.
3. Interview with Mike Podhorzer, AFL-CIO, March 1, 2001.
4. Participant, CFI Labor/Liberal Roundtable, April 11, 2001. Chuck Cunningham, director of federal affairs for the National Rifle Association (NRA), also sees his organization as being a replacement for bygone local parties. Interview with Chuck Cunningham, NRA, May 26, 2000.
5. Participants, CFI Labor/Liberal Roundtable, April 11, 2001; interview with SEIU official, June 28, 2001.
6. Interview with NEA official, July 3, 2001.

7. Interview with David Bounby, AFL-CIO, June 27, 2001.

8. Participant, AFL-CIO, CFI Labor/Liberal Roundtable, April 11, 2001.

9. Interview with Karen Ackerman, AFL-CIO, June 27, 2001. Similarly, Chuck Cunningham, director of federal affairs for the NRA, believes that it is more effective to show that a given candidate is anti-gun by showing his or her record rather than simply tell gun owners how to vote without such information. Interview with Chuck Cunningham, NRA, May 26, 2000.

10. Interview with David Bounby, AFL-CIO, June 27, 2001.

11. Interview with Mike Podhorzer, AFL-CIO, March 1, 2001.

12. Participant, CFI Labor/Liberal Roundtable, April 11, 2001.

13. Participant, CFI Labor/Liberal Roundtable, April 11, 2001.

14. Interview with Mike Podhorzer, AFL-CIO, March 1, 2001.

15. Interview with Mike Podhorzer, AFL-CIO, March 1, 2001.

16. Interview with Chuck Cunningham, NRA, May 26, 2000.

17. Interview with Chuck Cunningham, NRA, May 30, 2001.

18. Interview with Chuck Cunningham, NRA, May 30, 2001; interview with Glen Caroline, NRA, January 25, 2001.

19. Interview with Chuck Cunningham, NRA, May 30, 2001.

20. Interview with Chuck Cunningham, NRA, May 30, 2001.

21. Interview with Gloria Totten, NARAL, May 26, 2000.

22. Interview with Martin Burns, AARP, June 13, 2000.

23. Greg Casey, CFI Business/Conservative Roundtable, April 18, 2001.

24. Interview with Carol Long Tobias, National Right to Life Committee, April 30, 2001.

25. Interview with Chuck Cunningham, NRA, February 7, 2001.

26. Interview with Chuck Cunningham, NRA, February 7, 2001.

27. Interview with Mike Podhorzer, AFL-CIO, March 1, 2001.

28. Interview with Mary Crawford, NFIB, May 24, 2000.

29. Interview with Mary Crawford, NFIB, February 8, 2001.

30. Interview with Mary Crawford, NFIB, May 24, 2000.

31. Interview with Mary Crawford, NFIB, May 24, 2000.

32. Interview with Mary Crawford, NFIB, February 8, 2001.

33. Interview with Gloria Totten, NARAL, May 26, 2000.

34. Interview with Gloria Totten, NARAL, May 26, 2000.

35. Interview with Kim Haddow, Sierra Club, June 15, 2000.

36. www.emilyslist.org.

37. www.clubforgrowth.org/news/041103.php.

38. Personal communication from Adam Rozansky, Club for Growth, April 25, 2002.

39. Interviews with ATLA officials, February 28, 2001.

40. Interviews with ATLA officials, February 28, 2001.

41. Center for Responsive Politics.www.crp.org.

42. Interview with Chuck Cunningham, NRA, May 26, 2000.

8

Expertise

THE THIRD RESOURCE AVAILABLE TO GROUPS IS EXPERTISE. In this context, expertise consists of special abilities and knowledge that groups can bring to bear in order to win elections. While expertise is necessary to use the other resources effectively, and money and membership are needed to build expertise, expertise is still a separate and distinct resource. Longtime staffers may have skills, acquired from years of activity, that are not easy to duplicate—although political professionals do frequently change jobs, moving from group to group, working for this or that campaign. An organization may have established credibility with members or other voters that can be difficult to replicate. A group may have been closely identified with an issue through decades of activism, such as the Sierra Club and the environment or Planned Parenthood and sexual health. This can build a reputation among voters that can pay off at election time. Or a group may have built a close relationship with its members by advocating for their interests, as organized labor has. Expertise is not simply money transmuted into another form.

There are several types of expertise that an organization can employ in order to win elections. One is *issue credibility*, the ability to speak on a particular issue in a way than affects voters' decisions. Closely aligned with issue credibility is *targeting voters*, the ability to reach specific voters outside the organization, usually ones who care about a priority issue. Another form of expertise is *targeting races*, that is, selecting which races will receive priority involvement. Finally, some groups provide *campaign services*, such as polls, demographic research, candidate training, or fund-raising.

Issue Credibility

Perhaps the most important form of expertise is issue credibility, the ability to speak out on particular issues in a way that sways a significant number of voters. Issue credibility comes from years of activity, from public visibility, from ties to other organizations, and from spending money. Groups may aim their efforts at a particular segment of voters, often compiled in a computerized list, or at a much broader audience. Groups can use issue credibility not just to win elections, but to raise the salience and visibility of their issue. If politicians believe that a given issue sways voters, they will treat it as important.

Issue credibility has been the Sierra Club's stock-in-trade. In 1996, the Sierra Club spent $3.5 million on a Voter Education Project that distributed voter guides in twenty-eight House and seven Senate races. It also moved into the new arena of issue advocacy, attacking freshman Republicans such as Reps. Fred Heineman (NC) and James Longley (ME) (Cantor 1999; E. N. Carney 1997). All told, the Sierra Club spent $7.2 million on political activity in 1995–1996, of which $3 million went to issue advocacy, including broadcast ads, mailings, phone banks, and grassroots organizing. The Club's PAC spent $700,000, up from $430,000 in 1994. The club spent $100,000 on issue advocacy in 1994 (E. N. Carney 1997). Candidates received $372,000, with 94 percent of that amount going to Democrats (Foskett 1998). "We use issue advocacy as a tool to affect environmental policy and to increase congressional accountability—not to affect the outcome of elections," asserted Daniel J. Weiss, former political director of the Sierra Club (E. N. Carney 1997).

In 1998, the club targeted twenty-four races; its favored candidates won in twenty-two of them. It targeted seventeen races in 2000 (Foskett 2000). Its major targets included Senators Al D'Amato (R-NY) and Lauch Faircloth (R-NC), who both lost. The club conducted voter turnout efforts in twenty states (Magleby 2000). But its most visible weapon has been issue ads, which allow the club to use its treasury funds without dipping into its PAC money. Generally speaking, the club has preferred to run issue ads early during campaigns, so it can make the environment a priority issue for candidates and to avoid being drowned out by ads by candidates or by richer interest groups (Marcus 1998b; Magleby 2000). *National Journal* estimated the club's overall spending in the 2000 elections as between $9 million and $9.5 million (E. N. Carney 2000; Kriz 2000).

Perhaps the most visible aspect of its 2000 efforts was the Environmental Voter Education Campaign, an $8 million issue advocacy campaign. EVEC targeted mostly Republicans, including Senators Spencer Abraham (MI), Conrad Burns (MT), and Slade Gorton (WA) as well as Reps. Don Sherwood (PA), Tom Tancredo (CO), Anne Northup (KY), and Clay Shaw (FL). Abraham and Gorton lost; the others were reelected. The club also thanked eleven members for their environmental records; most of these members were Democrats, but they did include Rep. Christopher Shays (R-CT). Most Sierra Club ads focused on local issues; for example, one ad thanked Dennis Moore (D-KS) for supporting cleaning up the Kansas River, while another criticized Republican Senate candidate George Allen (VA) for his record on the Chesapeake Bay during his term as governor (Samuels 2000; Broder 2000; Galvin 2000; NationalJournal.com 2000). In 2000, EVEC included mailings, broadcast ads, "video voter guides," and a website. The club targeted women ages twenty-five to forty-five who have children; the club's staff believed that they are more likely to care about environmental issues such as clean air and water. For the first time, the club also produced Spanish-language ads; one former club official argued that Hispanic families have the same concerns as their Anglo counterparts, especially recreation.[1]

The club tried to capitalize on its issue credibility by having volunteers distribute handouts at baseball games and other events. Some of these handouts were meant to catch voters' attention in unusual ways; these included the "Spence Abraham Dollar," showing the senator's support from polluting corporations, and the "Slade Gorton Scorecard"(distributed at baseball games), illustrating Gorton's voting record on environmental issues.[2]

Since the environment is an issue with broad public appeal, the Sierra Club has mostly pursued highly visible methods of getting out its message, as opposed to the "under-the-radar" techniques used by other groups. But, with their fund-raising down and the environment off the public agenda after 9/11, the Sierra Club mostly shifted to "ground war" techniques in 2002, particularly in Senate races in Colorado, Minnesota, New Hampshire, and Missouri (Edsall 2002a; Magleby and Tanner 2004). The Sierra Club continued this approach in 2004.

The Sierra Club's staff believe that they have greatest credibility when they speak about local issues and when they attack an incumbent for a poor voting record, rather than praising a good one. Local issues mean more to voters than abstract concerns about the Amazon rain forest or global warming. In addition, local issues allow the club to speak to voters in areas not usually seen as sympathetic to environmentalists; for example, pollution from hog farms has become an important issue in the rural Midwest and South. Going negative works better than going positive because voters expect officials to protect the environment, and are shocked when they do not.[3]

Deanna White, deputy political director of the Sierra Club, said that her group's greatest success in 2000 was

> the increased visibility of the environment as an issue. And ultimately that's the goal of our program—to get people to talk about the environment. Because the

more visibility it gets, the more aware decision makers are that people care about the environment and the more they will be held accountable for what they do.[4]

Other groups capitalize on issue credibility in order to move voters. But many of these groups target their efforts far more than the Sierra Club does. Activists who are interested in "hot-button" issues such as abortion and gun control know that their issues are not salient to many or even most voters. (For example, in four meetings with NRA staff, at no time did they mention contacting voters who do not own guns.) They also know that their opponents care passionately about these issues, and could be activated by a broadcast campaign. So groups concerned with these issues usually target their efforts narrowly at identified supporters.

The National Rifle Association (NRA) mostly eschews broadcast advertising; its main television campaign in 2000 was a series of infomercials aimed at encouraging gun owners to join the organization. Instead of "broadcasting" its message, the NRA "narrow-casts" to a selected audience of gun owners. The National Right to Life Committee (NRLC) also avoids broadcast advertising; instead, it and its state affiliates focus on those voters who share their antiabortion commitment. (The exceptions to these rules are telling. The NRA has broadcast some advertisements on cable outlets such as the Outdoor Life Network and in rural TV markets. In both cases, few unsympathetic voters are likely to see the spots. Similarly, Right to Life occasionally runs advertisements on Christian radio.) NARAL has sponsored broadcast advertising before, especially in 1992, a year of unusually high activism by abortion rights advocates. But in 2000, it switched to communicating with identified pro-choice voters by phone, mail, and e-mail. An official with Planned Parenthood suggested that NARAL made its switch because it had exhausted its credibility with "swing" voters because it appeared too partisan and too focused on the single issue of abortion. By contrast, Planned Parenthood, which had built up credibility and a nonpartisan "public service" image over many decades, was able to capitalize on these assets in 2000. It conducted a $7 million television campaign decrying George W. Bush's views on abortion and sex education that was targeted at such key states as Florida and Pennsylvania.[5]

These groups may target their pitches to sympathetic audiences because they do not want to risk mistakenly activating the opposition: a pro-choice Republican who sees a Right to Life advertisement backing an antiabortion GOP candidate may decide to vote Democratic this year. It may also allow the groups to use tougher, more persuasive pitches than they could if their messages were going to the general public. Finally, it may simply be more efficient to spend their money on phone banks or mass mailings rather than TV time for ads that will reach many voters who are apathetic or antagonistic on the groups' issues.

Targeting Voters

In order to target voters, it is necessary to find them first, usually by combining money and expertise. Creation of a list of targeted voters (usually including addresses and phone numbers) is vital for groups that want to contact just those voters who are likely to respond favorably. In 2000, one of the most ambitious efforts at targeting voters was NARAL's creation of a list of 2.9 million pro-choice-identified voters. According to deputy political director Chris Mather, NARAL created this list through the use of phone banks and through buying lists compiled by others.[6] NARAL also was able to build on lists that it and its state affiliates had built during previous campaigns. This was especially helpful in states that have seen repeated battles over abortion, such as Michigan and Missouri.[7] NARAL can contact the voters on the lists by mail and phone for persuasion and turnout. The lists are also used to determine which communities will be targeted for "visibility and outreach" activities. NARAL made a race a priority only where its voter list included at least 3 percent of projected voter turnout.[8] Rather than focus on its members, who are already highly politicized, NARAL aims its turnout activity at these voters.[9]

According to political director Gloria Totten, NARAL put 80 percent of its spending into get-out-the-vote and voter contacting, rather than into media. Most of the voters listed in the file are women; the majority are political independents. (Totten admitted that NARAL had difficulty moving Republican women; she pressed the organization to focus more on independents.) After the election, NARAL was able to use its list to activate voters to oppose the nomination of John Ashcroft to the position of attorney general.[10] One race where NARAL used its voter file extensively was Adam Schiff's (D) successful drive to oust Rep. Jim Rogan (R-CA), one of the managers of Bill Clinton's impeachment. NARAL targeted potential Schiff supporters from its voter file for both persuasion and GOTV phone calls; about seven-eighths of those contacted ended up voting for Schiff (Linzer and Menefee-Libey 2003). In 2004, NARAL put together a list of 4 million pro-choice voters (Rosenberg 2003).

Another group that relied heavily on a voter list was the NAACP National Voter Fund, created in 2000 to increase political participation by African Americans. It used a voter file of 3.8 million black voters; the fund staff decided to concentrate on infrequent voters because most groups preferred to contact those likely to vote. According to Heather Booth, director of the fund, only about one-fifth of the people included in the list voted frequently. Almost half rarely voted. The fund assembled the file in cooperation with other groups and with a vendor. The vendor acted as a broker, helping the fund buy the best lists in targeted states. The list could be broken down by state, congressional district, age, gender, or marital status.[11] By contacting these voters, the NAACP could translate the issue credibility built through decades of advocating for African Americans into results at the ballot box.

Lists can also be compiled from publicly available sources. While the National Rifle Association boasts more than 4 million members, that is only a small percentage of the estimated 80 million Americans who own a gun. (Polls have shown that about two out of five American adults own a firearm; for example, a 1999 Louis Harris survey found that 39 percent of respondents reported having a gun in their home or garage. See "Increased Gun Control" 1999.) Since there is no national registry of gun owners—thanks in part to the NRA's efforts—the organization has to put together its own list for voter contact. The NRA buys some lists that are likely to contain many gun owners, for example, subscribers to outdoor-sports magazines such as *Field and Stream, Guns and Ammo,* and *Outdoor Life.* But the NRA also uses many publicly available lists: those of licensed hunters and holders of concealed weapon permits, for example. NRA volunteers attend gun shows and visit gun stores, where they obtain lists of customers.[12] The NRA can then add these names to its lists of gun owners targeted for voter turnout.

Groups can also reach voters through existing organizations. Right to Life organizations have long relied on Protestant and Catholic churches and the social networks they create. These churches help add to the Right to Life movement's formidable grassroots strength. While churches may not formally endorse candidates, clergy can speak out on issues, including abortion. Churches can also distribute voter guides. Right to Life activists also often leaflet outside churches or in church parking lots, thereby reaching people likely to be sympathetic to their cause. Carol Long Tobias, political director of the National Right to Life Committee, explained that activists can leaflet in the parking lots because they are "generally open to the public, the church, it's mainly not controlled unless they're inviting people to come to their services, the lot is open. So that would have a different legal standard than actually inside the church building."[13]

Missouri has long been a center of pro-life activism. In 2000, Right to Life worked to elect Bush, Senator John Ashcroft (R), and Republican gubernatorial nominee James Talent. Bush carried the state, but Ashcroft and Talent lost. Kropf et al. (2001) reported that Missouri Right to Life spent over $45,000 on mailings and phone banks in support of Ashcroft. During two weekends in October, Missouri Right to Life volunteers distributed 175,000 flyers in the St. Louis area at parking lots outside Catholic churches. Missouri Right to Life also planned to dispense "hundreds of thousands" of leaflets outside "sympathetic" Protestant and Catholic churches across the state (Mannies 2000). Such churches also provided Right to Life with volunteers (Dao 2000).

In 2002, Right to Life was once again active in Missouri, assisting Talent in his successful race against Senator Jean Carnahan (D). Both the NRLC and Missouri Right to Life sent mailings to lists of pro-life voters. The NRLC used advertisements to reach voters likely to be sympathetic to its message, airing radio spots on Christian radio and placing a full-page advertisement in a free newspaper distributed to Catholic parishioners (Kropf et al. 2004). In South Dakota, another traditional center of antiabortion activism, the NRLC and other socially conservative groups sent so many pieces of mail attacking Senator Tim Johnson (D) that their efforts may have backfired, alienating voters and painting Rep. John Thune, the Republican nominee, as an extremist (Bart and Meader 2004). Two years later, Thune successfully challenged Senate Minority Leader Tom Daschle, in a campaign in which Thune frequently highlighted his evangelical faith and his opposition to abortion (Brokaw 2004).

Reaching Voters

Once groups have targeted voters, they have to reach them. The most common means of contacting voters are phone, mail, and e-mail. Usually, reaching voters by phone simply means using phone banks, whether staffed by volunteers or paid workers, whether in-house or outside. But telemarketers have worn out Americans' patience for being called at home. So groups have had to get more creative. One of the most distinctive means of reaching voters by phone is "robo-calling." This is the use of a taped message sent out by computer to thousands of potential voters, usually on the eve of an election, with the purpose of reminding them to vote (Porter 1999). Often the message is intended more for being recorded on an answering machine rather than being heard directly by the recipient. The message is frequently recorded by a celebrity or by a politician. NARAL used messages recorded by Sarah Jessica Parker, star of HBO's *Sex and the City*, while Planned Parenthood used Barbra Streisand. The NAACP National Voter Fund used Bill Clinton. (Interestingly, the fund found that the infrequent voters it targeted welcomed phone calls at home; unlike more politically active people, they were not used to people asking for their votes.) By contrast, and perhaps illustrating the importance of grassroots organization, the National Education Association used the leaders of the local affiliates. While robo-calls seem cutting edge, the evidence of their effectiveness is mixed at best. Certainly they are no substitute for more personal means of contacting voters (see Gerber and Green 2000; Green and Gerber 2004).

The other classic means of reaching targeted voters is by mail. The NRA has long sent distinctive orange postcards reminding gun owners of its endorsements. It also mails bumper stickers that serve as visible evidence of the NRA's support for a candidate. The Sierra Club sends voter guides to its members and others. While its mailings are not as focused as some other groups', they are primarily sent to its primary target audience of women ages twenty-five to forty-five who are registered to vote.[14] The lists have been purchased from vendors.[15]

With the growth of the Internet, most politically active groups have developed an online presence. All of the groups included in this study have sophisticated websites where visitors can get lists of endorsements and statements on public issues and sign up for e-mail lists. On the AFL-CIO's site, workers could download flyers that could then be printed and distributed.[16] The Sierra Club experimented with banner ads on popular Internet sites, but did not find them particularly helpful.[17] The National Rifle Association is collecting e-mail addresses from its members to supplement "snail mail" addresses and telephone numbers. In May 2001, NRA federal affairs director Chuck Cunningham estimated that his organization had collected about 200,000 e-mail addresses, but hoped to have 2 million within a year.[18] NARAL collects e-mail address through mail and its website.[19] Planned Parenthood also uses e-mail to contact its activists, and the e-mails may even include links to streaming video. But one top official expressed skepticism about e-mail, since it is not organized geographically.[20] The National Education Association also e-mails its members, and it has the added difficulty that it is not allowed to send e-mail to teachers' work addresses.[21]

Problems Reaching Voters

There are a variety of problems that can confront groups trying to reach voters outside their memberships. Other issues may take precedence in voters' minds; loyalty to a party or a personal affinity with a candidate may be more important than ideological fidelity. Truman (1971) notes that overlapping group memberships can create great difficulty for organizations. For example, union officials were often frustrated by the support that many of their members gave to Ronald Reagan, who had dealt the labor movement a savage blow through his firing of striking air traffic controllers.[22]

Opponents may soft-pedal an issue to make it less salient. In 2000, NARAL staffers found that George W. Bush's confusing utterances on the abortion issue made it difficult for them to sway Republican women away from their allegiance to their party's nominee.[23] Gloria Totten, then political director for NARAL, explained the difficulty:

> Bush obfuscated his position throughout his campaign. He toned down his rhetoric. He said, "I'm not a threat to the right to choose. I won't use litmus tests. I'm

not going to overturn *Roe v. Wade.* You know, blah blah blah. And Gore quite frankly ... never drew a stark enough comparison between himself and Bush on the issue. And it hurt him with Republican women, it hurt him with women of a higher economic class, with white women in general. It was a problem because exit polling showed that Republican women listed choice as one of the top two issues that they cared about, but they never fully believed that Bush was a threat to the issue.[24]

Even candidates supported by a group may avoid that particular issue in a campaign if they believe that it could cost them votes. Officials of the Sierra Club, NARAL, and Handgun Control all complained that Al Gore down-played their issues during his 2000 presidential campaign.[25] Gore's campaign evidently worried that his socially liberal and environmentalist views were hurting him among rural, blue-collar voters. (Given Gore's surprising defeats in West Virginia and Tennessee, those concerns may have been valid.)

In 2004, the Sierra Club's efforts to arouse voters about the Bush adminis-tration's environmental record were thwarted by a lack of interest by both the presidential candidates and by the general public. Rather than speak to voters as a whole through the airwaves, the Sierra Club instead sought to turn out about a half million targeted voters identified as environmentally aware. The club sent staffers to eleven targeted states, and mobilized thousands of volun-teers who went door-to-door (Kay 2004; A. C. Smith 2004b; Barringer 2004b; Eilperin 2004b).

Targeting Races

Most of the participants in this study did not believe that they had special ex-pertise in targeting races. Several respondents cited the same sources: *Roll Call, The Hotline, The Cook Political Report, The Rothenberg Political Report.* They all swim in the same sea of information. Some attended briefings by party officials for PAC directors; they often also reported meeting with candi-dates who were visiting Washington to raise money.

Some groups did report receiving information from their grass roots about particular candidates. Chuck Cunningham of the NRA recalled reallocating re-sources between races due to information from the field on the competitiveness of races.[26] Unions receive reports from their locals about promising candidates.

There is a class of organizations, known as "lead PACs," that provide cues to their ideological allies about which candidates to support. The two most prominent are the Business Industry Political Action Committee (BIPAC) and the AFL-CIO's Committee on Political Education (COPE), which furnish di-rection to conservative and liberal groups, respectively. Donations from either group can serve as a cue for further support; in addition, BIPAC prepares re-ports on top races around the country. But both organizations have been moving away from their lead PAC function. Since 1995, the AFL-CIO has been de-emphasizing PAC giving in favor of member contact and broadcast-issue advocacy (Francia 2000); since 2000, BIPAC has been conducting programs to help corporations communicate with their employees.[27] While these groups have not abandoned their lead PAC function, they have discovered that they possess other areas of expertise that are just as valuable (Wilcox 1994; Nelson 1994; Nelson and Biersack 1999; Gerber 1999).

EMILY's List also acts as a lead PAC of sorts for a much narrower class of candidates: pro-choice Democratic women. Indeed, EMILY's List's very name implies its lead PAC function: EMILY stands for "Early Money is Like Yeast"—it makes the dough rise. But EMILY's List primarily exercises its cuing func-tion by encouraging its members to give to endorsed candidates. By encour-aging its members to give early, EMILY's List helps favored candidates prove their viability to potential donors. In one 2004 race, EMILY's List conspicu-ously preferred one pro-choice Democratic woman over others. After con-ducting polls in Wisconsin's Fourth District, EMILY's List endorsed Gwen Moore for the Democratic nomination; its surveys had shown her to be the most viable of the female candidates in the race. Moore went on to be elected as Wisconsin's first black member of Congress (Sandler 2004).

Campaign Services

Groups can also use their expertise to help friendly candidates by providing them with campaign services, which are often tied to specific issues advo-cated by the groups and ultimately to the incentives they offer to members. NARAL and the Sierra Club provide staffers to campaigns to help mobilize their targeted constituencies. NARAL and EMILY's List train candidates; NARAL, in particular, holds seminars for candidates on how to turn the "choice" issue to their advantage, using such examples as Gray Davis's suc-cessful 1998 campaign for governor of California.[28] EMILY's List and the Na-tional Women's Political Caucus both conduct training workshops for women seeking office. EMILY's List also produces a manual for female can-didates focusing on the special challenges they face. In addition, both groups recruit women to run for office (Rozell 2000). EMILY's List also trains young activists through its Campaign Corps; recent college graduates attend a weeklong Campaign School, and then are placed on targeted, progressive campaigns for the three months leading up to election day (Campaign Corps 2005). The American Medical Association (AMA) and EMILY's List provide polls to candidates (Rozell and Wilcox 1999). The AMA, EMILY's List, the Sierra Club, the NFIB, and NARAL all help candidates with fund-raisers, whether by hosting them themselves or by encouraging their members to do so (Edsall 2000; Gusmano 1999).[29]

While groups do provide a variety of campaign services, many interview subjects commented that this was an area that the groups tended to leave to candidates, consultants, and parties. An ATLA official explained:

> Most of the time the candidates we support I would say have good advice—good polling, good media, good direct mail, good fund-raising people. . . . If the race is viable but there are problems, the party committees are going to step in and at least say, look, if you want party money, you better do something about this. So it's not like we have to give advice of that nature.[30]

Gloria Totten of NARAL said that her organization rarely did polling for candidates:

> Skinner: Do you provide polls to candidates? (*Totten shakes her head.*) They can get their own poll.

> Totten: Candidates do a hell of a lot more polling than we do anyway. No we don't. We give them some polling info. But, particularly our political polls, we usually don't release [them]. We use it to shape our internal strategy.[31]

Groups generally do not see providing such services as their primary role. Instead, they leave this to other members of the party networks. Groups have their own jobs to do. EMILY's List has been something of an exception to this. Longtime political director Mary Beth Cahill often demanded that campaigns follow her advice if they wanted EMILY's List's support (Rosin 2004). In 2004, EMILY's List helped Betty Castor (D-FL), a member of the group herself, raise more than $1 million for her Senate race, but it also provided her with extensive campaign advice (Kumar 2004; Kumar and Bousquet 2004).

Expertise and Lobbying

The expertise that groups build during campaigns can also be used when they lobby on public policy issues. Both NARAL and the National Right to Life Committee reported using voter files during the campaign to contact people during the battle over the nomination of John Ashcroft to the post of attorney general.[32] More generally, the clout that groups build through campaigns can persuade candidates that their issues move voters. Daniel J. Weiss of the Sierra Club gave the example of his group's intervention in the January 1996 special election for a Senate seat in Oregon: "It made the environment a much more politically dangerous issue for people in Congress to mess with"(Kriz 2000).

Expertise and the Political World

Interest groups possess expertise that is not easily transferred and that is not simply an outgrowth of spending. While unions can contribute millions of dollars to Democratic candidates and committees, they cannot so easily transfer their expertise at turning out their members to vote. The NRA has invested years of work and treasure in building its credibility with gun owners; a start-up organization could not expect to duplicate the NRA's clout, even if it could match its spending. The Sierra Club, the NAACP, and Planned Parenthood all have "brand names" that may be as relevant to voters as Coca-Cola, Kellogg, and Budweiser are to consumers.

For many organizations, their political expertise helps justify their very existence. Group leaders can boast of their effectiveness to potential members, to journalists, to other political activists. Belonging to a group that has shown political prowess can itself be an incentive for members to join.

Groups' areas of expertise allow them to fulfill different roles in the party networks. The NRA can mobilize gun owners, while Right to Life organizations can turn out antiabortion voters, both usually in support of Republican candidates. Arguably, both can speak to their constituencies more effectively than the party committees can. Similarly, unions can turn out their members, the Sierra Club can talk to "soccer moms" about the environment, and ATLA can encourage trial lawyers to contribute to Democratic candidates. While these webs of relationships are not precisely the same as formal party organizations, they are still essential parts of party politics today—"extended parties" or "party networks."

Notes

1. Interview with Daniel J. Weiss, Sierra Club, July 6, 2001.
2. Interview with Deanna White, Sierra Club, June 27, 2001.
3. Interview with Deanna White, Sierra Club, June 15, 2000; interview with Kim Haddow, Sierra Club, June 15, 2000.
4. Interview with Deanna White, Sierra Club, April 5, 2001.
5. Interview with Planned Parenthood official, July 9, 2001.
6. Interview with Chris Mather, NARAL, June 27, 2001.
7. Interview with Gloria Totten, NARAL, May 26, 2000. Totten later claimed that NARAL contacted 17 percent of Missouri voters for get-out-the-vote activity. Interview with Gloria Totten, NARAL, April 19, 2001.

8. Interview with Gloria Totten, NARAL, April 19, 2001.

9. Interview with Gloria Totten, NARAL, May 26, 2000.

10. Interview with Gloria Totten, NARAL, May 26, 2000.

11. Interview with NAACP National Voter Fund official, June 11, 2001.

12. Interview with Chuck Cunningham, NRA, May 26, 2000.

13. Interview with Carol Long Tobias, National Right to Life Committee, April 30, 2001.

14. Interview with Deanna White, Sierra Club, June 15, 2000.

15. Interview with Deanna White, Sierra Club, April 5, 2001.

16. Interview with David Bounby, AFL-CIO, June 27, 2001.

17. Interview with Daniel J. Weiss, Sierra Club, July 6, 2001.

18. Interview with Chuck Cunningham, NRA, May 30, 2001.

19. Interview with Chris Mather, NARAL, June 27, 2001.

20. Interview with Planned Parenthood official, July 9, 2001.

21. Interview with NEA official, July 3, 2001.

22. Union members have been cross-pressured on various issues for decades. In a 1949 mayoral election in Detroit, United Automobile Worker leaders were frustrated by the support that many of their members gave to a Republican businessman who defeated a labor-backed Democrat. The key issue was the Republican's opposition to building integrated public housing in predominately white neighborhoods. Whatever loyalties workers had to their union were overcome by conflicting identities as home owners protective of property values and as racists fearful of African Americans. See Sugrue 1996.

23. Interview with Gloria Totten, NARAL, April 19, 2001.

24. Interview with Gloria Totten, NARAL, April 19, 2001.

25. Interview with official of Brady Campaign to Prevent Handgun Violence (formerly Handgun Control), July 17, 2001; interview with Gloria Totten, NARAL, April 19, 2001; interview with Daniel J. Weiss, Sierra Club, July 6, 2001.

26. Interview with Chuck Cunningham, NRA, May 30, 2001.

27. Greg Casey, CFI Business/Conservative Roundtable, April 18, 2001.

28. Interview with Gloria Totten, NARAL, April 19, 2001.

29. Interview with Kim Haddow, Sierra Club, June 15, 2000; interview with Mary Crawford, NFIB, May 24, 2000; interview with Gloria Totten, NARAL, May 26, 2000.

30. Interview with ATLA official, February 28, 2001.

31. Interview with Gloria Totten, NARAL, May 26, 2000.

32. Interview with Chris Mather, NARAL, June 27, 2001; interview with Carol Long Tobias, National Right to Life Committee, April 30, 2001.

IV

THE CONTEXT

9

Groups' Relationships with Political Parties

A S HAS BEEN DISCUSSED EARLIER IN THIS WORK, political scientists have tended to view groups and parties as competing forms of political organization. Parties aggregate voters; groups disaggregate them. Parties serve to counteract the inegalitarian biases of the American system; groups exacerbate them. During the 1960s, 1970s, and 1980s, commentators decried the simultaneous decline of political parties and the proliferation of interest groups (Burnham 1982; Crotty 1984; Wattenberg 1998). On the fate of political parties, however, a new conventional wisdom is beginning to emerge: that parties have actually experienced a revival over the past two decades.

With this strengthening and polarization of political parties, we may be seeing an evolution by some interest groups toward closer ties to the parties. With the current atmosphere of polarization, it may no longer be as easy for groups to work with members of both parties. Narrow margins of control make every seat count. Close group party alliances, such as those between the Democrats and organized labor and between the Republicans and the Christian Right, have been flourishing. These ties may be growing strong enough that we can treat some groups as actual parts of a party network. As part of this party network, groups can perform valuable tasks that are beyond the capabilities of the party committees.

But there are limits to groups' participation in the party network. Obviously, pragmatic organizations, such as most corporate PACs (see Eismeier and Pollock 1988), will want to keep their distance. But even highly ideological groups, which have little ability to persuade policymakers who oppose their positions, may still want to maintain a nominally nonpartisan image. While both groups and parties may want their side to win control, party leaders may see it as an end in itself while group leaders seek it as a means to enact their agenda. (Of course, party leaders may have their own policy goals—Newt Gingrich may have thought "dismantling the welfare state" was key to his vision of the Republican Party, while Bob Dole probably would have disagreed.) As part of their mission, purposive groups may wish to highlight issues that party leaders would prefer to keep hidden. Due to the incentives they offer, groups usually cannot support candidates who do not share their positions. If groups did so, they would run the risk of alienating their supporters. For example, after pro-life Rep. Ron Klink defeated pro-choice state senator Allyson Schwartz for the Democratic nomination for U.S. Senate in Pennsylvania in 2000, the National Abortion and Reproductive Rights Action League (NARAL Pro-Choice America) could not rally behind Klink. While his race for the Senate proved crucial for party control, NARAL could not endorse a candidate who did not share its positions.

Groups Look at Parties

During interviews conducted in 2000 and 2001, not all interest group representatives saw an increasingly polarized environment. Greg Casey, president of the Business Industry Political Action Committee (BIPAC), actually argued that the parties were becoming less polarized on some economic issues, such as trade. Casey noted that some conservative Republicans, particularly those from a Christian Right background, have opposed normal trade relations with China, and some centrist "New Democrats" have supported it. While data does not generally support Casey's position, his observation may still hold some validity (Shoch 2001; Vita and Eilperin 2000). A Republican Party that is increasingly supported by blue-collar social conservatives and by Main Street small-business interests may become less disposed to supporting such traditional Wall Street issues as expanded trade. Certainly, such prominent conservatives as Pat Buchanan and Rep. Duncan Hunter (R-CA) have been critical of free-trade legislation. Similarly, while most access-oriented business PACs did increase their giving to Republicans after 1994, they usually still gave a healthy percentage to Democrats.[1] Nor have they increased their giving to challengers (see Boatright et al. 2003). Since these groups usually do not have a strong partisan preference, and are more concerned about getting along with incumbents than in changing the composition of Congress, they have little incentive to change their behavior.

   Not surprisingly, these groups generally have not engaged in substantial non-PAC-contribution activity. One exception has been the Business Roundtable, which sponsored advertisements in 2000 praising forty incumbent House members for their support for business's agenda, including expanded trade. While most of the ads supported Republicans, a few backed such Democrats as Cal Dooley (D-CA), Dennis Moore (D-KS), and Gregory Meeks (D-NY) (Eilperin 2000a). The pharmaceutical industry, which strongly supports Republicans in its PAC giving, has also funded the issue-advocacy groups Citizens for Better Medicare and the United Seniors Association, which spent millions on ads praising GOP candidates in 2000 and 2002. They have also funded broadcast campaigns by the U.S. Chamber of Commerce.

Unlike many trade associations, the National Federation of Independent Business (NFIB) has remained very close to the Republican Party. Its strong reliance on purposive incentives helps reinforce its partisan and ideological characteristics. Unlike many business groups, the NFIB cannot depend on a handful of large firms that would support it through good times and bad; it must provide a steady stream of purposive incentives to win new members. Its membership comes from a variety of economic sectors, so the NFIB must focus on issues that unite the small-business community—which tend to be the conservative perennials of opposing higher taxes and government regulations. (Industry-specific trade associations tend to focus on a narrower range of issues that are less likely to break along party lines.)

Mary Crawford, then communications director for the NFIB, remarked that "party control is very important" to her organization. Democrats find it difficult to receive a high rating from NFIB, since to do so they would need to frequently oppose their party leadership on such core issues as the minimum wage and workplace regulation. Unlike the Business Roundtable, the NFIB is not interested in foreign-trade issues; Crawford explained that the group's membership did not see permanent normal trade relations with China as a priority: "When you ask our members, 'What do you care about?' trade is like—down at the bottom of the list."[2] In 2000, the NFIB did not endorse a single Democrat for federal office. Crawford herself was a veteran of both the Republican National Committee and the National Republican Congressional Committee, and later joined the Department of Commerce under President George W. Bush.[3] Jack Faris, who revitalized the NFIB during the 1990s, had previously served as head of the Republican National Finance Committee (Shaiko and Wallace 1999). More so than its big-business counterparts, the NFIB has enjoyed a warm relationship with the Republican congressional leadership and the more conservative activist community (Balz and Brownstein 1996).

Organized labor has maintained its decades-long relationship with the Democratic Party, including close links at the grass roots. While staff at the AFL-CIO reported some dissatisfaction with the Democrats, they remained intensely anti-Republican: "The Republican takeover was rhetorically and really committed to doing as much damage to us as possible. . . . And it became important to demonstrate to Republican leadership that we weren't going to get annihilated fighting back."[4] On issue after issue, the AFL-CIO sees the Republican leadership as its enemy; there are only a few Republican members from the Northeast and Midwest who have good relationships with labor.[5]

Since 2000, two unions with special concerns, the International Brotherhood of Teamsters and the United Brotherhood of Carpenters and Joiners, have developed stronger ties with the Republicans. But their endorsements and PAC giving still heavily favor Democrats. From the 1997–1998 cycle through 2003–2004, the percentage of the Teamsters' PAC giving that went to Republicans rose from 7 percent to 11 percent; the comparable figures for the Carpenters were 7 percent and 27 percent.[6] While these are well above the figures for most other major unions, they still mark these two unions as strongly Democratic.

The Teamsters, a union that has long sought an amicable relationship with the GOP, tried to reach out to George W. Bush during and after the 2000 election. Judis (2002) argues that Teamsters leader James Hoffa wanted Bush to end federal supervision of his union (imposed to end decades of corruption), while Bush wanted Hoffa's support for his energy policies and political backing in key midwestern states. But the basic conservatism of the Bush administration and the Republican Party posed an insurmountable obstacle. In a February 2003 meeting with the AFL-CIO executive committee, Secretary of Labor Elaine Chao defended the Bush administration's imposition of stricter financial disclosure rules on labor unions. Many labor leaders (including Hoffa) felt insulted by Chao's speech, particularly her discussion of union corruption. Shortly afterward, House Majority Leader Tom DeLay (R-TX) wrote a fund-raising letter for the National Right to Work Legal Defense Fund that denounced "Big Labor Bosses," further alienating the Teamsters. Hoffa also joined other labor leaders in denouncing Bush administration policies on overtime rules and ergonomics regulation. Bush had also issued executive orders that made it more difficult for unions to use member dues for political purposes and ended a requirement that many federal contractors use union workers. He also opposed allowing employees of the Department of Homeland Security to bargain collectively. By March 2003, Hoffa had publicly broken with Bush (Barnes 2003; Greenhouse 2003a; Greenhouse 2003b; Murray 2003).

One faction of liberal interest groups that has steadily improved its relationship with the Democratic Party is composed of those organizations that focus on noneconomic issues, such as abortion and the environment. In the 1970s, when these groups were first becoming active in Democratic politics, they were regarded with skepticism by party regulars and union leaders, who saw them as fringe players who could only alienate the groups' blue-collar supporters. In return, many "new politics" activists disdained traditional Democrats as part of an "establishment" uninterested in change.

Today, the social-issue activists are full-fledged members of the party networks. For example, one interviewee at a pro-choice group later became the director of a liberal PAC with close ties to organized labor. With the growing polarization of the political parties, especially among activists, on social issues such as abortion and the environment, it makes sense for NARAL and the Sierra Club and similar organizations to build strong ties with the Democrats. Planned Parenthood broke with a tradition of political reticence by spending $7 billion on broadcast ads in 2000 attacking George W. Bush for his views on abortion and sex education. A high Planned Parenthood official reported that some Republican donors were upset by the organization's more partisan stance, but that staff felt that the differences were so great between Bush and Gore that the organization had to become more aggressive.[7] She said she had noticed a shift among liberal organizations in recent years to being more forthrightly partisan and seeking to build stronger coalitions.

Ties between such groups and organized labor have grown in recent years, symbolized by SEIU head Andrew Stern's onetime marriage to a leader of the left-wing environmentalist group Friends of the Earth, and by longtime AFL-CIO political director Steve Rosenthal's background as a student radical. They are not George Meany's kind of unionists.

On the conservative side, social-issue activists—notably the NRLC—have developed close ties to the Republican Party. Pro-lifers have become a potent force in Republican primaries. Representatives from the NRLC have attended Grover Norquist's weekly gatherings of conservative activists (Drew 1997). The National Republican Congressional Committee donated $250,000 to the National Right to Life Committee (NRLC) in October 1999, causing some moderate Republicans to complain (Leavitt 2000). The NRLC seems to be a classic example of an interest group that is deeply embedded in a party network.

During the 2000 Republican presidential primaries, the NRLC sent almost 2.5 million mailers and, along with its South Carolina affiliate, spent over $300,000 on phone calls. It reportedly spent $475,000 on independent expenditures during the presidential nomination season (Magleby 2000). During the New Hampshire and South Carolina primaries, the NRLC ran radio ads supporting George W. Bush and criticizing Senator John McCain (R-AZ) for his support of campaign finance reform and alleged lack of commitment to banning abortion (Fowler et al. 2000; Moore and Vinson 2000). A Republican staffer, asked if the NRLC had become a "de facto arm" of the Bush campaign, said, "I don't know why you say de facto, it's official" (Rees 2000). (It could be said that Bush was the "official" candidate of the Republican Party network, given the support he received from GOP officeholders and conservative interest groups, even Rush Limbaugh.) One study found that the Bush and McCain campaigns agreed that the pro-life groups and the Christian Coalition were the most effective of the outside groups involved in South Carolina because "they clearly presented to their supporters that McCain was not a pro-life, religious conservative, and was even a threat to these things" (Moore and Vinson 2000). One-third of South Carolina Republican primary voters were self-identified religious conservatives; they favored Bush over McCain by 67 percent to 10 percent. Overall, Bush defeated McCain by 53 percent to 42 percent.

Unlike many other areas of political activity, PAC donations generally do not reflect an increasing partisan polarization. Most single-issue groups have not changed the partisan distribution of their contributions; by 1992, most were already making their donations almost solely to candidates of one party. NARAL directed 92 percent of its money in 1992 toward Democrats, and 90 percent in 2002. The National Right to Life Committee channeled 86 percent of its funds to Republicans in 1992, compared with 98 percent in 2002. The National Rifle Association (NRA) is the exception to this rule, increasing from 64 percent to Republicans in 1992 to 88 percent in 2002 (Wilcox et al. 2001; Center for Responsive Politics).

But these official PAC figures obscure some important changes. Many of these PACs sometimes backed vulnerable candidates from the other party in 1992, but in 2000 gave virtually all of their cross-party money to safe incumbents (Wilcox et al. 2001). Additionally, usually the only effort on behalf of candidates of the other party was a financial contribution from the PAC; by contrast, voter contacting, issue advocacy, and other efforts were heavily partisan. It does not appear that the close margins and party polarization led these groups to abandon their token bipartisanship in 2000, but it does appear that the more partisan side of their activity was conducted at a far more intense level in 2000 than in years past (Wilcox et al. 2001).

The Republican takeover of Congress in 1994 forced many liberal groups to change their views of the political parties. No longer could they count on a friendly congressional leadership that would kill unfavorable bills in committee or keep them from ever coming to the floor. In its place was a militantly conservative Republican Party that threatened all their values and interests. In response, the AFL-CIO greatly expanded its political activity across the board but, after 1996, placed a special emphasis on grassroots mobilization. According to political director Gloria Totten, NARAL became less tolerant of Republicans with "mixed-choice" records: those who mostly favored abortion rights but voted for some restrictions. NARAL also reduced its assistance to those supporters who had safe seats, instead shifting resources to competitive races. In addition, NARAL also shifted its emphasis from lobbying to electoral activity, merging its PAC with its field department.[8] Although the environment is not as polarizing an issue as abortion, Kim Haddow, media consultant for the Sierra Club, commented that while the club's leadership was grateful for Republican support, they were aware of the importance of party control.[9]

Providing Aid to the Parties

Of all the interest groups included in this project, only organized labor and the National Rifle Association were major givers of "soft money" to the political parties. Unions were among the most important soft-money donors to the Democrats. In the 1999–2000 cycle, organized labor gave $30 million in soft money to Democratic committees, about one-eighth of the party's total soft-money intake. The American Federation of State, County and Municipal Employees (AFSCME), Service Employees International Union (SEIU), the Carpenters and Joiners, the Communications Workers of America, and the United Food and Commercial Workers were the Democrats' five largest single donors. The NRA gave nearly $1.5 million to the Republican Party in the 1999–2000 cycle and smaller amounts in earlier and later cycles.[10]

Despite the wide variety of activities they pursue, interest groups have not become the financial juggernauts that the political parties are. While some of these groups do have impressive political budgets, they cannot match the parties' resources. Semiatin and Rozell (2005) estimated the 2000 spending by the AFL-CIO, the NRA, and EMILY's List at $45 million, $25 million, and $20 million. Sometimes, group representatives will compare their groups' activities favorably to those pursued by the parties; indeed, more than one interviewee expressed the view that the political parties have become primarily mechanisms for fund-raising. But they admitted that the parties were better at performing many political tasks, such as recruiting candidates and providing targeting information. This finding is analogous to Dulio and Kolodny's (2001) discovery that political consultants tend to specialize in some fields such as polling and media strategy, while leaving others (fund-raising assistance, voter turnout) to the party committees.

Networking Among Groups

Groups on either side of the partisan divide are increasingly networking with one another, sharing information about candidates and techniques. Campaign finance regulations do limit the ability of groups to share information about specific races, since groups that are coordinating their activities with candidates cannot share information with groups that are doing independent expenditures in the same contests. Nevertheless, extensive networking does occur. The most conspicuous examples are the weekly meetings of conservative activists held by Grover Norquist and Paul Weyrich. The Business Industry Political Action Committee has long sought to coordinate political activity by businesses. Labor and liberal groups have their own networking activities. Personnel move between groups in the same party network. Chuck Cunningham served as field director for the Christian Coalition before he became the NRA's director of federal affairs. Margaret Conway, who is now political director for the Sierra Club, previously held similar positions at Planned Parenthood and the Human Rights Campaign. Before Mary Crawford served as communications director for the NFIB, she worked for the Republican National Committee and the National Republican Congressional Committee.[11] Mary Beth Cahill moved from running EMILY's List to directing John Kerry's presidential campaign. In 2004, America Votes, led by Cecile Richards, a onetime aide to House Minority Leader Nancy Pelosi, brought together twenty-nine liberal groups in order to coordinate their efforts (Barnes 2004; Hadfield 2004).

Ideas, as well as personnel, move between groups in the same party network. When the National Association for the Advancement of Colored People (NAACP) created the National Voter Fund to foster African American political participation, a top official with the fund consulted with staff at Handgun Control and the Sierra Club. She sought advice from them even though the fund's target audience was very different from those of the two organizations.[12] Gloria Totten reported regular meetings between leading liberal and labor organizations to share information about political developments, as well as consultation between NARAL and Planned Parenthood about activity in individual congressional races.[13] The parties themselves foster the sharing of information by holding regular briefings for sympathetic PACs.

During the 2004 campaign, America Votes, a coalition of pro-Democratic groups, held biweekly meetings of liberal activists to plot strategy. America Votes allowed member organizations to share voter files, survey data, and demographic information. This allowed America Votes staff to coordinate the efforts of groups such as the Sierra Club, NARAL Pro-Choice America, and the League of Conservation Voters in stimulating voter turnout and contacting swing voters. America Votes targeted thirteen battleground states; in some states, such as Michigan and Florida, the organization has been continuing its efforts for key 2006 races (Hadfield 2004).

The other two elements in the Democrats' "shadow party" of 527s also support the notion of a party network. After the passage of the Bipartisan Campaign Reform Act (BCRA), DNC chairman Terry McAuliffe established a Task Force on BCRA that included Harold Ickes, former deputy chief of staff to Bill Clinton; Michael Whouley, a longtime Democratic operative; John Podesta, former White House chief of staff for Clinton; and two top officials of the DNC. Ickes devised the Media Fund, which he subsequently led; before BCRA became effective, McAuliffe encouraged leading Democratic donors to give to the new organization (Weissman and Hassan, forthcoming; also see Skinner 2005).

Ickes also helped devise America Coming Together and America Votes through meetings with top members of the Democratic Party network. These included Sierra Club director Carl Pope, EMILY's List president Ellen Malcolm (who also serves on the DNC's executive committee), SEIU president Andrew Stern, and former AFL-CIO political director Steve Rosenthal. They agreed on the need to coordinate interest-group electoral operations; this became America Votes (Weissman and Hassan, forthcoming).

Stern and Rosenthal also discussed their desire to create a "ground war" operation funded by unions, and that would apply to the general public the voter turnout techniques used to mobilize union members. This eventually became America Coming Together (ACT); billionaire George Soros and insurance tycoon Peter Lewis pledged $20 million to fund ACT as long as Rosenthal controlled its operations (Weissman and Hassan, forthcoming). Malcolm and Ickes formed the Joint Victory Campaign to raise money for all three groups. With the assistance of Soros and Bill Clinton, Malcolm and Ickes wooed many of the party's top donors; Hollywood producer Steve Bing was among the many onetime soft-money givers who helped fund ACT and the Media Fund (Weissman and Hassan, forthcoming).

During the campaign, ACT, America Votes, and the Media Fund, along with two labor-backed 527s, were all headquartered in the same building in downtown Washington, across the street from the AFL-CIO's headquarters. By the fall of 2004, ACT had fifty-five offices in seventeen states, and 1,300 paid canvassers working to turn out Democratic voters (Dwyer, Walczak, and Woellert 2004). Not only was the leadership of the "shadow party" groups deeply embedded in the party networks, their staff was, too. Both the Media Fund and ACT hired the Thunder Road Group, run by former Kerry campaign manager Jim Jordan, to handle their communications. Larry Gold served as counsel for both ACT and the AFL-CIO. Bill Knapp served as a consultant for the Media Fund before he quit to work for the Kerry campaign (Drinkard 2004).

Progress for America (PFA), a leading Republican 527 group, was also run by people active in their party network. PFA was founded in 2001 by Tony Feather, political director of the 2000 Bush-Cheney campaign and an ally of Bush adviser Karl Rove; after a year of inactivity, Feather handed over PFA to Chris LaCivita, former political director for the NRSC. In the spring of 2004, Brian McCabe took over PFA; McCabe was a partner in the DCI Group, a political consulting firm. Even when LaCivita was running PFA, he was also doing work for DCI. DCI and its affiliate FLS-DCI both later did work for the Bush campaign. Tom Synhorst, a partner in both DCI and FLS-DCI, served as a strategic adviser and fund-raiser for PFA. Synhorst had worked as an adviser to the 2000 Bush campaign and helped run the 1996 and 2000 Republican national conventions (Weissman and Hassan, forthcoming). Benjamin Ginsberg served as counsel to PFA; he served in similar capacities for both the 2004 Bush reelection effort and Swift Boat Veterans for Truth. The Swift Boat organizers approached PFA, seeking advice; PFA personnel encouraged them to see LaCivita, who became an adviser to the group (Weissman and Hassan, forthcoming; Stone 2003a).

PFA became a 527 organization in May 2004, after the Federal Election Commission (FEC) decided not to regulate 527s; Bush-Cheney campaign chairman Marc Racicot and RNC chairman Ed Gillespie soon released a statement urging support for PFA and other sympathetic 527s. PFA quickly gained access to the financial resources of the Republican Party network, hiring some well-connected fund-raisers, holding a fund-raiser at the national convention, and gaining the assistance of such party stalwarts as San Diego Chargers owner Alex Spanos (Weissman and Hassan 2006; Drinkard 2004).

The Limits of the Party Network

While groups in the party networks may share an interest with party organizations in partisan control of Congress, they have different ultimate ends. Groups seek control to enact favorable policy; party leaders may see control as an end in itself. But in today's polarized environment, those goals are not easily disentangled. Totten recalled how pro-choice Democratic chairmen would kill antiabortion bills in committee, even when they might have commanded a majority on the floor. By contrast, Republican leaders have repeatedly spearheaded attempts to limit abortion rights, including a ban on "partial-birth" abortions. Totten expressed her frustration at leaders' ability to restrict abortion in low-visibility, technical ways; this allows Republicans to satisfy their right-to-life constituency without giving pro-choice activists easy grounds to rally support.[14]

Another source of conflict is groups' inability to support candidates that oppose them on their key issue, even if the race could make a difference in partisan control. In 2000, NARAL supported pro-choice state senator Allyson Schwartz for the Democratic nomination to oppose U.S. senator Rick Santorum (R-PA), a staunch abortion foe. When Schwartz lost to pro-life representative Ron Klink, NARAL pulled out of the race. Klink went on to lose to Santorum, in part because of the coolness of pro-choice voters and donors. Had Klink won, the Democrats would have immediately taken control of the Senate, rather than after Senator Jim Jeffords's leaving the Republican Party (Soskis 2000).

The National Rifle Association follows a different path. When both the Democratic and Republican candidates in a congressional race support gun control, the NRA does not support either one. But the NRA does send to its members what federal affairs director Chuck Cunningham calls a "RINO letter" (for Republicans In Name Only), which, while not endorsing the Republican, criticizes the Democrat much more vehemently. Cunningham explained that the NRA sends the RINO letters for two reasons: First, because the antigun Republican would still vote for GOP control of the House, which means a progun Speaker and progun committee chairmen. Second, because Cunningham believes that antigun Republicans are much less likely than their Democratic counterparts to sponsor or co-sponsor legislation, make hostile speeches, or otherwise promote the gun-control agenda:

> Cunningham: There will be some districts in which the Republican is no friend of ours and the Democrat would be even worse. And we will communicate with our members, not endorse the Republican, but really vilify the Democrat. In hopes that the antigun Republican will prevail over the more antigun Democrat. Because most of the Republicans who are antigun don't sponsor bills, don't speak out, and there is a difference.... Those are races where the Republicans are lousy, but the Democrats would be even worse. We're not going to lose credibility by saying, go out and support the Republican, but we're going to highlight how bad the Democrat would be.
>
> Skinner: Is that simply based on what that person would do in Congress or because they might be part of a Democratic majority?
>
> Cunningham: Both.[15]
>
> Because there wasn't much good to say about the Republican, we focused all of our discussion in those mailings, which hit on the weekend before the Tuesday election, about the details of how bad the Democrat candidate was. Because it is in our best interests that Lott be majority leader, and that Hastert would be Speaker, and that Sensenbrenner be chairman of Judiciary in the House and Hatch in the Senate.[16]

Through the use of "RINO letters," the NRA is able to help Republicans maintain control of Congress without losing credibility or alienating its highly ideological membership. Such low-key, low-visibility assistance is probably more acceptable than an overt endorsement, which would open the NRA to charges of hypocrisy and partisanship.

Groups can also conflict with parties' ultimate goal of gaining or holding control by supporting in primaries candidates who may not be the most electable. The Club for Growth, a small group of wealthy conservative donors, has supported conservative candidates in Republican primaries against the wishes of party leaders; in 2004, it heartily supported Rep. Pat Toomey's conservative challenge to Senator Arlen Specter (R-PA). NARAL has supported pro-choice candidates in culturally conservative districts who seem unlikely to win. While most groups confine their activities to primaries of either the Democrats or the Republicans, some have played roles in both. In 2002, the NRA played a significant role in two Democratic congressional primaries, helping to reelect Rep. John Dingell (D-MI), a longtime NRA ally, and to defeat Rep. Tom Sawyer (D-OH), a supporter of gun control. But those were the exception rather than the rule.

Finally, interest groups must be aware that their members are motivated much more by their specific issues than by party control of Congress. While Totten acknowledged that the Republican takeover in 1994 had a huge effect on the politics of abortion within Congress, it did not motivate pro-choice voters as much as the prospect of an actual ban on abortion. Between the 1989 *Webster* decision and the 1992 *Casey* decision, NARAL saw a dramatic increase in its membership; it did not see such an effect after the 1994 elections. Totten recounted the days after *Webster*:

> And then people started hearing . . . about *Webster*, you know, the threat was so real. Everybody believed that *Roe v. Wade* was going to be overturned. Upper-middle-class white women who could fly to London in a day and get an abortion if they needed one were threatened by what was happening. And so people were coming out of the woodwork; you would open the door, checks were coming in, money was coming in, people were becoming members. It was incredible.

> And then after the '92 election with the election of Clinton there was a complete and immediate drop-off. It's like somebody turned off the music. It just stopped. Our budget was cut first by a third, then by a half. We laid off a third of our staff, about a month after the '92 elections. A third of the people had to go. There was no more money. And that was that.[17]

By contrast, congressional Republicans omitted any discussion of abortion from the Contract with America. Since they took power, Republicans have mostly stuck to incremental changes in abortion policy; these satisfy their right-to-life constituency without arousing the ire of pro-choice swing voters:

> And so then of course in '92, they learned a big lesson with '92—the other side— because they couldn't again get that in-your-face of the American public. And so the '94 elections, even those with extreme views that they elected, like Steve Largent, know enough to not put up amendments to outlaw *Roe v. Wade*. Go after it, get it another way.

> So then the effect in '94, even without getting elected, was not, it did not galva- nize our folks at all. . . . They see this prize and we don't see [the] threat, that's the problem.[18]

Groups in the Party Network

Even given all these caveats, some interest groups clearly have developed closer relationships with the political parties. They are often part of the same parti- san and ideological networks of individuals and organizations (see Bedlington and Malbin 2003; Monroe 2001; Schwartz 1990; and Cohen et al., forthcom- ing for elaborations of this concept). These party networks not only include party committees and friendly interest groups, they include individual politi- cians and the leadership PACs under their control, think tanks, lobbyists, and perhaps even media figures. The Republican National Committee, the NFIB, Tom DeLay and his leadership PAC (Americans for a Republican Majority), the Heritage Foundation, Vin Weber (a onetime House Republican, now a well-connected lobbyist), and Rush Limbaugh are part of a Republican network. This network shares information and coordinates activity.

The professionalization of politics has allowed more individuals to both live "off" politics and live "for" politics. Rather than being rewarded with deputy postmasterships or sinecures in the city Parks Department, today's political professionals can instead seek jobs as chiefs of staff or communications directors, perhaps with an eye to an eventual corner office on K Street. As they move from position to position, professionals remain enmeshed in webs of relationships within their own partisan universes. Even when working as lobbyists or consultants, they remain active in support of their party and its candidates (see Kersh 2002 and Loomis 2003 for discussions of how lobbyists can remain politically active while being paid to serve their clients).

Individuals can build careers by moving through the network. Ralph Reed has, in turn, served as national leader of the College Republicans, executive director of the Christian Coalition, a political consultant working for Republican candidates, and chairman of the Georgia Republican Party. While not all of the positions involved working for Republican Party organizations, they were all part of an identifiable Republican Party network. Party networks are not monolithic. They can encompass groups and individuals that have their own interests, even whole subnetworks (such as organized labor within the Democratic network). But they do bring together actors with shared interests and values.[19]

Not every actor in American politics is part of a party network. Access-oriented corporations and trade associations can seek their particularistic benefits from legislators of either party—although Republican leaders have put pressure on trade associations to hire Republican lobbyists. But the atmosphere created by partisan polarization makes it difficult for more ideological groups to play on both sides of the aisle. This is true for single-issue groups interested in abortion and gun control; it is also true for organized labor, the NFIB, and similar groups with broad multi-issue agendas.

We need to expand our notion of what a political party is. It is not simply a series of committees. It is instead a matrix of relationships between politicians, whether they work in party organizations, in interest groups, in the media, in political action committees, in consulting firms, or in government itself. The activists at the Sierra Club, EMILY's List, or the AFL-CIO may not get their checks from the Democratic National Committee, but they are part of the same Democratic Party network. The people working for the NRA, the NFIB, or other Republican-leaning organizations are essential parts of the Republican Party network. Rather than tearing down the party system, they are among its most important pillars.

Notes

1. In 1992 and 1994, corporate PACs gave 48 percent of their contributions to Democrats. (Trade association PACs gave 57 percent in 1992 and 48 percent in 1994.) In 1996, corporate PACs gave only 27 percent to Democrats, but in 1998 and 2000, this proportion rose to roughly one-third. Trade association giving followed a similar pattern. Data from Norman J. Ornstein, Thomas E. Mann, and Michael J. Malbin, *Vital Statistics on Congress: 1999–2000.* Available at www.cfinst.org/studies/vital/3-11.htm.

2. Interview with Mary Crawford, National Federation of Independent Business, May 24, 2000.

3. Interview with Mary Crawford, National Federation of Independent Business, May 24, 2000; interview with Mary Crawford, National Federation of Independent Business, February 8, 2001.

4. Interview with Mike Podhorzer, AFL-CIO, March 1, 2001.

5. Interview with David Bounby, AFL-CIO, June 27, 2001.

6. Center for Responsive Politics. www.crp.org.

7. Interview with Planned Parenthood official, July 9, 2001.

8. Interview with Gloria Totten, NARAL, May 26, 2000.

9. Interview with Kim Haddow, Sierra Club, June 15, 2000.

10. Center for Responsive Politics. www.crp.org.

11. Interview with Mary Crawford, National Federation of Independent Business, May 24, 2000.

12. Interview with official of the NAACP National Voter Fund, June 11, 2001.

13. Interview with Gloria Totten, NARAL, April 19, 2001.

14. Interview with Gloria Totten, NARAL, May 26, 2000.

15. Interview with Chuck Cunningham, NRA, May 26, 2000.

16. Interview with Chuck Cunningham, NRA, February 7, 2001.

17. Interview with Gloria Totten, NARAL, May 26, 2000.

18. Interview with Gloria Totten, NARAL, May 26, 2000.

19. Burdett Loomis and Micheal Struemph have defined the Industry of Politics as including "corporations, labor unions, membership organizations, wealthy individuals, political parties, and the staff-based 'enterprises' of legislators. . . . So are fundraisers, consultants, public affairs firms, and producers of political advertising. Likewise, much of the media establishment qualifies, especially to the extent that it focuses on political content" (Loomis and Struemph 2003). Most of the members of this "industry" belong to the party networks. Indeed the party networks can be considered to be an aspect of the Industry of Politics. One could also speak of an "Industry of Ideology" that formulates a "party line" that is then transmitted by elites to rank-and-file voters.

10

Changes in Context

THE GROUPS INCLUDED IN THIS STUDY have shown an ability to respond to changing political and legal contexts. Changes in political context have included a growing polarization between the two political parties and a series of shifts in power in Washington. Changes in legal context have included more and less permissive environments for issue advocacy, the rise and fall of "soft money," and the growth of PACs.

Reaganism and Its Repercussions

The election of Ronald Reagan as president in 1980 climaxed the rise of the "New Right" and began a new era of partisan polarization in American politics. The 1950s, 1960s, and 1970s saw a decline in party-line voting both in Congress and in the electorate. Particularly in the 1960s and 1970s, congressional party leaders saw their power dissipate as first committee and then subcommittee chairmen exercised increasing clout. Presidents of this era often sought a nonpartisan image, appealing to voters across ideological divides through an "objective" media. They built ad hoc coalitions of support in Congress without regard to party lines; for example, Lyndon Johnson relied heavily on Republican votes to pass civil rights legislation. They presided over an executive branch staffed by nonpartisan experts who were more interested in policy than politics. Presidents such as Dwight Eisenhower and Jimmy Carter showed little interest in their party's performance in down-ballot races, let alone its long-term fate. Eisenhower, Carter, and Richard Nixon all had difficult relationships with their congressional parties, and often could not count on them for steadfast support (see Skinner 2006).

All of this changed after 1980. Party-line voting exploded first in Congress and then in the electorate. Tip O'Neill and Jim Wright reinvigorated party government in the House of Representatives. Ronald Reagan governed in a frankly ideological manner and sought to build the GOP into a majority party. As often as not, his successors followed his lead. They also turned to their congressional parties for support and often endured difficult, even toxic, relationships with the opposition. Both Reagan and George W. Bush have sought to put a stronger partisan imprint upon the executive branch, centralizing personnel decisions, and favoring ideological loyalists or spinmeisters over career civil servants or nonpartisan experts. Reagan and his successors have actively campaigned for their party's candidates and sought to use the national party committees as tools of governance. (Compare to Eisenhower's apathy toward the GOP, or Johnson's and Nixon's distrust of their national party committees.) Reagan, Bill Clinton, and George W. Bush have all shown an interest in their party's long-term fortunes that escaped, say, Jimmy Carter.

While groups did much to bring this new state of affairs about, they also had to respond to it. The "New Right" of the 1970s, including the antiabortion movement, had been suspicious of the Republican Party, believing it to be dominated by complacent country-clubbers, advocates of détente, and Nelson Rockefeller loyalists. The social movements that arose in the 1960s, including feminism and environmentalism, often distrusted the Democratic establishment, accusing it of coddling segregationists, oppressing antiwar activists, and toadying to big-city bosses and corrupt union leaders. In addition, the heavily Catholic leadership of the Democratic Party in many states was often uncomfortable with the movement for abortion rights.

Even the economic interests that had been clearly aligned along party lines since the New Deal did not always see politics in purely partisan terms. Organized labor—particularly the building trades that then dominated the AFL-CIO leadership—had always sought friends among Republicans. George Meany had enjoyed a friendship with Nelson Rockefeller that dated back to the construction of Rockefeller Center, which created valuable jobs for Meany's New York constituents during the Great Depression. While Meany never felt such warm emotions for Richard Nixon, he did have an amicable enough relationship with Nixon's administration. More importantly, Meany despised Nixon's enemies in the antiwar movement, and withheld the AFL-CIO's endorsement from George McGovern. Similarly, while the business community consistently preferred the GOP, there was a long history of corporate lobbyists getting along with prominent Democrats, especially southern pragmatists such as Wilbur Mills and Russell Long. Even as liberals came to dominate the Democratic Party in the 1980s and 1990s, the power of the gavel kept corporate PAC contributions flowing to Democrats.

Groups have had to adapt to an environment in which it became increasingly difficult to find friends on the other side of the aisle, but where stronger party leadership made close ties to a party more viable. The Reagan administration's unabashed conservatism drew the New Right more securely into the Republican Party; while Reagan alienated liberals, his policies helped their organizations raise money and gain a higher public profile.

Unions were also affected by the growing polarization between the parties. Much more than their Republican predecessors Dwight Eisenhower and Richard Nixon, Presidents Ronald Reagan and George H. W. Bush were hostile to organized labor and its agenda. Most conspicuously, Reagan broke an illegal strike by air traffic controllers by firing the workers. This hostility forced the AFL-CIO to revamp its political activity. This consisted, to a great extent, of adapting to the reforms of the 1970s—responding to another major change in political context. Congressional reform had reduced the power of committee chairmen, weakening the kind of cozy relationships longtime AFL-CIO boss George Meany had preferred. But it also created the opportunity for stronger party leadership and Speakers Thomas P. O'Neill Jr. and Jim Wright, both strong labor allies, used their powers to the greatest possible extent.

The McGovern-Fraser reforms had reduced party conventions to a formality, ending the days when labor bosses could confer with party bigwigs to pick a nominee. But the primaries and caucuses that now determined the nomination placed a premium on money and volunteers, resources that unions (especially the UAW and AFSCME) had in abundance. In the 1980s, the Democrats chose presidential nominees with strong labor ties: Walter Mondale and Michael Dukakis. George Meany had long made clear his lack of regard for antiwar activists, feminists, and black militants. But after Meany retired in 1979, the AFL-CIO built bridges to other liberal groups, including those with a "New Politics" heritage; they were able to rally around a platform of strong opposition to Reagan-Bush policies. But the AFL-CIO was not able to turn around the declining rate of membership in labor unions, especially the industrial unions that were devastated by the recession of 1981–1982. AFL-CIO president Lane Kirkland helped heal ideological wounds and bring back wayward affiliates (the UAW, UMW, and Teamsters all rejoined the federation during his time in office). But he did not provide the kind of strong leadership that many thought necessary to revive labor's fortunes (Dark 1998).

Labor unions split during the 1992 nomination season, with public employee unions embracing Bill Clinton and industrial unions flirting with Tom Harkin until his candidacy proved untenable. (The building trades mostly remained neutral.) After Clinton was nominated, the AFL-CIO strongly supported him in the general election. It generally enjoyed a good relationship with the Clinton administration, except on the issue of foreign trade. But the AFL-CIO was hit hard by the results of the 1994 congressional elections. Not only did Republicans take control of Congress for the first time in forty years, but the new congressional leadership was adamantly antiunion (Dark 1998; Gerber 1999; Asher et al. 2001; Francia 2005).

The atmosphere of heightened polarization also drew new groups more securely into the Democratic coalition. The pro-choice movement had struggled in the years after *Roe v. Wade.* A string of pro-life victories in 1978 and 1980 made the downside of supporting abortion rights all too apparent. By contrast, pro-choice voters assumed that *Roe* guaranteed that abortion would remain legal, so they did not see the issue as important. But victories in 1982 by several Democratic challengers who had been endorsed by the National Abortion and Reproductive Rights Action League (NARAL) helped convince many candidates that backing from the group could be an asset. Pro-choice politicians, especially Democrats, became more comfortable accepting a NARAL endorsement. Opposition to the nomination of Judge Robert Bork to the Supreme Court in 1987 helped revive public interest in NARAL and other pro-choice organizations (O'Connor 1996; Craig and O'Brien 1993; Thomas 1994 [AQ: Not on ref list.], 1999). The evolution of NARAL into a respectable member of the Democratic coalition can be seen in the changing stand of Tom Harkin of Iowa, a state where the pro-life movement began its rise to prominence. In 1984, when Harkin was first running for Senate, he returned a NARAL contribution after it received negative press. Six years later, when Harkin was waging a difficult campaign for reelection, he accepted NARAL's endorsement and contribution. In fact, one postelection analysis attributed Harkin's defeat of Rep. Tom Tauke (R), in part, to Tauke's opposition to abortion (Thomas 1994; Barone and Ujifusa 1991).

The trend toward partisan polarization extended well beyond traditional splits between labor and management and "hot-button" concerns such as abortion to previously bipartisan issues such as the environment. Lodato (2004) demonstrates the evolution of the Senate Environment and Public Works Committee from a bastion of bipartisan comity to a body divided fiercely along party lines. In the 1970s and 1980s, Democrats such as Edmund Muskie (ME) worked easily with Republicans such as Howard Baker (TN) and Robert Stafford (VT). Many Republican members were ardent environmentalists, while Democratic chairmen Jennings Randolph (WV) and Quentin Burdick (ND) were mostly interested in sending public works projects to their low-income states. But in the 1990s, Republicans on the committee increasingly opposed environmental legislation, as conservative stalwarts like James Inhofe (OK) and Robert Bennett (UT) replaced more moderate members.

Meanwhile, Democrats on the committee were no longer Randolph-Burdick–style pragmatists, but liberal crusaders from the coasts such as Barbara Boxer (CA) and Frank Lautenberg (NJ). As a result, the committee has become as fiercely polarized as the rest of Congress.

In 1992, Bill Clinton was elected president, ending twelve years of Republican dominance of the White House. While he was a "New Democrat" on many issues, Clinton enjoyed warm relationships with most members of the Democratic coalition. Paradoxically, but in accordance with the predictions of interest-group theory, Clinton's ascendance actually demobilized liberal groups such as NARAL and reinvigorated the conservative movement.

The National Rifle Association had fared well under the Reagan administration, eventually achieving its goal of rolling back some provisions of the Gun Control Act of 1968. But this record of success, followed by a much more uneven relationship with the administration of George H. W. Bush, demobilized gun owners and demoralized the NRA. Gun control advocates scored a series of victories, climaxing with the passage of the Brady law and an assault weapons ban under President Bill Clinton. This newly hostile environment allowed the NRA to recruit many new members and to more broadly mobilize gun owners for political action. The NRA gained a million members between 1991 and 1994, reaching a new high of 3.5 million (Patterson and Singer 2002). In 1994, the NRA played a major role in winning Congress for the Republicans for the first time in forty years; an exit poll showed that 69 percent of gun owners voted Republican for the House. The NRA enjoyed a good relationship with Newt Gingrich and other Republican leaders both before and after the takeover (Balz and Brownstein 1996). Other conservative groups, including Right to Life, the Christian Coalition, and the NFIB, experienced rapid growth during the early years of the Clinton administration.

The Republican takeover of 1994 drastically altered the environment for organized labor and liberal interest groups. No longer could they rely on Democratic committee chairmen to kill unfriendly legislation, or on the Democratic floor leadership to help pass favorite bills. Most of the newly elected Republicans were deeply conservative; their leaders went out of their way to antagonize organized labor, feminists, and environmentalists. It was against this background that AFL-CIO leader Lane Kirkland resigned October 1995; he was facing a campaign for his removal led by the Service Employees International Union (SEIU) and American Federation of State, County and Municipal Employees (AFSCME). Kirkland was replaced by John Sweeney, president of the SEIU. Sweeney had close relationships with other liberal activists and his union was one of the few to have gained members in recent years. While Sweeney's core support came from public-employee and service unions, he gained some backing from industrial and craft unions, including the UAW and the Teamsters. Sweeney soon announced the launching of a $35 million campaign to elect a Democratic Congress that included $25 million in "issue ads" as well as $10 million on grassroots organization. (Outside estimates of labor's total spending put the figure much higher.) Labor's grassroots activity included voter registration, voter education, get-out-the-vote drives, and training for local activists. Labor's campaign contributed to the defeat of several Republicans, but it failed to deliver control to the Democrats (Dark 1998; Gerber 1999).

After a period of complacency, the Sierra Club increased its political activity following the 1994 Republican takeover, which had devastated its influence on the congressional agenda. Indeed, some Republican leaders took pride in their disdain for the environmental movement (Cantor 1999). During the 1995–1996 cycle, the club boosted its political activity in a variety of ways. It increased its fund-raising: its yield from direct mail doubled as eco-conscious donors responded to the Republican takeover. It became more partisan in its giving, favoring many Democratic challengers. It increased its independent spending and its voter education.

The 1994 elections were not only a big defeat for Democrats, but also a disaster for pro-choice activists. They lost five seats in the Senate and thirty-nine in the House, wiping out all their gains in 1990–1992. Pro-choicers still have not recouped these losses. While Republicans had not mentioned abortion in their Contract with America, they soon passed a series of restrictions on abortion, particularly on federal funding. This defeat was a wake-up call for NARAL, leading it to revamp its political operations. As was the case for many liberal groups, the January 1996 special election to fill the seat of Senator Bob Packwood (R-OR) marked the beginning of a new activism for NARAL. But NARAL was unable to increase its fund-raising. Many of the abortion restrictions passed by the Republican Congress were complex and difficult to understand; they did not easily translate into fund-raising appeals. NARAL adapted to the new environment by channeling its PAC funds to challengers and open-seat candidates; it also decreased its overall PAC giving in favor of increased spending on voter education (Thomas 1999).

The National Rifle Association experienced a period of drift and division after the Republican takeover in 1994. But the NRA revitalized itself during the 2000 elections. The threat of further gun control legislation helped the NRA mobilize gun owners. Bill Clinton called for new gun licensing requirements while Al Gore and Bill Bradley, competing for the Democratic presidential nomination, both called for gun registration (Eilperin 2000b).

By election eve, the NRA's membership had reportedly hit a new high of 4.1 million. The NRA reportedly spent a total of $20 million on political activity in 2000 (Eilperin 2000b; MacPherson 2000; Miller and Miller 2000).

The NRA gave $1.5 million in soft money to the Republican Party (it gave nothing to the Democrats), making it the fourth-biggest donor organization to the GOP.[1] The NRA's PAC gave $1.5 million to candidates, with 86 percent going to Republicans.[2] Federal Election Commission data show that the NRA spent just under $2.2 million on independent expenditures supporting Bush and attacking Gore.

It seems that George W. Bush's election in 2000 should have spurred a new wave of growth for liberal interest groups. For all his self-labeling as a "compassionate conservative," Bush had little use for the agenda of feminists, environmentalists, or organized labor. He slashed taxes on high-income earners, rolled back regulations on business, and catered to the agenda of the Christian Right. This would appear to provide a golden opportunity for liberal groups to increase their clout. Indeed, such organizations as the Sierra Club and Planned Parenthood have seen their membership increase during the George W. Bush administration. Bush has also proven to be quite unpopular among liberal voters.

But the terrorist attacks of September 11 and the subsequent wars in Afghanistan and Iraq swept domestic issues off the public agenda. This made it difficult for liberal groups to highlight their concerns or expand their membership. Bush's phenomenal popularity among conservative voters proved to be a potent tool in driving up GOP turnout in key races. Many liberal donors flocked to MoveOn.org, an Internet-based group originally created to oppose Bill Clinton's impeachment. Especially as the Iraq war enraged opponents of the Bush administration, MoveOn.org became one of the leading voices on the left.

Besides the dominance of national-security issues, the political environment in 2002 and 2004 changed in other ways that limited the influence of many politically active interest groups. The number of competitive seats continues to shrink. G. C. Jacobson (2003) notes that the post-2000 redistricting decreased the number of Gore-majority districts from 207 to 198 and increased the number of Bush-majority districts from 228 to 237. Redistricting also significantly reduced the number of competitive districts: only four incumbents were defeated by challengers. Of the 389 House incumbents who sought reelection, 83 percent won with at least 60 percent of the vote; in 1992, only 66 percent of incumbents won by such a margin (Cohen 2003).

Democrats were hurt by redistricting, in part, because of the cautious paths followed by Democratic redistricters in states such as California while Republicans in Florida, Michigan, and Pennsylvania maximized their advantages. In part, these were aftershocks of the 1994 earthquake; in Michigan and Pennsylvania, the GOP had won complete control of state government in 1994, but lost it in 2002 with the election of Democratic governors (Cohen 2003).

Jacobson argues that the decrease in the number of competitive districts makes it more difficult for Democrats to regain control of the House, while the tendency of the Democrats to run better in larger states weakens them in the Senate. Cohen (2003) also suggests that redistricting may have placed control of the House out of Democrats' reach for the remainder of the decade. He quotes one Democratic lawyer as stating that redistricting could keep the Democrats "in the minority for the next five Congresses—even if, nationally, Democrats repeatedly capture more congressional votes than do Republicans."

The year 2002 also saw a continuation of the trend to partisan consistency between presidential and congressional voting that began in 1992. The number of "split-result" districts fell to its lowest level in more than fifty years (G. C. Jacobson 2003). Oppenheimer (2005) notes that over the past thirty years, congressional districts have become increasingly polarized along party lines; incumbents today owe much more of their security to partisanship than to any services they may provide.

In 2002, business dominated interest group activity. The Business Industry Political Action Committee (BIPAC) continued its efforts to help corporations communicate with their workers about politics; one official claimed the effort reached 11 million voters. Several business organizations, including the Business Roundtable, contracted with BIPAC to develop materials for their members. But the pharmaceutical industry was the most active of all business interests, giving $14 million to candidates, three-quarters of them Republicans, and mobilizing volunteers for voter turnout drives (Weisman 2002). The United Seniors Association, largely funded by the pharmaceutical industry, spent at least $8.7 million on TV ads in 2002. Americans for Job Security, another business-funded group, spent $1.5 million ("One Billion Dollars Spent" 2002). On election eve, the U.S. Chamber of Commerce planned to send out over 2 million pieces of mail and make 1 million get-out-the-vote phone calls (Kirchhoff and Kornblut 2002).

Meanwhile, liberal groups such as NARAL and the Sierra Club saw two of their top Senate candidates, Tom Strickland (D-CO) and Jeanne Shaheen (D-NH), go down to defeat, as Republicans streamed to the polls to support George W. Bush. With their heavy reliance on a small number of big donors, liberal groups were especially hurt by the decline in the stock market. Most notably, the fall in the value of shares of AOL Time Warner prevented Jane Fonda from repeating her 2000 performance of channeling more than $11 million to Planned Parenthood and other groups (Edsall 2002a). They also saw the visibility of their issues diminish, in the wake of the post-9/11 emphasis on homeland security.

Unions continued to be politically active. Steve Rosenthal, political director of the AFL-CIO, estimated that there were 225,000 union members involved in turning out the vote (Kiely 2002). The AFL-CIO spent at least $3.6 million on TV advertising ("One Billion Dollars Spent" 2002).

Overall levels of spending were down; some attributed this to a weaker economy, competition for donors from candidates and parties, and a small number of competitive races. Many groups instead chose to use mail and phone banks to turn out voters (Drinkard 2002). This continued a pattern spotted by Wilcox et al. (2001) of groups turning away from heavy spending on media in favor of grassroots mobilization.

Republican gains in 2004, to a great extent, occurred in regions where liberal interest groups are quite weak. Republicans picked up Senate seats in North Carolina, South Carolina, Georgia, Louisiana, and South Dakota; these are among the most socially conservative states in the nation and have very low rates of unionization. (North Carolina is the least unionized state in the nation.) Republicans also successfully defended a contested open Senate seat in Oklahoma and picked up five U.S. House seats (thanks to a new redistricting plan) in Texas; these are two other conservative states that have a limited union presence. (Republicans did win a Senate seat in Florida, a less socially conservative state that, while it has relatively few union members, is home to many union retirees from the Northeast and Midwest.)

Republicans now control twenty-two of the twenty-six Senate seats from the South (including Kentucky and Oklahoma), which is the only region where the party has actually gained seats since 1994. Democrats have made gains in the Northeast and on the West Coast. Similar patterns hold in the House, where Democrats have gained four seats in the East and thirteen seats in the West (concentrated in California), while Republicans have gained eighteen seats in the South. Much of the GOP gains have come at the expense of moderate and conservative "Blue Dog" Democrats, further widening the gap between the parties. Republicans benefit from the structure of both the Senate and the House. In 2000, while losing the popular vote, Bush carried 30 of 50 states and 228 of 435 congressional districts (Dodd and Oppenheimer 2005).

Interest groups have also shown a remarkable ability to adapt to changes in the legal context. After the passage of the 1974 Federal Employees Compensation Act (FECA) amendments, and subsequent rulings by the courts and the FEC, corporations and trade associations rapidly set up PACs, which had previously been dominated by labor unions and the American Medical Association (AMA). A series of court rulings, culminating with the *Christian Action Network* case in 1995, created a much more permissive environment for issue advocacy. Beginning with the AFL-CIO in 1996, groups adapted to this environment with relish.

The Bipartisan Campaign Reform Act (BCRA) has also changed the playing field for interest groups. No longer will they be able to donate soft money to the national parties. Their ability to run "issue ads" will be severely curtailed.

Wilcox et al. (2001, 2002) found that many groups were reorienting their strategies to focus more on targeted communication, which would accelerate a preexisting trend. Others may choose to run broadcast advertisements earlier in the cycle, before the 30-60 "window." Many activists already expressed dissatisfaction with television, because of high advertising costs, audience fragmentation, and the rise of the Internet (Boatright et al. 2003). Some group representatives predicted a revival of PAC activity. Boatright et al. (2003) suggest that some soft money that corporations gave at the request of politicians may leave the political system entirely. One new group formed in the wake of BCRA, America Coming Together, spent $76 million on voter education and registration in seventeen key states; it was funded by unions and wealthy liberals (Weissman and Hassan, forthcoming).

Notes

1. Center for Responsive Politics. www.crp.org.
2. Center for Responsive Politics. www.crp.org.

11

Theoretical Conclusions

ORGANIZATIONS ARE SHAPED BY THE INCENTIVES THEY OFFER to members to join. Purposive incentives attract memberships that are homogeneous, motivated, ideological, and relatively small. Material incentives attract memberships that are heterogeneous, apathetic, nonideological, and relatively large. Some business organizations are an exception to this rule, since they can attract memberships that are small in number but impressive in resources. Purposive organizations may encourage their members to donate money to candidates or volunteer on campaigns, while material organizations can amass much larger treasuries through their memberships. These resources then affect groups' capacity for political action. Groups with many members can turn them out to vote. Groups that can accumulate large treasuries can use them to pay for broadcast ads or mail and phone campaigns. They can also use them to build staffs that develop areas of expertise helpful to sympathetic politicians. (Of course, some groups are well endowed in all three resources.)

The issues on which a group focuses—in essence, the form that its purposive incentives take—can also affect its political activity. A group that emphasizes an issue that appeals to a wide variety of voters, such as the Sierra Club and the environment, will seek to get its message out widely. But groups that focus on issues that are narrower or more polarizing, such as abortion or gun control, will seek to target their messages to those voters already known to be sympathetic. Purposive organizations, which have smaller, ideologically committed memberships, will focus their messages on nonmembers. Material organizations, which have larger, less ideological memberships, will focus their messages on members.

Most of the hypotheses of this work have been confirmed. Partisan groups have led the way in innovating campaign techniques and finding ways to go beyond FEC limits. While they have shifted their PAC contributions toward Republicans, nonpartisan, access-oriented groups have not significantly changed their activities since 1994. They have generally avoided broadcast advertising, voter mobilization, and other paths of increasing their electoral impact.

Groups use their political resources much as was predicted. Business groups, which may have few political assets besides money, funnel contributions into "front groups." Purposive groups, especially those with some appeal to the general public, use money to exploit their "issue credibility." While the AFL-CIO has formidable financial resources, its leadership has come to believe that its money is best spent in exploiting its relationship with its members. Its membership is a potent resource, but one that is shrinking (at least, relative to the population as a whole) and has limited applicability (especially geographically).

This study has produced some surprising results. Money, when not backed up by "issue credibility," may not have the all-powerful influence that some perceive. Groups' fields of expertise are often limited. Few groups see themselves as particularly adept at providing campaign services such as polling or media advice. Party committees and political consultants do these things better. The "issue credibility" that some groups possess is often narrowly focused: the National Rifle Association (NRA) is primarily able to speak to gun owners and the National Right to Life Committee (NRLC) focuses on mobilizing identified antiabortion voters.

As expected, membership incentives have a powerful influence on groups' political resources, on their internal organization, and ultimately on their political activity. But other institutional characteristics can shape the behavior of political organizations. For decades, the AFL-CIO's federated structure has influenced its political power. At times, it has been united under strong leadership, as under George Meany in the 1960s or John Sweeney in the late 1990s. But during the 1970s, it was bitterly fragmented; it achieved greater unity in the 1980s, but without much power at the center. Institutional culture can matter, too. Surely, the ease of exit is not the only reason for the great difference in the political behavior of the AFL-CIO and the AARP. The first has been highly political from its beginnings; the second only gradually entered the political arena, years after its creation. Such differences shape an organization's public image and the type of staff it is likely to attract. The decentralized, grassroots nature of the right-to-life movement gives the NRLC opportunities not available to the far more centralized National Abortion and Reproductive Rights Action League (NARAL Pro-Choice America).

Groups and the Party Networks

Generally speaking, my findings have tended to confirm the view that ties have grown stronger between *some* groups and the political parties and that these groups are part of broader party networks. But these groups have their own interests separate from the parties. Their ultimate goals—which include organizational maintenance, achievement of favorable public policy, advancement of staff's careers—are not always compatible with the party's goals. But traditional party organizations also included factions of "Stalwarts" and "Half-Breeds," "Hunkers" and "Locofocos," as well as scores of self-interested politicians. A party network will always include individuals and organizations that do not agree on everything. That does not mean that the party network does not exist. In the real world (as opposed to econometric models), actors usually have multiple motives, which can include both furthering party success and advancing career objectives, pursuing ideological causes and seeking material gain.

Evidence for increased partisanship is mixed. Most of the increase in non-PAC activity is clearly on one side or the other of the party divide. With the notable exception of the AARP, most of the organizations included in the case studies report stronger ties to one party, and that those ties are growing stronger. But many of these groups already had very close links to the parties before 1994, as the PAC data show. Perhaps a "new partisan era" has begun, one of greater polarization and ideological conflict, but it may have started in 1980 as much as in 1994.

It is highly partisan groups that have led the way in innovating campaign techniques and in stepping up groups' overall involvement. This includes the mobilization by the NRA and the National Federation of Independent Business (NFIB) in 1994 and the Sierra Club and AFL-CIO's reaction to the Republican takeover of Congress. These are groups with very close ties to one party or the other; personnel frequently flow between these groups and the parties, or between groups in the same party network. Staff at these groups see very sharp differences between the parties; there may be a few people on the other side with whom they have decent relations, but only a few.

By contrast, nonpartisan groups—access-oriented corporations, most trade associations—have not fundamentally changed their behavior in recent years. They make PAC contributions and give soft money on both sides of the aisle. They steer away from controversial issues and try to keep a low profile. They rarely help challengers. Nor do they usually go "beyond the limits" —except to give soft money in the same access-oriented fashion in which they make PAC contributions.

The findings of this study cast some doubt on the more extravagant claims made by supporters of the Bipartisan Campaign Reform Act (BCRA). If political parties can be best understood as networks of relationships, then money that is forbidden to the party committees may well shift to other entities enmeshed in the same webs. The same politicians who sought contributions for the parties' nonfederal accounts may steer money to newer, "independent" organizations. But evidence also contradicts the more simplistic "hydraulic" predictions that contributors of "soft money" would simply find other avenues for their donations. Much of the corporate money that had been solicited by the parties during the "soft money" era remained outside of politics in 2004 (Weissman and Hassan, forthcoming).

The concept of a party network has validity across time, although it probably applies better to today's politics than to that of a generation ago. There have always been interest groups that had close relationships with the political parties. But there have been changes in recent decades that have made the parties more "network-y" and simultaneously more polarized. These include:

- Legal changes in the 1970s that favored the creation of political action committees
- A long series of legal changes, administrative decisions, and judicial rulings that encouraged the rise of issue advocacy and soft money
- The rise of political consultants
- The rise of more openly partisan media and think tanks
- The creation of leadership PACs and similar operations controlled by party leaders
- Adaptation by existing groups (such as the AFL-CIO and the NRA) that have made them more purposive or more politically effective or both
- The rise of strongly purposive interest groups and their subsequent integration into party networks
- A general trend toward purposive (often highly ideological) incentives throughout our political system
- The growing partisan polarization in both voting in Congress and by the electorate

One essential difference between today's party networks and those of, say, the 1950s is that contemporary networks are more fundamentally based on purposive incentives. As the histories of the NRA and NARAL show, purposive groups are dependent on sharp policy conflict for their very survival. (They are not the only ones—where would Rush Limbaugh or Sidney Blumenthal be without enemies to demonize?) Perhaps this is the age of the institutionalized ideologue and the professional amateur. Our political system tends to overrepresent the views of intense minorities and amplify the most strident voices. Many of the groups included in this study, by definition, respond to such opinions.

Groups that are dependent on purposive incentives have to maintain a degree of ideological purity in order to hold on to old members and win new ones. They are also likely to attract staff who share those values. To the extent that they are involved in party networks, they are likely to push the parties toward ideological extremes. NARAL and the National Right to Life Committee exert great power with the Democratic and Republican parties, respectively, over abortion policy. But there is no organization of people who, for example, believe that abortion should remain legal but be more greatly restricted. While there are business groups that follow a nonideological path, they generally do not play the political role that the NFIB, the Club for Growth, and other purist groups do. The Republican Party network (e.g., the congressional leadership, the National Right to Life Committee, Rush Limbaugh) backed George W. Bush throughout the 2000 presidential primaries and excoriated John McCain for his ideological heresies. While purism is usually tempered with pragmatism, the net effect of the involvement of these groups is probably to heighten the polarization between the parties—a polarization that leaves out many Americans. The general trend by groups to focus more on encouraging turnout among targeted voters, rather than on persuading undecided voters, probably also accentuates this polarization (Boatright et al. 2003).

How Are Groups Shaping Parties?

There are two fundamentally different ways of conceptualizing the roles that political parties should play in our system. One is known as the "responsible," or "programmatic" school; it was given fullest expression in the 1950 report "Toward a More Responsible Two-Party System," issued by the APSA Committee on Political Parties. The doctrine of responsible parties argues that political parties should adopt binding, programmatic doctrines on a wide range of issues. They should have strong centralized leadership, both in government and in party organizations. Parties should base their appeals primarily on ideological differences, rather than on personality or patronage. Both Woodrow Wilson and Franklin Roosevelt seemed to have held this view of political parties (Ceaser 1979; Milkis 1999). Although most of the Founding Fathers disdained them, parties arose within a few years of the Constitution. To the extent that the Federalists and Republicans accepted political parties, it was a temporary strategem until the opposition was overcome. But to that extent, they saw parties as stemming from profound philosophical differences with little respect due to those who disagreed (Hofstadter 1969).

The other school of thought might be called the doctrine of "integrative parties." In this view, parties should encompass a variety of views. Rather than consistently stake out bold views on matters of principle, party leaders should play down controversial issues. Parties should work to bring together people of various perspectives in a common pursuit of office. Opposition should be tolerated and treated as legitimate; politicians of differing parties should have amicable relations. This view is most associated with Martin Van Buren, eighth president and principal founder of the Democratic Party. The party organization that Van Buren created in the 1820s was decentralized and nonideological, interested more in securing patronage than in seeking programmatic change (Ceaser 1979; Hofstadter 1969).

In recent years, the political parties have, in some ways, been evolving toward the responsible party model. The parties have become ideologically coherent. The party networks have become more centralized in Washington; "top-down" parties have replaced "bottom-up" ones. Party unity in Congress has increased. Party voting among the public has increased, at least among those who identify with a party. Party identification appears to be based more on perceived issue differences than on inherited loyalties than it was in the 1950s and 1960s. Ideological activists have mostly replaced patronage hacks as the lead players in party politics. The national party organizations spend more money and play increased roles in elections. Even state and local parties have revived, to a limited extent. But there are few signs of an increased role for rank-and-file voters; indeed, a party-defining document like the Contract with America was conceived by a few insiders, while most voters remained unaware (Green and Herrnson 2002; Weisberg 2002; Pomper and Weiner 2002).

In some ways, the 2004 election continued the trend toward party responsibility. The parties were relatively unified, and George W. Bush provided the GOP with the type of strong, centralized leadership that Woodrow Wilson and Franklin Roosevelt had sought. Dodd and Oppenheimer (2005) note the continued trend toward partisan consistency in presidential and congressional voting.

The Internet helped fulfill another aspect of party responsibility, allowing wider participation in party politics, as thousands of Americans contributed to campaigns and to party committees online. Howard Dean raised $13 million on the Internet; after his triumph in the Iowa caucuses, John Kerry raised $65 million. Blogs and meetups helped transform many Americans from passive observers to active participants. Many bloggers blurred the line between journalism and activism, including the liberal, Howard Dean-supporting Daily Kos and the conservatives behind Powerline, which helped bring down Dan Rather. Both parties placed a greater emphasis on "ground war" operations, with the GOP encouraging supporters to contact friends and coworkers (Green and Gerber 2004 appears to have influenced many political operatives).

Not all of the consequences of this evolution have been salutary. Fiorina (2001) muses that the American political system has become too responsive to unrepresentative ideologues, whether in government, the political parties, or interest groups. As purposive incentives have replaced material benefits as the main motivation for political actors, officeholders now have "deeper policy commitments than their counterparts of a generation ago." As the parties have polarized and the number of competitive constituencies shrunk, candidates have become less concerned with the "median voter" and more attuned to activists at the extremes. As the parties become more internally homogeneous, only the ideologically faithful are able to advance politically.

Fiorina sees interest-group involvement as adding to this trend:

> As traditional patronage-based organizations withered, a wide variety of groups stepped into the space unoccupied. Increasingly such groups generate candidates and take an important role in organizing and funding campaigns. But the reason for belonging to such groups is commitment to group goals, and that is also a prerequisite for gaining group support.... It seems likely that members increasingly motivated by policy goals would be more likely to establish records rich in policy content, to emphasize issues as part of their personal political image, and to attract the notice of groups and individuals with similar policy commitments. (Fiorina 2001)

Some observers might hail these developments; the parties finally stand for something, they would say. But Fiorina worries that Congress has become simultaneously "less insulated" and more "out of touch." Less insulated, because members are more subject to influence by activists outside the institution. Out of touch, because those activists are highly atypical of the American public. With both officeholders and activists driven by purposive incentives and holding strongly ideological views, compromise becomes almost impossible (Fiorina 2001).

Despite the polarization among elites, the American public remains essentially moderate. Politicians have instead become responsive to ideological activists; many officeholders are themselves driven more by their own strong policy preferences than by the often-fuzzy views of ordinary citizens. Strong partisans—who are most likely to vote in primaries, contribute money, and knock on doors—have increasingly diverged from the general public. While voters often make clear their disdain for ideological extremism, politicians pursue it when they can. For example, during the aftermath of the 1994 election, many Republican freshmen made clear their lack of regard for public opinion, preferring to follow their own conservative convictions. As voters see their own centrist views being ignored, they lose trust in government (Fiorina 2005; Jacobs and Shapiro 2000).

In a very different era, Wilson (1962) praised the American political system for serving as a means of "social integration rather than of political cleavage." Parties tended to stick to a "politics of interest" that played down divisive issues, except when external influences forced them temporarily into a "politics of principle." He feared the effects of converting "the two party system from an integrative to a divisive agency":

> The need to employ issues as incentives and to distinguish one's party from the opposition along policy lines will mean that political conflict will be intensified, social cleavages will be exaggerated, party leaders will tend to be men skilled in the rhetorical arts, and the party's ability to produce agreement by trading issue-free resources will be reduced.

There are worse ways of describing the political system of the early twenty-first century.[1]

It is not an insult to the interest-group activists interviewed for this study to say that they often aggravate this tendency toward ideological polarization. The "politics of principle" is their job, after all. But as they help push the party networks into greater programmatic coherence, one must ask, If parties are to be responsible, to whom should they be responsible? Ideological activists? Officeholders? "The people"? The "public interest"?

Alexis de Tocqueville has his own terminology for differentiating between "responsible" and "integrative" parties, or the "politics of principle" or the "politics of interest." He called them "great" and "small" parties. Ceaser (1979) suggests a third middle path: "Burkean" parties that are principled but moderate, energetic but civil. Perhaps such parties are more compatible with our system than purely "great" parties. (Van Buren-style "small" parties are probably gone forever. In an era of television and the Internet, who needs armies of patronage workers to reach voters?) But too often our party system produces a fun-house reflection of the American electorate, distorting the extremes and shrinking the middle. In recent years, the dependence of the parties—especially the Republicans—on unrepresentative groups of activists has helped produce some strikingly countermajoritarian outcomes: the impeachment of Bill Clinton, the 2001 Bush tax cuts, the Terri Schiavo affair.

This study also raises some questions about equality and representativeness. With the notable exception of the AFL-CIO, the groups examined here represent members who tend to be more affluent and more intense in their preferences than the average American. Our political system already privileges such citizens. These groups certainly encourage their members to participate. But most of them already are.

Methodological Appendix

The interviews for this study were conducted by the author during 2000 and 2001. The first series was conducted during May and June 2000, the second—meant to review the 2000 election—was conducted during February and March 2001. These two batches of interviews are supplemented by work done by the author and others for the Campaign Finance Institute. Two roundtables were held by CFI during the spring of 2001 that included representatives from leading interest groups. I was partially responsible for selecting participants for these events. The roundtables were followed by a series of interviews that summer; I conducted all the interviews, either on my own or in cooperation with Mark Rozell and Clyde Wilcox. I thank CFI, Rozell, and Wilcox for giving me permission to use these interviews.

All interviews were conducted in Washington, D.C. Subjects were all high-ranking officials with interest groups active in congressional elections. Interviews were requested in writing about two months in advance of the anticipated date. I usually requested interviews with both the group's political director and communications director; when one or the other was not available, I met with deputy directors or other political staff.

Interviews were all conducted at the groups' Washington offices. (The CFI roundtables took place at CFI's office in downtown Washington.) They usually lasted for between thirty and ninety minutes; one interview lasted for more than two hours. Interviews were tape-recorded; they were later transcribed by professionals.

Certain questions were asked of all subjects. These included:

Does your group engage in independent expenditures? What techniques do you use?

Does your group engage in issue advocacy within ninety days of an election? What techniques do you use?

How does your group mobilize its members to vote? Does it encourage them to engage in other political activity, such as volunteering for campaigns? What does your group do to encourage this participation?

Does your group encourage sympathetic nonmembers to vote? What techniques does it use? Whom does it target?

Does your group provide services to candidates such as polling, demographic research, or campaign training?

How do you decide to support a candidate? What factors are important? Do you consider the competitiveness of the race? Do you consider a member's support for your positions? Do you consider a candidate's political party?

How important is a candidate's political party to a decision to make an endorsement? What percentage of your endorsed candidates are Democrats? What percentage are Republicans?

How much does the $10,000 limit affect your role in elections? Does it
hamper your ability to affect the outcome of elections?

How did the Republican takeover of Congress in 1994 affect your political
involvement?

What advantages do you receive from direct communication in congressional campaigns? Does it allow you highlight particular issues? Do you
benefit from the lack of limits on spending?

Other questions were more specific to particular groups. For example, AFL-
CIO staff were asked several questions about member mobilization. Staff at

TABLE 8
Top Groups for Independent Expenditures in Congressional Races, 2004

Name	Amount ($)	% Republican	% Democratic
National Association of Realtors	2,603,143	88	12
Club for Growth	1,471,293	100	0
National Right to Life Committee	1,119,802	97	3
American Medical Association	1,057,332	97	3
National Rifle Association	685,083	97	3
American Society of Anesthesiologists	405,049	83	17
American Association of Orthopaedic Surgeons	320,440	100	0
League of Conservation Voters	227,210	67	33
EMILY's List	170,105	0	100
American Neurological Surgery PAC	129,613	100	0

Source: Center for Responsive Politics.

TABLE 9
Top Groups for Independent Expenditures in Congressional Races, 2002

Name	Amount ($)	% Republican	% Democratic
League of Conservation Voters	2,386,651	88	12
NARAL	2,370,630	0	100
American Medical Association	1,957,100	85	15
National Right to Life Committee	1,846,609	97	3
Service Employees International Union	1,811,242	100	0
National Education Association	1,558,357	0	100
National Rifle Association	1,306,882	92	8
National Association of Realtors	1,023,783	50	50
Sierra Club	265,772	17	83
Associated Builders and Contractors	171,500	100	0

Source : Center for Responsive Politics.

TABLE 10
Top Groups for Independent Expenditures in Congressional Races, 2000

Name	Amount ($)	% Republican	% Democratic
National Rifle Association	4,173,351	100	0
League of Conservation Voters	3,234,703	12	88
National Education Association	2,501,093	2	98
NARAL	2,268,779	0	100
American Medical Association	1,810,798	75	25
Handgun Control	1,243,567	0	100
National Right to Life Committee	749,781	100	0
Sierra Club	330,461	6	94
Associated Builders and Contractors	200,000	100	0
Susan B. Anthony List	171,500	100	0

Source: Center for Responsive Politics.

TABLE 11
Top Groups for Independent Expenditures in Congressional Races, 1998

Name	Amount	% Republican	% Democratic
American Medical Association	1,758,132	96	4
National Rifle Association	1,676,808	98	2
National Education Association	1,412,718	5	95
League of Conservation Voters	1,332,343	15	85
National Right to Life Committee	708,181	99	1
Campaign for Working Families	646,431	100	0
NARAL	576,743	0	100
Campaign for America	466,028	0	100
EMILY's List	112,550	0	100
Sierra Club	112,109	0	100

Source Center for Responsive Politics.

both NARAL and the National Right to Life Committee were asked questions about the impact of specific abortion-related issues, such as the abortion-inducing drug RU-486 and "partial-birth" abortion. There were also, of course, numerous follow-up questions.

Notes

1. Wilson's statement is consistent with high party voting in Congress; first, the high degree of ideological cohesion within the parties makes the use of "issue-free resources" less important; second, the House majority leadership's control of the floor (and increasing dominance of the committees) makes it easier to control voting in such a way as to reduce the need for such resources. See Sinclair 2000b. Even in this highly polarized Congress, members continue to desire such issue-free resources as highway funding; the Republican leadership has shown great skill in using such items to reward party loyalists.

Bibliography

AARP-VOTE, "Election Rules and Regulations That Impact AARP Election Activities."

Abramson, Jill. 1998. "Republican National Committee Funding $20 Million Advertising Campaign." *New York Times*, October 26.

Abramson, Paul, John H. Aldrich, and David W. Rohde. 1999. *Change and Continuity in the 1996 and 1998 Elections*. Washington, DC: CQ Press.

Aldrich, John H. 1995. *Why Parties? The Origin and Transformation of Political Parties in America*. Chicago: University of Chicago Press.

Aldrich, John H., and David W. Rohde. 2000. "The Consequences of Party Organization in the House." In *Polarized Politics: Congress and the President in a Partisan Era*, ed. Jon R. Bond and Richard Fleisher. Washington, DC: CQ Press.

Allen, Mike. 2004. "Cheney Tells NRA Kerry Will Target Guns; Speech, In Effort to Regain Momentum Lost in Dispute Over Assault Weapons." *Washington Post*, April 18.

Alpert, Bruce. 2004. "Landrieu, Opponents Divided on Abortion; They Agree on Other Issues." *New Orleans Times-Picayune*, October 13.

Anderson, Nick. 2004. "NRA Starts Ads Critical of Kerry." *Los Angeles Times*, October 5.

Annenberg Public Policy Center of the University of Pennsylvania. 2001. "Issue Advertising in the 1999–2000 Election Cycle." Washington, DC: Annenberg Public Policy Center of the University of Pennsylvania.

Apollonio, D. E., and Raymond J. La Raja. 2004. "Who Gave Soft Money? The Effect of Interest Group Resources on Political Contributions." *Journal of Politics* 66:1134–54.

Asher, Herbert B., Eric S. Heberlig, Randall B. Ripley, and Karen Snyder. 2001. *American Labor Unions in the Electoral Arena*. Lanham, MD: Rowman & Littlefield.

Association of Trial Lawyers of America. Undated pamphlet. *What Happens in Congress Matters to You and Your Clients*.

Babcock, Charles R., and Ruth Marcus. 1997. "For Their Targets, Mystery Groups' Ads Hit Like Attacks From Nowhere." *Washington Post*, March 9.

Baker, Anne Nibley and David B. Magleby. 2003. "Interest Groups in the 2000 Congressional Elections." In *The Other Campaign: Soft Money and Issue Advocacy in the 2000 Congressional Elections*, David B. Magleby, ed. Lanham, MD: Rowman & Littlefield.

Balz, Dan. 2000. "NARAL Targets Voters in 15 States." *Washington Post*, September 26.

Balz, Dan, and Ronald Brownstein. 1996. *Storming the Gates: Protest Politics and the Republican Revival*. Boston: Little, Brown.

Barnes, Fred. 2001. "Conservatives Love George W. Bush; But Will the Romance Last?" *Weekly Standard*, March 5.

Barnes, James A. 2003. "The Prince of Labor." *National Journal*, May 17.

———. 2004. "Where Democrats Might Have an Edge." *National Journal*, May 8.

Barone, Michael. 1990. *Our Country: The Shaping of America from Roosevelt to Reagan*. New York: The Free Press.

Barone, Michael, and Grant Ujifusa. 1991. *The Almanac of American Politics 1992*. Washington, DC: National Journal.

Barringer, Felicity. 2004a. "Establishment Candidates Defeat Challengers in Sierra Club Voting." *New York Times*, April 22.

———. 2004b. "From Cascades to the Everglades, A Struggle for Conservationist Votes." *New York Times*, October 23.

Bart, John, and James Meader. 2004. "The More You Spend, The Less They Listen: The South Dakota U.S. Senate Race." In *The Last Hurrah? Soft Money and Issue Advocacy in the 2002 Congressional Elections*, ed. David Magleby and J. Quin Monson. Washington, DC: Brookings Institution Press.

Bartels, Larry M. 2000. "Partisanship and Voting Behavior, 1952–1996." *American Journal of Political Science* 44:1.

Bartels, Lynn. 2004. "Clashing Over Abortion; Salazar Favors Some Choice, Coors Takes Opposing Stance." *Denver Rocky Mountain News*, October 21.

Beck, Deborah, Paul Taylor, Jeffrey B. Stanger, and Douglas G. Rivlin. 1997. *Issue Advocacy Advertising During the 1996 Campaign: A Catalog*. Philadelphia: Annenberg Public Policy Center of the University of Pennsylvania.

Bedlington, Anne, and Michael J. Malbin. 2003. "The Party as an Extended Network: Members Giving to Each Other and to Their Parties." In *Life After Reform: When the Bipartisan Campaign Reform Act Meets Politics*, ed. Michael J. Malbin. Lanham, MD: Rowman & Littlefield.

Berinsky, Adam J., and Susan S. Lederman. 2003. "The 2000 New Jersey Twelfth Congressional District Race." In *The Other Campaign: Soft Money and Issue Advocacy in the 2000 Congressional Elections*, ed. David Magleby. Lanham, MD: Rowman & Littlefield.

Berke, Richard L. 1998a. "Interest Groups Prepare to Spend on Campaign Spin." *New York Times*, January 10.

———. 1998b. "Late-Term Abortion Issue Pulls Republicans in Two Directions." *New York Times*, January 15.

Bernstein, Aaron. 2004. "Can This Man Save Labor?" *Business Week*, September 13.

Bernstein, Aaron, Paula Dwyer, and Lorraine Woellert. 2004. "Inside the Dems' Shadow Party." *Business Week*, March 22.

Bernstein, Jonathan, and Raymond J. La Raja. "Independent Expenditures and Partisanship in House Elections." Paper presented at the 1999 American Political Science Association Annual Meeting, Atlanta, GA.

Berry, Deborah Burfield. 2004. "Seniors Flex Their Muscles." *Newsday*, July 24.

Berry, Jeffrey M. 1977. *Lobbying for the People: The Political Behavior of Public Interest Groups*. Princeton, NJ: Princeton University Press.

———. 1997. *The Interest Group Society*. 3rd ed. New York: Longman.

Biersack, Robert, Paul S. Herrnson, and Clyde Wilcox, eds. 1994. *Risky Business? PAC Decisionmaking in Congressional Elections*. Armonk, NY: M. E. Sharpe.

———. 1999. *After The Revolution: PACs, Lobbies and the Republican Congress*. Boston: Allyn & Bacon.

Biersack, Robert, and Marianne H. Viray. 2005. "Interest Groups and Federal Campaign Finance: The Beginning of a New Era." In *The Interest Group Connection: Electioneering, Lobbying, and Policymaking in Washington*, ed. Paul S. Herrnson, Ronald G. Shaiko, and Clyde Wilcox. 2nd ed. Washington, DC: CQ Press.

"Biographies of the New Members of Congress and Governors." *National Journal*, November 6.

Birnbaum, Jeffrey H. 2001. "Fat and Happy in D.C." *Fortune*, May 28.

Birnbaum, Jeffrey H., and Thomas B. Edsall. 2004. "Interest Groups Seek New Faces for Top Ranks." *Washington Post*, March 29.

Boatright, Robert E., Michael J. Malbin, Mark J. Rozell, Richard M. Skinner, and Clyde Wilcox. 2003. "BCRA's Impact on Interest Groups and Advocacy Organizations." In *Life After Reform: When the Bipartisan Campaign Reform Act Meets Politics*, ed. Michael J. Malbin. Lanham, MD: Rowman & Littlefield.

Brady, Henry E., Kay Lehman Schlozman, Sidney Verba, and Laurel Elms. 2002. "Who Bowls? The (Un) Changing Stratification of Participation." In *Understanding Public Opinion*, ed. Barbara Norrander and Clyde Wilcox. 2nd ed. Washington, DC: CQ Press.

Brennan Center for Justice. 2000. "2000 Presidential Race First in Modern History Where Political Parties Spend More on TV Ads Than Candidates." News release, December 11.

———. 2001. "Tens of Millions of Sham Issue Ads Escaped Disclosure Laws in 2000." News release, March 14.

Brewer, Mark D. 2004. "Stability or Change? Party Images in America." Paper presented at the 2004 Northeastern Political Science Association, Boston.

Broder, David S. 1999a. "Stakes High in 2000; Voters Can Redirect 3 Federal Branches." *Washington Post*, June 21.

———. 1999b. "Weapons of Choice in 2000." *Washington Post*, June 23.

———. 2000. "The Battle for the Senate: Wash. Democrats Look Back in Anger; Cantwell Throws Tenure at Gorton, Who Beat Senate Power in '80 on Same Issue." *Washington Post*, October 28.

Broder, David S., and Haynes Johnson. 1997. *The System: The American Way of Politics at the Breaking Point*. Boston: Little, Brown.

Broder, John M. 2000. "Emotional Appeal Urges Blacks to Vote." *New York Times*, November 2.

Brokaw, Chet. 2004. "Religion Plays Prominent Role in South Dakota's Senate Race." Associated Press State & Local Wire, October 29.

Brown, David. 1999. "Medical Journal Editor Fired; Study on Defining Sex is 'Political,' AMA Boss Says." *Washington Post,* January 16.

Bureau of Labor Statistics. 2003. "Union Members in 2002." www.bls.gov/news.release/union2.toc.htm.

Burnham, Walter Dean. 1982. *The Current Crisis in American Politics.* New York: Oxford University Press.

Business Industry Political Action Committee. 1997. *Forward Thinking: What the Business Community Can Learn from the 1996 Elections To Preserve Its Majorities in Congress in 1998 and Beyond.* Washington, DC: BIPAC.

———. 1998. *Thinking Anew: How Business Can Win In the 1998 Elections by Being in the Right Places, on Behalf of the Right Candidates, and with the Right Techniques.* Washington, DC: BIPAC.

Campaign Corps. 2005. "Overview." www.campaigncorps.org/about.

Campaign Finance Institute. 2001. *Issue Ad Disclosure: Recommendations for a New Approach.* Washington, DC: Campaign Finance Institute. www.cfinst.org/disclosure/report1/toc.htm.

Campbell, Andrea Louise. 2003. *How Policies Make Citizens: Senior Political Activism and the American Welfare State.* Princeton, NJ: Princeton University Press.

Campbell, James E. 2003. "The Stagnation of Congressional Elections." In *Life After Reform: When the Bipartisan Campaign Reform Act Meets Politics,* ed. Michael J. Malbin. Lanham, MD: Rowman & Littlefield.

Candisky, Catherine. 2004. "Targeted Mailings Saturating Ohio Voters." *Columbus Dispatch,* October 28.

Cannon, Lou. 1998. "Democrats Boosted by Capps' Win in California." *Washington Post,* March 12.

Cantor, David. 1999. "The Sierra Club Political Committee." In *After the Revolution: PACs, Lobbies and the Republican Congress,* ed. Robert Biersack, Paul Herrnson, and Clyde Wilcox. Boston: Allyn & Bacon.

Carlton, Jim. 2000. "Sierra Club Faces a Revolt from Radicals." *Wall Street Journal,* March 15.

Carmines, Edward G., and James A. Stimson. 1989. *Issue Evolution: Race and the Transformation of American Politics.* Princeton, NJ: Princeton University Press.

Carney, Dan. 2000. "Mr. Class Action Goes to Washington." *Business Week,* September 11.

Carney, Eliza Newlin. 1997. "Stealth Bombers." *National Journal,* August 16.

———. 2000. "Big Bucks, Tiny State." *National Journal,* December 2.

———. 2004. "A Call to Arms." *National Journal,* January 17.

Carney, Eliza Newlin, Peter H. Stone, and James A. Barnes. 2003. "New Rules of the Game." *National Journal,* June 28.

Catanzaro, Michael. 2001. "What's Up, Docs?" *National Review,* May 14.

Ceaser, James W. 1979. *Presidential Selection: Theory and Development.* Princeton, NJ: Princeton University Press.

Center for Responsive Politics. www.crp.org.

Clark, Peter B., and James Q. Wilson. 1961. "Incentive Systems: A Theory of Organization." *Administrative Science Quarterly* 6:129–66.

Cleeland, Nancy. 2004. "Unions Confront Post-Election Reality." *Los Angeles Times*, November 10.

Clines, Francis X. 1996. "Abortion Rights League Plans to Challenge 15 Freshmen." *New York Times*, July 14.

Clymer, Adam. 1996. "House Approves Increase to $5.15 in Minimum Wage." *New York Times*, May 23.

Cohen, Adam. 2000. "Are Lawyers Running America?" *Time*, July 17.

Cohen, Marty, David Karol, Hans Noel, and John Zaller. 2001. *Beating Reform: The Resurgence of Parties in Presidential Nominations*. Chicago: University of Chicago Press.

———. 2003. "What Drives Presidential Nominations: Pols or Polls?" *Brookings Review* (Summer).

Cohen, Richard E. 2003. "Broken Barometer." *National Journal*, July 12.

Confessore, Nicholas. 2003. "Welcome to the Machine; How the GOP disciplined K Street and Made Bush Supreme." *Washington Monthly*, July/August.

Connelly, Joel. 2000. "Women Honor Gorton as Great Boss." *Seattle Post-Intelligencer*, October 21.

Connelly, Timothy J. 1996. "Dems' Old Coalition Came Back to Life." *Worcester (MA) Sunday Telegram*, November 17.

Connolly, Ceci. 2003. "Democratic Candidates Criticize AARP; Seniors Lobby's Backing of Medicare Drug Benefit Angers Presidential Hopefuls." *Washington Post*, November 19.

Cook, David. 2003. "The Point Man on AARP's Controversial Medicare Move." *Christian Science Monitor*, December 11.

Cook, Elizabeth, Clyde Wilcox, and Ted G. Jelen. 1993. "Generational Differences in Attitudes Toward Abortion." *American Politics Quarterly* 21:31–53.

Corrado, Anthony. 1997. "Party Soft Money." In *Campaign Finance Reform: A Sourcebook*, ed. Anthony E. Corrado, Thomas E. Mann, Daniel R. Ortiz, Trevor Potter, and Frank J. Sorauf. Washington, DC: Brookings Institution Press.

Cox, Gary W., and Mathew D. McCubbins. 1993. *Legislative Leviathan: Party Government in the House*. Berkeley: University of California Press.

Crabtree, Susan. 2001. "AMA Pains Republicans; Group's Giving Suddenly Tilts to Democrats." *Roll Call*, July 23.

Craig, Barbara Hinkson, and David M. O'Brien. 1993. *Abortion and American Politics*. Chatham, NJ: Chatham House Publishers.

Crotty, William. 1984. *American Parties in Decline*. 2nd ed. Boston: Little, Brown.

Crowley, Brian E. 2000. "McCollum, Nelson Air Their Many Differences." *Palm Beach Post*, October 24.

Dao, James. 2000. "Ringing Phones, Chiming Doorbells, Stuffed E-Mailboxes: The Great Voter Roundup." *New York Times*, November 7.

Dark, Taylor E. 1998. *The Unions and the Democrats: An Enduring Alliance*. Ithaca, NY: Cornell University Press.

———. 1999. "Organized Labor in the 1998 Elections." members.aol.com/OS-CURO/1998update.html.

Davidson, Osha Gray. 1993. *Under Fire: The NRA and the Battle for Gun Control.* New York: Henry Holt and Company.

Davis, Julie Hirschfeld. 2004. "Kerry Aims to Bag Gun Owners." *Baltimore Sun,* September 15.

Day, Christine L. 1990. *What Older Americans Think: Interest Groups and Aging Policy.* Princeton, NJ: Princeton University Press.

"Declining Professions; Just Another Way to Make a Living." 1998. *Economist,* March 14.

DiBacco, Thomas V. 1998. "The Rise and Fall of the AMA; Missteps Have Helped Erode Doctors' Power." *Washington Post,* June 2.

Dine, Philip. 2000. "Labor Leaders Launch Political Organization for Retired Workers." *St. Louis Post-Dispatch,* May 24.

Dionne, E. J. 1992. *Why Americans Hate Politics: The Death of the Democratic Process.* New York: Simon & Schuster.

Dodd, Lawrence C., and Bruce I. Oppenheimer. 2005. "Perspectives on the 2004 Congressional Elections." In *Congress Reconsidered,* ed. Lawrence C. Dodd and Bruce I. Oppenheimer. 8th ed. Washington, DC: CQ Press.

Dreazen, Yochi J. 2000. "Voter Turnout Stays Low Despite Ad Barrage, Close Race." *Wall Street Journal,* November 9.

Dressing, Dennis L. 1999. "Wisconsin's First District." In *Outside Money: Soft Money and Issue Ads in Competitive 1998 Congressional Elections,* ed. David Magleby. Lanham, MD: Rowman & Littlefield.

Drew, Elizabeth. 1997. *Whatever It Takes: The Real Struggle for Political Power in America.* New York: Viking Penguin.

———. 1998. "Get Ready for the 'Issue Ads.'" *Washington Post,* May 17.

Dreyfuss, Robert. 1998. "Which Doctors?" *New Republic,* June 22.

———. 2001. "Gephardt Gets Strategic." *American Prospect,* June 4.

Drinkard, Jim. 2002. "Special-Interest Money Floods Races." *USA Today,* November 4.

———. 2004. "'Outside' Political Groups Full of Party Insiders." *USA Today,* June 28.

Dulio, David A., and Robin Kolodny. 2001. "Political Parties and Political Consultants: Creating Alliances for Electoral Success." Paper presented at the Western Political Science Association Convention, Las Vegas.

Dulio, David A. and Robin Kolodny. 2003. "Political Party Adaptation in Congressional Campaigns: Why Political Parties Use Coordinated Expenditures to Hire Political Consultants." *Party Politics* 9: 729–46.

Dwyer, Paula, Lee Walczak, and Lorraine Woellert. 2004. "The Invisible Campaign; Bush vs. Kerry: For Both Campaigns, It's All About the Turnout." *Business Week,* September 13.

Dwyre, Diana. 1997. "Pushing the Campaign Finance Envelope: Parties and Interest Groups in the 1996 House and Senate Elections." Paper presented at the American Political Science Association Annual Meeting, Washington, DC.

Dwyre, Diana, and Robin Kolodny. 2001. "Party Financing of the 2000 Elections." Paper presented at the Western Political Science Association Convention, Las Vegas.

Edsall, Thomas B. 1996. "Issues Coalitions Take On Political Party Functions; Alliances on Left, Right Gain Power." *Washington Post*, August 8.

———. 1998. "Grass-Roots Organizing Tops TV Ads in AFL-CIO Political Agenda." *Washington Post*, May 20.

———. 2000. "Unions in High-Tech Fight for Their Future." *Washington Post*, October 31.

———. 2002a. "Drug Industry Financing Fuels Pro-GOP TV Spots; Spending Swamps Donations for Liberal Ads by 3-1 Margin." *Washington Post*, October 23.

———. 2002b. "EMILY's List Makes a Name for Itself." *Washington Post*, April 21.

———. 2003a. "Democrats Go to Bat With 2 Strikes; Bush Fundraising, Loss of Soft Money Hurt Party in '04." *Washington Post*, January 12.

———. 2003b. "Liberals Form Fund to Defeat President; Aim is to Spend $75 Million for 2004." *Washington Post*, August 8.

———. 2004. "Union Leader Urges AFL-CIO Reform; Federation Is Outdated, SEIU Head Says." *Washington Post*, June 22.

Edsall, Thomas B., and Juliet Eilperin. 2002. "PAC Attack II: Why Some Groups Are Learning to Love Campaign Finance Reform." *Washington Post*. August 18.

Edsall, Thomas B., James V. Grimaldi, and Alice R. Crites. 2004. "Redefining Democratic Fundraising: Kerry Has Amassed Record Sums From Disparate Groups Opposed to Bush." *Washington Post*, July 24.

Edsall, Thomas B., and Devon Spurgeon. 1998. "Abortion Rights Group's Ad Doesn't Mention Candidates." *Washington Post*, March 2.

Eilperin, Juliet. 2000a. "Flush with Cash, Business Groups Going on Air to Tout GOP Hopefuls, Mostly." *Washington Post*, October 15.

———. 2000b."Health Care Issue Tested in Costly Kentucky Race." *Washington Post*, May 9.

———. 2000c. "A Pivotal Election Finds NRA's Wallet Open." *Washington Post*, November 1.

———. 2000d. "Rejuvenated NRA Arms for Election-Year Showdown; Group's Influence Rises Again as Guns Become a Hot Campaign Issue." *Washington Post*, March 5.

———. 2002. "After McCain-Feingold, A Bigger Role for PACs; Groups May Be 'Soft Money' Conduits." *Washington Post*, June 1.

———. 2004a. "Immigration Issue Sparks Battle at Sierra Club; Groups Vie to Reshape Nonprofit's Board." *Washington Post*, March 22.

———. 2004b. "Reaching to the Converted; Environmental Groups Canvass Environmentalist Voters." *Washington Post*, August 21.

Eismeier, Theodore J., and Philip H. Pollock III. 1988. *Business, Money, and the Rise of Corporate PACs in American Elections*. New York: Quorum Books.

EMILY's List. 2004. "EMILY's List Election 2004 Update." Press release, November 4. www.emilyslist.org/newsroom/releases/20041104a.html.

"Enviros Thank 11 Members, Bash One." 2000. NationalJournal.com, April 27. nationaljournal.com/members/adspotlight/2000/04/0427sc1.htm.

Eversley, Melanie. 2000. "NAACP Establishes Group for Registering Black Voters." *Atlanta Journal-Constitution*, September 21.

Farhi, Paul. 2003. "Dean Works to Be Labor's Man: Candidate Trails Gephardt in Union Endorsements." *Washington Post*, November 23.

Federal Election Commission. www.fec.gov

Fields, Julie. 2000. "Small Business, Big Spender." *Business Week,* December 4.

Fineman, Howard. 1999. "Under Fire." *Newsweek,* May 31.

Fiorina, Morris. 2001. "Keystone Reconsidered." In *Congress Reconsidered,* ed. Lawrence C. Dodd and Bruce I. Oppenheimer. 7th ed. Washington, DC: CQ Press.

———. 2005. *Culture War? The Myth of a Polarized America.* Pearson Education: New York.

Fischer, Karen. 2000. "Unions, NRA Fight for Voters." *Charleston Daily Mail,* October 20.

Flanigan, William H., Joanne M. Miller, Jennifer L. Williams, and Nancy H. Zingale. 2004. "From Intensity to Tragedy: The Minnesota U.S. Senate Race." In *The Last Hurrah? Soft Money and Issue Advocacy in the 2002 Congressional Elections,* ed. David Magleby and J. Quin Monson. Washington, DC: Brookings Institution Press.

Fleisher, Richard, and Jon R. Bond. 2001. "Evidence of Increasing Polarization Among Ordinary Citizens." In *American Political Parties: Decline or Resurgence?* ed. Jeffrey E. Cohen, Richard Fleisher, and Paul Kantor. Washington, DC: CQ Press.

Fletcher, Michael A. 2000. "NAACP Makes Leap to Big-Money Political Activism." *Washington Post,* August 4.

Flynn, Kevin. 1998. "Schumer Showed Strength Across the State, Even in Some of D'Amato's Strongholds." *New York Times,* November 5.

Foskett, Ken. 1998. "Sierra Club a Tough Team on Environmental Turf; Protecting Natural Resources, Not Partisan Politics Is the Name of the Game, Leader Says." *Atlanta Journal-Constitution,* June 29.

———. 2000. "Sierra Club Earmarks $8 Million for 17 U.S. Races." *Atlanta Journal-Constitution,* April 26.

Fowler, Linda L., Constantine J. Spiliotes, and Lynn Vavreck. 2001. "Group Advocacy in the 2000 New Hampshire Primary." *PS: Political Science and Politics* 34: 272.

Francia, Peter L. 2000. *Awakening the Sleeping Giant: The Renaissance of Organized Labor in American Politics.* PhD diss., University of Maryland, College Park.

———. 2005. "Protecting America's Workers in Hostile Territory: Unions and the Republican Congress." In *The Interest Group Connection: Electioneering, Lobbying, and Policymaking in Washington,* ed. Paul S. Herrnson, Ronald G. Shaiko, and Clyde Wilcox. Washington, DC: CQ Press.

Francia, Peter L., John C. Green, Paul S. Herrnson, Lynda W. Powell, and Clyde Wilcox. 2003. *The Financiers of Congressional Elections: Investors, Ideologues, and Intimates.* New York: Columbia University Press.

Franck, Matthew. 2004. "What Does GOP Win Mean For Missouri?" *St. Louis Post-Dispatch,* November 7.

Freeman, Gregory. 2000. "Campaign to Get Out the Vote Among Black Voters is Likely to Help Gore More Than Bush," *St. Louis Post-Dispatch,* October 22.

Galvin, Kevin. 2000. "Sierra Club TV Ad Targets Gorton." *Seattle Times,* April 26.

Garrow, David J. 1994. *Liberty and Sexuality: The Right to Privacy and the Making of Roe v. Wade.* New York: Macmillan.

Gerber, Alan, and Donald P. Green. 2000. "The Effects of Canvassing, Telephone Calls, and Direct Mail on Voter Turnout: A Field Experiment." *American Political Science Review* 94:653–63.

Gerber, Robin. 1999. "Building to Win, Building to Last: AFL-CIO COPE Takes On The Republican Congress." In *After The Revolution: PACs, Lobbies and the Republican Congress*, ed. Robert Biersack, Paul S. Herrnson, and Clyde Wilcox. Boston: Allyn & Bacon.

Germond, Jack W., and Jules Witcover. 2000. "Who'd Ya Rather Have a Beer With?" *National Journal*, October 28.

Gerth, Joseph. 2000. "Doctors' PAC Shuns GOP Congressman." *Louisville (KY) Courier-Journal*, April 22.

Gigot, Paul. 2001. "Growth Club: How to Enforce a Tax Cut." *Wall Street Journal*, February 9.

Godwin, R. Kenneth, and Barry J. Selden. 2002. In *Interest Group Politics*, ed. Allan J. Cigler and Burdett A. Loomis. 6th ed. Washington, DC: CQ Press.

Goldstein, Amy. 1998. "Rebel Candidacy Roils Ailing AMA; D.C. Doctors Seeking Presidency of Divided Medical Lobby." *Washington Post*, June 15.

Goodliffe, Jay. 1999. "Utah's Second District." In *Outside Money: Soft Money and Issue Ads in Competitive 1998 Congressional Elections*, ed. David Magleby. Lanham, MD: Rowman & Littlefield.

Green, Donald P., and Alan S. Gerber. 2004. *Get Out the Vote! How to Increase Voter Turnout*. Washington, DC: Brookings Institution Press.

Green, John C., and Paul S. Herrnson. 2002. "Party Development in the Twentieth Century: Laying the Foundations for Responsible Party Government?" In *Responsible Partisanship? The Evolution of American Political Parties Since 1950*, ed. John C. Green and Paul S. Herrnson. Lawrence: University Press of Kansas.

Greenhouse, Steven. 1999. "Republicans Credit Labor for Success by Democrats." *New York Times*, November 6.

——. 2001. "A.F.L.-C.I.O. Forms Retiree Advocacy Group." *New York Times*, May 24.

——. 2003a. "DeLay Denies Role in Letter Riling Union." *New York Times*, February 8.

——. 2003b. "Labor Leader Backs Away From Bush." *New York Times*, March 16.

——. 2003c. "Sweeney to Seek New 4-Year Term as Head of AFL-CIO." *New York Times*, September 18.

——. 2004a. "As Labor Leadership Gathers, Head of Largest Union Issues Call for Major Changes." *New York Times*, November 10.

——. 2004b. "Labor Is Feeling Embattled as Union Leaders Convene." *New York Times*, March 9.

Gross, Donald A., and Penny M. Miller. 1999a. "Kentucky's Sixth District." In *Outside Money: Soft Money and Issue Ads in Competitive 1998 Congressional Elections*, ed. David Magleby. Lanham, MD: Rowman & Littlefield.

——. 1999b. "Profile of Kentucky Senate." In *Outside Money: Soft Money and Issue Ads in Competitive 1998 Congressional Elections*, ed. David Magleby. Lanham, MD: Rowman & Littlefield.

Gugliotta, Guy. 2001. "AMA Chooses Head of Drug Association as Chief Executive; Consumer Groups Note Policy Conflicts." *Washington Post*, November 20.

Gugliotta, Guy, and Ira Chinoy. 1997. "Outsiders Made Erie Ballot a National Battle." *Washington Post*, February 10.

Gunn, Roland. 1994. "A New Political Pragmatism? The National Right to Life PAC." In *Risky Business? PAC Decisionmaking in Congressional Elections*, ed. Robert Biersack, Paul Herrnson, and Clyde Wilcox. Armonk, NY: M. E. Sharpe.

Gusmano, Michael. 1999. "The Doctors' Lobby." In *After the Revolution: PACs, Lobbies and the Republican Congress*, ed. Robert Biersack, Paul Herrnson, and Clyde Wilcox. Boston: Allyn & Bacon.

Guth, James L., Lyman A. Kellstedt, John C. Green, and Corwin E. Smidt. "A Distant Thunder? Religious Mobilization in the 2000 Elections." 2002. In *Interest Group Politics*, ed. Allan J. Cigler and Burdett A. Loomis. 6th ed. Washington, DC: CQ Press.

Hadfield, Joe. 2004. "Shifting Gears; Where Will America Votes Go After the Vote?" *Campaigns and Elections*, December.

Halbfinger, David M. 2004. "Democrats Give Republicans a Fight for the Elderly." *New York Times*, August 11.

Haley, Jean. 1994. "AARP Learned Some Key Lessons Since Health-Care Debate." *Kansas City Star*, October 26.

Hallow, Ralph Z. 1998. "Party Pulling Out All Stops to Back Bordonaro in Special House Race." *Washington Times*. March 8.

Hamburger, Tom. 2000. "Battling to Win; in Kentucky, Business Makes Bold Bid to Play a Grass-Roots Game." *Wall Street Journal*, November 2.

———. 2001. "Business Groups Move to Increase Political Clout." *Wall Street Journal*, January 24.

———. 2004. "Workplace New Terrain of Politics." *Los Angeles Times*, October 29.

Handler, Edward, and John R. Mulkern. 1992. *Business in Politics: Strategies of Corporate Action Committees*. Lexington, MA: Lexington Books.

Hansen, John Mark. 1985. "The Political Economy of Group Membership." *American Political Science Review* 79:79–96.

"Happenings Monday in the 2000 Campaign." 2000. Associated Press State & Local Wire, October 2.

Harris, John F., and Jim VandeHei. 2004. "AFL-CIO Backing Gives Kerry a Boost; Meanwhile, Edwards Weighs In on Trade, Jobs." *Washington Post*, February 20.

Harwood, John. 1998. "'Partial-Birth' Abortion Ban May Be a Bit Closer." *Wall Street Journal*, November 27.

Herrnson, Paul S. 1998. *Congressional Elections: Campaigning at Home and in Washington*. Washington, DC: CQ Press.

———. 2005. "Interest Groups and Campaigns: The Electoral Connection." In *The Interest Group Connection: Electioneering, Lobbying, and Policymaking in Washington*, ed. Paul S. Herrnson, Ronald G. Shaiko, and Clyde Wilcox. 2nd ed. Washington, DC: CQ Press.

Hetherington, Marc J. 2001. "Resurgent Mass Partisanship: The Role of Elite Polarization." *American Political Science Review* 95:619–31.

Hirschman, Albert O. 1971. *Exit, Voice and Loyalty: Responses to Decline in Firms, Organizations and States*. Cambridge, MA: Harvard University Press.

Hitt, Greg, and Helene Cooper. 2000. "Big Sky's the Limit: For Sale House Seat, Montana is Swamped with Special Interests." *Wall Street Journal*. November 7.

Hofstadter, Richard. 1969. *The Idea of a Party System: The Rise of Legitimate Opposition in the United States, 1780–1840*. Berkeley: University of California Press.

Holmes. Steven A. 2001. "The World According to AARP: Repositioning for the Boomers." *New York Times*, March 21.

Holsworth, Robert, Stephen K. Medvic, Harry L. Wilson, Robert Dudley, and Scott Keeter. 2003. "The 2000 Virginia Senate Race." In *The Other Campaign: Soft Money and Issue Advocacy in the 2000 Congressional Elections*, ed. David B. Magleby. Lanham, MD: Rowman & Littlefield.

"Increased Gun Control Not Necessarily a Cure-All." 1999. *The Public Perspective* (June/July).

"Insider Commentary: NARAL's Michelman on the Election." 1996. *Abortion Report.* October 31.

Jacobs, Lawrence R., and Robert Y. Shapiro. 2000. *Politicians Don't Pander: Political Manipulation and the Loss of Democratic Responsiveness*. Chicago: University of Chicago Press.

Jacobson, Gary C. 1997. *The Politics of Congressional Elections*. 4th ed. New York: HarperCollins.

———. 1999. "The Effect of the AFL-CIO's Voter Educational Campaign on the 1996 Hourse Elections." *Journal of Politics.* 61:185–94.

———. 2000. "Party Polarization in National Politics: The Electoral Connection." In *Polarized Politics: Congress and the President in a Partisan Era*, ed. Jon R. Bond and Richard Fleisher. Washington, DC: CQ Press.

———. 2003. "Terror, Terrain, and Turnout: Explaining the 2002 Midterm Elections." *Political Science Quarterly* 118:1–22.

Jacobson, Gary C., and Samuel Kernell. 1983. *Strategy and Choice in Congressional Elections*. New Haven, CT: Yale University Press.

Jacobson, Louis. 2000. "Business Mobilizes for a Ground War." *National Journal*, September 23.

Janofsky, Michael. 2003. "Foes of Bush Form PAC in Bid to Defeat Him." *New York Times*, August 8.

Johnson, Dennis. 2001. *No Place for Amateurs: How Political Consultants Are Reshaping American Democracy*. New York: Routledge.

Judis, John B. 2002. "What the Teamsters Want From George W." *The New Republic*, April 1.

Justice, Glen. 2004. "In Final Days, Attacks Are in the Mail and Below the Radar." *New York Times*, October 31.

Kasindorf, Martin. 1998. "Calif. Winner Sees Victory Over Outsiders; Congress-woman-Elect Says Voters Rejected Interest Groups." *USA Today*, March 12.

Kay, Jane. 2004. "Environment Clearly Divides Bush and Kerry; Senator's Record Sits Well with Conservation Groups." *San Francisco Chronicle*, October 7.

Keller, Amy. 2001. "Billion-Dollar Mark Broken; Fundraising Hit New Peak in Last Cycle." *Roll Call*, May 17.

Kelly, Jack. 2004. "NRA Campaigns Against Kerry." *Pittsburgh Post-Gazette*, October 14.

Kersh, Rogan. 2002. "Corporate Lobbyists as Political Actors." In *Interest Group Politics*, 6th edition. Edited by Allan Cigler and Burdett Loomis. Washington, DC: *CQ Press.*

Kiely, Kathy. 2002. "Strategy that Spelled Success for GOP: Get Ours to the Polls." *USA Today*, November 7.

King, David C., and Jack L. Walker. 1992. "The Provision of Benefits by Interest Groups in the United States." *Journal of Politics* 54:394–426.

Kinnard, Meg. 2004. "Abortion, Cuban-American Interests Top New Issue Ads." NationalJournal.com, October 1.

Kirchhoff, Sue. 2001. "United in Retirement; AFL-CIO Puts Clout behind Alliance for Retired Workers." *Boston Globe*, June 22.

Kirchhoff, Sue, and Anne E. Kornblut. 2002. "Republicans Strive to Top Democrats in Getting Voters to Polls." *Boston Globe*, November 2.

Kolodny, Robin. 1998. *Pursuing Majorities: Congressional Campaign Committees in American Politics*. Norman, OK: University of Oklahoma Press.

Kolodny, Robin, and David Dulio. 2001. "Where the Money Goes: Party Spending in Congressional Elections." Paper presented at the Annual Meeting of the Midwestern Political Science Association, Chicago.

Kolodny, Robin, Sandra Suarez, and Michael Rodrigues. 1999. "Pennsylvania's Thirteenth District." In *Outside Money: Soft Money and Issue Ads in Competitive 1998 Congressional Elections*, ed. David Magleby. Lanham, MD: Rowman & Littlefield.

Kondracke, Morton. 2001. "AARP's Agenda At Odds with Bush Priorities." *Roll Call*, February 19.

Kriz, Margaret. 2000. "The Green Team Backing Al Gore." *National Journal*, September 2.

Kropf, Martha E., Anthony Simons, E. Terrence Jones, Dale Neuman, Allison Hayes, and Maureen Gilbride Mears. 2001. "The 2000 Missouri Senate Race." In *Election Advocacy: Soft Money and Issue Advocacy in the 2000 Congressional Elections*, ed. David B. Magleby. Provo, UT: Center for the Study of Elections and Democracy, Brigham Young University.

Kropf, Martha E., E. Terrence Jones, Matt McLaughlin, and Dale Neuman. 2004. "Battle for the Bases: The Missouri U.S. Senate Race." In *The Last Hurrah? Soft Money and Issue Advocacy in the 2002 Congressional Elections*, ed. David Magleby and J. Quin Monson. Washington, DC: Brookings Institution Press.

Kumar, Anita. 2004. "Castor's Ties to Group Draw Fire." *St. Petersburg Times*, July 12.

Kumar, Anita, and Steve Bousquet. 2004. "Martinez, Castor Foes Claim Campaign Fouls." *St. Petersburg Times*, August 3.

Lawrence, David G. 2001. "On the Resurgence of Party Identification in the 1990s." In *American Political Parties: Decline or Resurgence?* ed. Jeffrey E. Cohen, Richard Fleisher, and Paul Kantor. Washington, DC: CQ Press.

Lawrence, Jill. 2000. "Aggressive NAACP Urged African-Americans to Polls." *USA Today*, December 8.

Layman, Geoffrey C. 2002. "Party Polarization and 'Conflict Extension' in the American Electorate." *American Journal of Political Science* 46:786–802.

Leavitt, Paul. 2000. "GOP Moderates Question Party's Campaign Spending." *USA Today*, July 6.

Lee, Frances E., and Bruce I. Oppenheimer. 1999. *Sizing Up the Senate: The Unequal Consequences of Equal Representation*. Chicago: University of Chicago Press.

Lefkowitz, Joel. "Explaining the 1998 Congressional Elections: Re-election Strategies, Challenger Campaigns and Mobilization Against Incumbents." Paper presented at the 1999 American Political Science Association Annual Meeting, Atlanta.

Levy, Clifford J. 2000. "Campaign's Endgame: Getting Your Voters to Vote." *New York Times*, November 4.

Lewin, David. 1986. "Public Employee Unionization in the 1980s: An Analysis of Transformation." In *Unions in Transition; Entering the Second Century*, ed. Seymour Martin Lipset. San Francisco: ICS Press.

Light, Paul. 1985. *Artful Work: The Politics of Social Security Reform*. New York: Random House.

Lightman, David. 2004. "The Quiet Issue: Abortion; Debate Is Alive in Campaign but under the Surface." *Hartford Courant*, October 12.

Linzer, Drew A., and David Menefee-Libey. 2003. "Opening the Floodgates: Campaigning Without Scarcity in the 2000 California 27th Congressional District Race." In *The Other Campaign: Soft Money and Issue Advocacy in the 2000 Congressional Elections*, ed. David Magleby. Lanham, MD: Rowman & Littlefield.

Lodato, Raymond M. 2004. "Where the Grass Was Always Greener: The Changing Nature of the Senate Environment and Public Works Committee, 1990–2000." Paper presented at the 2004 annual meeting of the Midwest Political Science Association, Chicago.

Loomis, Burdett. 2003. "Doing Well, Doing Good and (Shhh!) Having Fun: A Supply-Side Approach to Lobbying." Paper presented at the 2003 annual meeting of the American Political Science Association, Philadelphia.

Loomis, Burdett, and Micheal Struemph. 2003. "Organized Interests, Lobbying, and the Industry of Politics." Paper presented at the 2003 annual meeting of the Midwest Political Science Association, Chicago.

Luker, Kristin. 1984. *Abortion and the Politics of Motherhood*. Berkeley: University of California Press.

MacManus, Susan A. 1996. *Young vs. Old; Generational Combat in the 21st Century*. Boulder, CO: Westview Press.

MacPherson, Karen. 2000. "NRA's Election Spending Has Mixed Results." *Pittsburgh Post-Gazette*, November 10.

Magleby, David. 1999. *Outside Money: Soft Money and Issue Ads in Competitive 1998 Congressional Elections*. Lanham, MD: Rowman& Littlefield.

———. 2000. "Issue Advocacy in the 2000 Presidential Primaries." www.byu.edu/outsidemoney/2000primary/overview.htm.

———. 2001a. *Dictum Without Data: The Myth of Issue Advocacy and Party Building*. Provo, UT: Center for the Study of Elections and Democracy, Brigham Young University.

———. 2001b. "Election Advocacy: Soft Money and Issue Advocacy in the 2000 Elections," In *Election Advocacy: Soft Money and Issue Advocacy in the 2000 Congressional Elections*, ed. David B. Magleby. Provo, UT: Center for the Study of Elections and Democracy, Brigham Young University.

———. 2004. "The Importance of Outside Money in the 2002 Congressional Elections." In *The Last Hurrah? Soft Money and Issue Advocacy in the 2002 Congressional Elections*, ed. David Magleby and J. Quin Monson. Washington, DC: Brookings Institution Press.

Magleby, David, and Jason Richard Beal. "Independent Expenditures and Internal Communications in the 2000 Congressional Elections." 2003. In *The Other Campaign: Soft Money and Issue Advocacy in the 2000 Congressional Elections*, ed. David Magleby. Lanham, MD: Rowman & Littlefield.

Magleby, David, and J. Quin Monson. 2004. In *The Last Hurrah? Soft Money and Issue Advocacy in the 2002 Congressional Elections*, ed. David Magleby and J. Quin Monson. Washington, DC: Brookings Institution Press.

Magleby, David, and Jonathan W. Tanner. 2004. "Interest Group Electioneering in the 2002 Congressional Elections." In *The Last Hurrah? Soft Money and Issue Advocacy in the 2002 Congressional Elections*, ed. David Magleby and J. Quin Monson. Washington, DC: Brookings Institution Press.

Mannies, Jo. 2000. "Debate over Social Issues Heats Up as Election Nears." *St. Louis Post-Dispatch*, October 15.

———. 2003. "Abortion Could Play Crucial Role in 3rd District Race." *St. Louis Post-Dispatch*, June 22.

———. 2004a. "As Gephardt Exists, Question Is: What Are District Voters' Values?" *St. Louis Post-Dispatch*, June 28.

———. 2004b. "Labor Unions Here Remain a Force Come Election Time." *St. Louis Post-Dispatch*, September 20.

———. 2004c. "Miscounts Delay City Vote Tallies." *St. Louis Post-Dispatch*, August 5.

March, William, and Michael Fechter. 2000. "Ads, Tactics Growing More Shrill as Election Day Showdown Nears." *Tampa Tribune*, November 3.

Marcus, Ruth. 1998a. "Issue Groups Hold Their Fire; Spending on Advocacy Ads Falls but Candidates Still Feel Heat." *Washington Post*, October 23.

———. 1998b. "When the Opposition Isn't on the Ballot; Candidates Expect Another Fall of 'Issue Advocacy' Spots; Outside Groups Anxious, Too." *Washington Post*, June 30.

Marinucci, Carla. 2004. "Huge Abortion Rights Rally; Hundreds of Thousands in D.C. Pledge to Take Fight to Polls." *San Francisco Chronicle*, April 24.

Mayhew, David. 1974. *Congress: The Electoral Connection*. New Haven, CT: Yale University Press.

McCarthy, Robert J. 1998. "D'Amato Hoping Pataki's Numbers Rub Off." *Buffalo News*, October 28.

McGinley, Laurie. 1999. "In Other Wards: Republicans Don't Feel Too Good as Doctors Cut Across Party Lines." *Wall Street Journal*, September 28.

Medvic, Stephen K., and Matthew M. Schorson. 2004. "When Incumbents Clash, Fundamentals Matter; Pennsylvania Seventeen." In *The Last Hurrah? Soft Money and Issue Advocacy in the 2002 Congressional Elections*, ed. David B. Magleby and J. Quin Monson. Washington, DC: Brookings Institution Press.

Milkis, Sidney. 1999. *Political Parties and Constitutional Government: Remaking American Democracy*. Baltimore: Johns Hopkins University Press.

Miller, Alan C., and T. Christian Miller. 2000. "Election Was Decisive in Arena of Spending: Ever-Higher Sums." *Los Angeles Times*, December 8.

Miller, Penny M., and Donald A. Gross. 2001. "The 2000 Kentucky Sixth Congressional District Race." *PS*, June.

Mintz, John. 2000. "The Interest Groups; Liberals Mobilize Against Bush, GOP." *Washington Post*, November 3.

Moe, Terry M. 1980. *The Organization of Interests: Incentives and the Internal Dynamics of Political Interest Groups*. Chicago: University of Chicago Press.

Monroe, J. P. 2001. *The Political Party Matrix: The Persistence of Organization*. Ithaca: State University of New York Press.

Monson, J. Quin. 2004. "Get On TeleVision vs. Get On The Van." In *The Last Hurrah? Soft Money and Issue Advocacy in the 2002 Congressional Elections*, ed. David B. Magleby and J. Quin Monson. Washington, DC: Brookings Institution Press.

Monson, J. Quin, and Jonathan W. Tanner. 2004. "Interest Group Electioneering in the 2002 Congressional Elections." In *The Last Hurrah? Soft Money and Issue Advocacy in the 2002 Congressional Elections*, David B. Magleby and J. Quin Monson, eds. Washington, DC: Brookings Instituion Press.

Moore, Bill, and Danielle Vinson. 2000. "The South Carolina Republican Primary." www.byu.edu/outsidemoney/2000primary/southcarolina.htm.

Morgan, Dan. 2000. "From Courtroom to Campaign Trail." *Washington Post*, June 25.

Mundo, Philip A. 1992. *Interest Groups: Cases and Characteristics*. Chicago: Nelson-Hall Publishers.

Munro, Neil. 2004. "Promise Keeper." *National Journal*, August 21.

Murakami, Kery. 1996. "Women, Seniors Key in Tate's Defeat." *Seattle Times*, November 6.

Murray, Mark. 2003. "On The Ropes." *National Journal*, March 8.

Mutch, Robert E. 1994. "AT&T PAC: A Pragmatic Giant." In *Risky Business? PAC Decisionmaking in Congressional Elections*, ed. Robert Biersack, Paul S. Herrnson, and Clyde Wilcox. Armonk, NY: M. E. Sharpe.

———. 1999. "AT&T PAC: The Perils of Pragmatism." In *After the Revolution: PACs, Lobbies, and the Republican Congress*, ed. Robert Biersack, Paul S. Herrnson, and Clyde Wilcox. Armonk, NY: M. E. Sharpe.

Nangle, Richard. 1996. "McGovern 'Choice' Stance Cited in Win." *Worcester (MA) Sunday Telegram*, November 17.

Nasser, Haya El. 1996. "As Special Interests Take Stock, Labor Finds Its Blitz Was a Bust." *USA Today*, November 7.

NationalJournal.com. 2001. "Environmentalist Thank 11 Members, Bush One." April 27.

Neal, Terry M. 1997. "N.Y. House Seats Stay with G.O.P.; Pitched Battle for Off-Year Vacancy Featured Big Spending by Party." *Washington Post*, November 5.

Nelson, Candice J. 1994. "The Business-Industry PAC: Trying to Lead in an Uncertain Climate." In *Risky Business? PAC Decisionmaking in Congressional Elections*, ed. Robert Biersack, Paul S. Herrnson, and Clyde Wilcox. Armonk, NY: M. E. Sharpe.

Nelson, Candice J., and Robert Biersack. 1999. "The Business-Industry PAC: Working to Keep a Pro-Business Congress." In *After the Revolution: PACs, Lobbies and the*

Republican Congress, ed. Robert Biersack, Paul Herrnson, and Clyde Wilcox. Boston: Allyn & Bacon.

Nelson, Randolph. 2000. "Candidates for U.S. Senate Draw Contrasts." *Jacksonville Florida Times-Union*, October 9.

Nie, Norman, and Sidney Verba. 1972. *Participation in America: Political Democracy and Social Equality*. New York: Harper and Row.

Novak, Robert D. 2004. "In the End, Democrats Wrong about Those 'Loony Rightists.'" *Chicago Sun-Times*, November 11.

O'Connor, Karen. 1996. *No Neutral Ground? Abortion Politics in an Age of Absolutes*. Boulder, CO: Westview Press.

O'Donnell. Norah M. 1998. "Abortion Debate Moves into the Campaign Arena." *Roll Call*, October 8.

Olson, Mancur. 1965. *The Logic of Collective Action*. Cambridge, MA: Harvard University Press.

"One Billion Dollars Spent on Political Television Advertising in 2002 Midterm Election, Says New Report." 2002. Press release, Wisconsin Advertising Project. December 5.

Oppenheimer, Bruce I. 2005. "Deep Red and Blue Congressional Districts; The Causes and Consequences of Declining Party Competitiveness." In *Congress Reconsidered*, ed. Lawrence C. Dodd and Bruce I. Oppenheimer. 8th ed. Washington, DC: CQ Press.

Page, Susan. 2001. "Norquist's Power High, Profile Low; Tax Fighter May Be the Most Influential Washingtonian Below the Radar." *USA Today*, June 1.

"Partial Birth Abortion Debate Has Limited Election Impact." 1996. *Congress Daily*, November 12.

Patterson, Kelly D. 1999. "Political Firepower: The National Rifle Association." In *After the Revolution: PACs, Lobbies and the Republican Congress*, ed. Robert Biersack, Paul Herrnson, and Clyde Wilcox. Boston: Allyn & Bacon.

Patterson, Kelly D., and Matthew M. Singer. 2002. "The National Rifle Association in the Face of the Clinton Challenge." In *Interest Group Politics*, ed. Allan J. Cigler and Burdett A. Loomis. 6th ed. Washington, DC: CQ Press.

Persico, Joseph E. 1982. *The Imperial Rockefeller*. New York: Simon & Schuster.

Peterson, Steven A., and Albert Somit. 1994. *The Political Behavior of Older Americans*. New York: Garland Publishing.

Phelps, Timothy M. 2004. "Thousands March For Rights; At Least 500,000 Attend Election-Year Rally for Abortion Rights Targeting Bush and the Makeup of the Supreme Court." *Newsday*, April 26.

Pomper, Gerald M., and Marc D. Weiner. 2002. "Toward a More Responsible Two-Party Voter: The Evolving Bases of Partisanship." In *Responsible Partisanship? The Evolution of American Political Parties Since 1950*, ed. John C. Green and Paul S. Herrnson. Lawrence: University Press of Kansas.

Porter, Rick. 1999. "The Magic Campaign Combination in the Age of Access." *Campaigns and Elections*, October/November.

Potter, Trevor E. 1997. "Issue Advocacy and Express Advocacy." In. *Campaign Finance Reform: A Sourcebook*, ed. Anthony E. Corrado, Thomas E. Mann, Daniel R. Ortiz, Trevor Potter, and Frank J. Sorauf. Washington, DC: Brookings Institution Press.

Pratt, Henry J. 1983. "National Interest Groups among the Elderly: Consolidation and Constraint." In *Aging and Public Policy: The Politics of Growing Old in America*, ed. William P. Browne and Laura Katz Olson. Westport, CT: Greenwood Press.

———. 1993. *Gray Agendas: Interest Groups and Public Pensions in Canada, Britain and the United States.* Ann Arbor: University of Michigan Press.

Purdum, Todd S. 1998. "Interest Groups Run Own Race in California." *New York Times*, March 7.

Ratnesar, Romesh. 1998. "The New Money Game; Issue Ads are the Parties' Latest Ploy For Skirting Campaign-Finance Laws." *Time*, November 2.

Rees, Matthew. 2000. "'Independent' Expenditures?" *Weekly Standard*, January 13.

Riskind, Jonathan. 2004. "AARP Striving to Regain Members Opposed to Medicare Law." *Columbus Dispatch*, March 14.

Rohde, David W. 1991. *Parties and Leaders in the Postreform House.* Chicago: University of Chicago Press.

Romano, Michael. 2001. "Failed Mission; AMA Loses Members, Revenue Despite Ambitious Recruiting Drive." *Modern Healthcare*, March 5.

Rosenberg, Debra. 2003. "In Roe's Shadow." *Newsweek*, January 27.

Rosenblatt, Robert A. 2000. "AARP Members See Investment as Option." *Los Angeles Times*, May 21.

Rosenstone, Steven J., and John Mark Hansen. 1993. *Mobilization, Participation and Democracy in America.* New York: Macmillan.

Rosenstone, Steven J., and Raymond Wolfinger. 1980. *Who Votes?* New Haven, CT: Yale University Press.

Rosin, Hanna. 2004. "The Motor in Kerry's Bandwagon; With His Campaign Lagging, the Senator Turned to Mary Beth Cahill to Rev it Up." *Washington Post*, March 17.

Rothenberg, Lawrence S. 1988. "Organizational Maintenance and the Retention Decision in Groups." *American Political Science Review* 82:1129–52.

Rozell, Mark J. 2000. "Helping Women Run and Win: Feminist Groups, Candidate Recruitment and Training." *Women and Politics.* 21:101–16.

Rozell, Mark J., and Clyde Wilcox. 1999. *Interest Groups in American Campaigns: The New Face of Electioneering.* Washington, DC: CQ Press.

Sabato, Larry J. 1981. *The Rise of Political Consultants: New Ways of Winning Elections.* New York: Basic Books.

———. 1984. *PAC Power: Inside the World of Campaign Finance.* New York: Norton.

Sabato, Larry J., and Glenn R. Simpson. 1996. *Dirty Little Secrets: The Persistence of Corruption in American Politics.* New York: Times Books.

Salisbury, Robert. 1969. "An Exchange Theory of Interest Groups." *Midwest Journal of Political Science.* 13:1–32.

Samuels, Julie. 2000. "For the Airwaves, for the Environment." NationalJournal.com, September 5. nationaljournal.com/members/adspotlight/2000/09/0905sc1.htm.

Sandler, Larry. 2004. "National Woman's Group Boosts Moore in House Primary Race." *Milwaukee Journal-Sentinel*, June 17.

Sangillo, Gregg. 2003. "Going Global." *National Journal*, January 11.

Sayre, Wallace S., and Herbert Kaufman. 1960. *Governing New York City: Politics in the Metropolis.* New York: W. W. Norton & Company.

Scarrow, Susan E. 1996. *Parties and Their Members: Organizing for Victory in Britain and Germany.* New York: Oxford University Press.

Schattschneider, E. E. 1942. *Party Government.* New York: Holt, Rinehart and Winston.

———. 1948. *The Struggle for Party Government.* College Park: University of Maryland Press.

———. 1960. *The Semisovereign People: A Realist's View of Democracy in America.* New York: Holt, Rinehart and Winston.

Schier, Steven E. 2000. *By Invitation Only: The Rise of Exclusive Politics in the United States.* Pittsburgh: University of Pittsburgh Press.

Schlesinger, Joseph A. 1985. "The New American Political Party." *American Political Science Review* 79:1152–69.

Schlozman, Kay Lehman, and John T. Tierney. 1986. *Organized Interests and American Democracy.* New York: Harper & Row.

Schwartz, Mildred A. 1990. *The Party Network: The Robust Organization of Illinois Republicans.* Madison: University of Wisconsin Press.

Semiatin, Richard J., and Mark J. Rozell. 2005. "Interest Groups in Congressional Elections." In *The Interest Group Connection: Electioneering, Lobbying, and Policymaking in Washington,* ed. Paul S. Herrnson, Ronald G. Shaiko, and Clyde Wilcox. Washington, DC: CQ Press.

Serafini, Marilyn Werber. 2000a. "Congressional Drug Runs." *National Journal,* March 4.

———. 2000b. "K Street for May 13, 2000." *National Journal,* May 13.

———. 2002. "AARP's New Direction." *National Journal,* January 5.

———. 2003. "No Cure-All; Key Provisions of the Medicare Bill." *National Journal,* November 22.

———. 2004a. "A Prescription for Defeat." *National Journal,* August 30.

———. 2004b. "Still Counting Votes on Malpractice Caps." *National Journal,* November 13.

Shaiko, Ronald A., and Marc Wallace. 1999. "From Wall Street to Main Street: The National Federation of Independent Business and the New Republican Majority." In *After the Revolution: PACs, Lobbies and the Republican Congress,* ed. Robert Biersack, Paul Herrnson, and Clyde Wilcox. Boston: Allyn & Bacon.

Shefter, Martin. 1992. *Political Crisis—Fiscal Crisis: The Collapse and Renewal of New York City.* New York: Columbia University Press.

Shoch, James. 2001. *Trading Blows: Party Competition and U.S. Trade Policy in a Globalizing Era.* Chapel Hill: University of North Carolina Press.

Shogren, Elizabeth. 1994. "Members Lash Out at AARP's Support for Health Plans." *Los Angeles Times,* August 12.

"Sierra Club Launches Unearthly Campaign." 2000. NationalJournal.com, April 26. nationaljournal.com/members/adspotlight/2000/04/0426sc1.htm.

Sinclair, Barbara. 2000a. "Hostile Partners: The President, Congress, and Lawmaking in the Partisan 1990s." In *Polarized Politics: Congress and the President in a Partisan Era,* ed. Jon R. Bond and Richard Fleisher. Washington, DC: CQ Press.

———. 2000b. *Unorthodox Lawmaking: New Legislative Processes in the U.S. Congress.* 2nd ed. Washington, DC: CQ Press.

Skinner, Richard M. 2005. "Do 527's Add Up to a Party? Thinking About the 'Shadows' of Politics." *Forum* 3:3. www.bepress.com/forum/vol3/iss3/art5.

———. 2007. "The Partisan Presidency." In *The State of the Parties*, 5th edition, John C. Green and Daniel J. Coffey, eds. Lanham, MD: Rowman & Littlefield.

Smith, Adam C. 2000. "Senate Hopefuls Defy Easy Labeling." *St. Petersburg Times*, November 5.

———. 2004a. "Democrats Divide Old, New Unions." *St. Petersburg Times*, January 16.

———. 2004b. "Many More Have Signed Up, but Will They Vote." *St. Petersburg Times*, October 18.

Smith, Daniel A. 2004. "Strings Attached; Outside Money in Colorado's Seventh District." In *The Last Hurrah? Soft Money and Issue Advocacy in the 2002 Congressional Elections*, ed. David Magleby and J. Quin Monson. Washington, DC: Brookings Institution Press.

Smith, Richard Norton. 1982. *Thomas E. Dewey and His Times*. New York: Simon & Schuster.

Sorauf, Frank J. 1992. *Inside Campaign Finance: Myths and Realities*. New Haven, CT: Yale University Press.

Soskis, Benjamin. 2000. "A Tale of Two Cities." *New Republic*, September 28.

Sousa, David J. 1993. "Organized Labor in the Electorate, 1960–1988." *Political Research Quarterly* 46:741–58.

Spitzer, Robert J. 1995. *The Politics of Gun Control*, 2nd edition. Chatham, NJ: Chatham House Publishers.

"Spotlight Story—Post-Election: More Fallout on the Abortion Issue." 1996. *Abortion Report*, November 8.

Stanger, Jeffrey D., and Douglas G. Rivlin. 1999. *Issue Advocacy Advertising During the 1997–1998 Election Cycle*. Washington, DC: Annenberg Public Policy Center of the University of Pennsylvania.

Stanton, John. 2003. "Green Groups Fertilize Their Grassroots." *National Journal*, June 28.

Starr, Alexandra. 2004. "Desperately Seeking Single Women Voters." *Business Week*, June 21.

Steers, Stuart. 2004. "It's Not Easy Being Green; Look Who's Mad at Dick Lamm Now?" *Denver Westword*, March 18.

Stolberg, Sheryl Gay. 2003. "A Bill Signed, But It's Not Picture Perfect." *New York Times*, November 9.

———. 2004. "A Swing to the Middle on Gun Control." *New York Times*, March 7.

Stone, Peter H. 1997. "Business Strikes Back." *National Journal*, October 25.

———. 2000. "Business Confronts Labor's Clout." *National Journal*, January 8.

———. 2003a. "A Catalog of Key Groups." *National Journal*, December 20.

———. 2003b. "Trial Lawyers on Trial." *National Journal*, July 12.

Strom, Stephanie. 2003. "A Deficit of $100 Million is Confronting the NRA." *New York Times*, December 21.

Sugrue, Thomas J. 1996. *The Origins of the Urban Crisis*. Princeton, NJ: Princeton University Press.

Swoboda, Frank. 1999. "AFL-CIO Plots a Push for Democratic House; Union Allots $46 Million For 2-Year Effort." *Washington Post*, February 18.

Taft, Philip. 1964. *Organized Labor in American History*. New York: Harper & Row.

Teixeria, Ruy. 2003. "Deciphering the Democrats' Debacle." *Washington Monthly*, May.

Thomas, Stephen W. 1980. "Interest Groups: Inside Perspectives." In *Parties, Interest Groups and Campaign Finance Laws*, ed. Michael J. Malbin. Washington, DC: American Enterprise Institute.

Thomas, Sue. 1994. "The NARAL PAC: Reproductive Choice in the Spotlight." In *Risky Business: PAC Decisionmaking in Congressional Elections*, Robert Biersack, Paul S. Herrnson, and Clyde Wilcox, eds. Armonk, NY: M. E. Sharpe.

————. 1999. "NARAL PAC: Battling for Women's Reproductive Rights." In *After the Revolution: PACs, Lobbies and the Republican Congress*, ed. Robert Biersack, Paul Herrnson, and Clyde Wilcox. Boston: Allyn & Bacon.

"Tobacco, Abortion, Gun Groups See Gains and Losses." 2000. *Wall Street Journal*, November 9.

Tobias, Carol Long. 2004. "Statement by Carol Tobias, National Right to Life Political Director." November 4. www.nrlc.org/Post/Tobias110404.html.

Toner, Robin. 2004. "Abortion's Opponents Claim the Middle Ground." *New York Times*, April 25.

Traugott, Michael. 2001. "The 2000 Michigan Senate Race." In *Election Advocacy: Soft Money and Issue Advocacy in the 2000 Congressional Elections*, ed. David B. Magleby. Provo, UT: Center for the Study of Elections and Democracy, Brigham Young University.

Trowbridge, Gordon. 2000. "GOP's Strength in Oakland Threatened." *Detroit News*, November 10.

Truman, David. 1971. *The Governmental Process*. 2nd ed. New York: Knopf.

Turner, Douglas. 1998. "Schumer Puts Big Dent in State GOP Machine Built by D'Amato." *Buffalo News*, November 4.

Tye, Larry. 1999a. "AMA's Firing of Editor Draws Barbs Worldwide." *Boston Globe*, January 25.

————. 1999b. "AMA in Danger of Vanishing from Scene." *Boston Globe*, May 10.

Uhlaner, Carole J. 1989. "Rational Turnout: The Neglected Role of Groups." *American Journal of Political Science* 33:390–422.

Underwood, James E., and William J. Daniels. 1982. *Governor Rockefeller in New York: The Apex of Pragmatic Liberalism in the United States*. Westport, CT: Greenwood Press.

Vaida, Bara. 2004. "AARP's Big Bet." *National Journal*, March 13.

Vaida, Bara, and Peter H. Stone. 2004. "Business, Conservative Groups Win Big." *National Journal*, November 6.

Verba, Sidney, Kay Lehman Schlozman, and Henry E. Brady. 1995. *Voice and Equality: Civic Voluntarism and American Politics*. Cambridge, MA: Harvard University Press.

Victor, Kirk. 2004. "Trial Lawyers Suppress Their Glee." *National Journal*, July 26.

Vita, Matthew, and Juliet Eilperin. 2000. "House Passes China Trade Bill; Measure to Normalize Ties Wins Easily in the End, 237 to 197." *Washington Post*, May 25.

Von Drehle, David. 2000. "No Stone Is Left Unturned for Turnout; Tight Contest Fires Up Faithful in Record Push for Votes." *Washington Post*, November 7.

Waldman, Amy. 1998. "Killing of Doctor Who Performed Abortions Becomes a Factor in Political Races." *New York Times*, October 27.

Walker, Jack L. 1983. "The Origins and Maintenance of Interest Groups in America." *American Political Science Review* 77:390–406.

———. 1991. *Mobilizing Interest Groups in America: Patrons, Professions and Social Movements*. Ann Arbor: University of Michigan Press.

Walsh, Edward. 2003. "Two Big Unions Announce Dean Endorsement." *Washington Post*, November 13.

Wattenberg, Martin. 1998. *The Decline of American Political Parties: 1952–1998*. Cambridge, MA: Harvard University Press.

Weisberg, Herbert F. 2002. "The Party in the Electorate as a Basis for More Responsible Parties." In *Responsible Partisanship? The Evolution of American Political Parties Since 1950*, ed. John C. Green and Paul S. Herrnson. Lawrence: University Press of Kansas.

Weisman, Jonathan. 2002. "Lobbies Hope the Elephants Won't Forget." *Washington Post*, November 8.

Weisskopf, Michael. 1994. "AARP Becomes First Major Organization to Support Mitchell Health Bill." *Washington Post*, August 11.

Weissman, Steve, and Ruth Hassan. Forthcoming. "BCRA and the 527 Groups." In *The Election After Reform: Money, Politics and the Bipartisan Campaign Reform Act*, ed. Michael Malbin. Lanham, MD: Rowman & Littlefield.

Whitley, Tyler. 2000. "The Stars Aligned for George Allen." *Richmond Times-Dispatch*, November 12.

Wilcox, Clyde. 1994. "Coping With Increased Business Influence: The AFL-CIO's Committee on Public Education." In *Risky Business? PAC Decisionmaking in Congressional Elections*, ed. Robert Biersack, Paul Herrnson, and Clyde Wilcox. Armonk, NY: M. E. Sharpe.

Wilcox, Clyde, Alexandra Cooper, Peter Francia, John C. Green, Paul S. Herrnson, Lynda Powell, Jason Reifler, Mark J. Rozell, and Benjamin A. Webster. 2003. "With Limits Raised, Who Will Give More? The Impact of BCRA on Individual Donors." In *Life After Reform: When the Bipartisan Campaign Reform Act Meets Politics*, ed. Michael J. Malbin. Lanham, MD: Rowman & Littlefield.

Wilcox, Clyde, Mark Rozell, Michael Malbin, and Richard Skinner. 2001. "Interest Group Campaign Adaptations in the Elections of 2000." Paper presented at the Annual Convention of the Southern Political Science Association, Atlanta.

———. 2002. "New Interest Group Strategies—A Preview of Post-McCain-Feingold Politics." Campaign Finance Institute paper.

Williams, Vanessa. 2004. "Democrats Aim to Organize the Union Vote; Labor Leaders Predict Record Turnout as They Rally Members for Kerry in Battleground States." *Washington Post*, October 23.

Wilson, James Q. 1962. *The Amateur Democrat: Club Politics in Three Cities—New York, Chicago, Los Angeles*. Chicago: University of Chicago Press.

———. 1973. *Political Organizations*. New York: Basic Books.

Wilson, Craig. 2001. "The 2000 Montana Senate Race." *PS: Political Science and Politics* 34: 272.

Woellert, Lorraine. 2004. "A Battle for the Sierra Club's Soul." *Business Week*, March 1.

Wolfe, Warren. "AARP's Broader Vision Includes Minnesota." *Minneapolis Star Tribune*, November 6

Wolinsky, Howard. 1999. "AMA Membership Keeps Shrinking." *Chicago Sun-Times*, June 16.

Zaller, John R. 1992. *The Nature and Origins of Mass Opinion.* New York: Cambridge University Press.

Zeller, Shawn. 2003. "Tort Reform's Massive War Chest." *National Journal*, March 29.

Zuger, Abigail. 1997. "After Bad Year for A.M.A., Doctors Debate Its Prognosis." *New York Times*, December 2.

Index

About the Author

Richard M. Skinner teaches political science at Williams College. He has also taught at Bowdoin College, Hamilton College, and SUNY Geneseo. He has served as a research analyst at the Campaign Finance Institute. His essay, "The Partisan Presidency," appeared in the most recent edition of *The State of the Parties* (also published by Rowman & Littlefiled); his work has also appeared in *The Journal of Politics*, *The Public Perspective*, and *Forum*.

9412